Biotechnology and Bioethics

Biotechnology and Bioethics

Editor

Vasiliki Mollaki

MDPI

Basel • Beijing • Wuhan • Barcelona • Belgrade • Novi Sad • Cluj • Manchester

Editor
Vasiliki Mollaki
Hellenic National Bioethics
Commission
Athens
Greece

Editorial Office
MDPI
St. Alban-Anlage 66
4052 Basel, Switzerland

This is a reprint of articles from the Special Issue published online in the open access journal *BioTech* (ISSN 2673-6284) (available at: https://www.mdpi.com/journal/biotech/special_issues/Biotechnology_Bioethics).

For citation purposes, cite each article independently as indicated on the article page online and as indicated below:

Lastname, A.A.; Lastname, B.B. Article Title. *Journal Name* **Year**, *Volume Number*, Page Range.

ISBN 978-3-7258-0105-3 (Hbk)
ISBN 978-3-7258-0106-0 (PDF)
doi.org/10.3390/books978-3-7258-0106-0

Cover image courtesy of Vasiliki Mollaki

Contents

About the Editor

Vasiliki Mollaki

Vasiliki Mollaki is a Geneticist and Ethics Expert. She is currently a Scientific Officer at the National Commission for Bioethics and Technoethics in Greece, an Ethics Expert at the European Commission, and an Adjunct Professor at the International Hellenic University in Greece and at the Open University of Cyprus. She has a broad interest in science, genetics, and ethics. She studied Genetics at Cardiff University, UK, and received her postgraduate degree in Molecular and Genetic Medicine and her doctorate in Genetics from Sheffield University, UK. She has been a postdoctoral research fellow at the Institute of Biomedical Research of the Academy of Athens, the National and Kapodistrian University of Athens, and the National Centre of Scientific Research "Demokritos" in Athens, in which she played a key role in research projects investigating the genetic basis of human diseases. She has been teaching Biology, Molecular Biology, Genetics, and Bioethics as an Adjunct professor at the Technological Institute of Athens (Greece), the University of West Attica (Greece), the International Hellenic University (Greece), and the Open University of Cyprus (Cyprus). She has been appointed as external Ethics Expert at the European Commission, where she has carried out ethics evaluations for EU-funded research programs, participating in more than 65 Ethics Panels and chairing 14 of them. She is a member of the Research Ethics Committee (REC) of the University of Patras, University of West Attica, and the International Hellenic University in Greece. She is a member of the National Committee for the Protection of Animals Used for Scientific Purposes, Greece. She is also a member of the Editorial Board of the journal Bioethica. She has published 3 monographs, 1 e-book, 17 articles in international scientific journals, 4 articles in national scientific journals, and contributed 3 chapters in 3 collective books.

Preface

Biotechnology produces numerous and significant benefits for humanity and the environment, but is often controversial regarding its societal implications. Over the recent decades, traditional but also novel technologies in this field of study have raised complex ethical concerns, which—in certain cases—necessitate policy changes at the national and/or international level.

This Special Issue aims to discuss the ethical, legal, and societal challenges raised by biotechnological applications and highlights the interdisciplinary approach that needs to be adopted to responsibly address such problems. For this reason, it explores the ethical issues and potential legal and societal consequences generated by the use of genome editing, genetic testing, gene therapy, organoid technology, synthetic biology, and artificial intelligence by bringing together scholars from diverse fields—including medicine, law, genetics and genomics, agriculture, chemical engineering, policy science, philosophy, and environmental and social sciences.

This Special Issue is addressed to biomedical scientists, environmental and social scientists, lawyers, philosophers, and policy makers.

Vasiliki Mollaki
Editor

BioTech

MDPI

Review

Biosafety of Genome Editing Applications in Plant Breeding: Considerations for a Focused Case-Specific Risk Assessment in the EU

Michael F. Eckerstorfer [1,*], Marcin Grabowski [2], Matteo Lener [3], Margret Engelhard [4], Samson Simon [4], Marion Dolezel [1], Andreas Heissenberger [1] and Christoph Lüthi [5]

1 Umweltbundesamt–Environment Agency Austria (EAA), Landuse & Biosafety Unit, Spittelauer Lände 5, 1090 Vienna, Austria; marion.dolezel@umweltbundesamt.at (M.D.); andreas.heissenberger@umweltbundesamt.at (A.H.)
2 Ministry of Climate and Environment, Department Nature Conservation, GMO Unit, Wawelska 52/54, 00-922 Warszawa, Poland; marcin.grabowski@srodowisko.gov.pl
3 ISPRA (Italian Institute for Environmental Protection and Research), Department for Environmental Monitoring and Protection and for Biodiversity Conservation, Via Vitaliano Brancati, 48, 00144 Roma, Italy; matteo.lener@isprambiente.it
4 Federal Agency for Nature Conservation, Division of Assessment of GMOs/Enforcement of Genetic Engineering Act, Konstantinstr. 110, 53179 Bonn, Germany; Margret.Engelhard@BfN.de (M.E.); Samson.Simon@BfN.de (S.S.)
5 Federal Office for the Environment (FOEN), Biotechnology Section, Soil and Biotechnology Division, BAFU, CH-3003 Bern, Switzerland; Christoph.Luethi@bafu.admin.ch
* Correspondence: michael.eckerstorfer@umweltbundesamt.at; Tel.: +43-1-31304-3313

Citation: Eckerstorfer, M.F.; Grabowski, M.; Lener, M.; Engelhard, M.; Simon, S.; Dolezel, M.; Heissenberger, A.; Lüthi, C. Biosafety of Genome Editing Applications in Plant Breeding: Considerations for a Focused Case-Specific Risk Assessment in the EU. *BioTech* **2021**, *10*, 10. https://doi.org/10.3390/biotech10030010

Academic Editor: Vasiliki Mollaki

Received: 14 May 2021
Accepted: 15 June 2021
Published: 22 June 2021

Abstract: An intensely debated question is whether or how a mandatory environmental risk assessment (ERA) should be conducted for plants obtained through novel genomic techniques, including genome editing (GE). Some countries have already exempted certain types of GE applications from their regulations addressing genetically modified organisms (GMOs). In the European Union, the European Court of Justice confirmed in 2018 that plants developed by novel genomic techniques for directed mutagenesis are regulated as GMOs. Thus, they have to undergo an ERA prior to deliberate release or being placed on the market. Recently, the European Food Safety Authority (EFSA) published two opinions on the relevance of the current EU ERA framework for GM plants obtained through novel genomic techniques (NGTs). Regarding GE plants, the opinions confirmed that the existing ERA framework is suitable in general and that the current ERA requirements need to be applied in a case specific manner. Since EFSA did not provide further guidance, this review addresses a couple of issues relevant for the case-specific assessment of GE plants. We discuss the suitability of general denominators of risk/safety and address characteristics of GE plants which require particular assessment approaches. We suggest integrating the following two sets of considerations into the ERA: considerations related to the traits developed by GE and considerations addressing the assessment of method-related unintended effects, e.g., due to off-target modifications. In conclusion, we recommend that further specific guidance for the ERA and monitoring should be developed to facilitate a focused assessment approach for GE plants.

Keywords: novel genomic techniques; genome editing; CRISPR/Cas; plant modification; GMO; environmental risk assessment; biosafety regulation

1. Introduction

The ruling of the European Court of Justice (ECJ) in the case C-528/16 delivered in July 2018 clarified that plants developed by novel genomic techniques for directed mutagenesis are considered genetically modified organisms (GMOs) in the EU in accordance with Directive 2001/18/EC on the deliberate release and placing on the market of GMOs. The ruling also confirmed they are not exempt from regulations according to Article 3 in conjunction with Annex IB of the Directive (i.e., the "mutagenesis exemption") [1]. In a broader sense, the decision established that organisms which are developed by methods of directed mutagenesis such as GE are subject to the current EU regulatory framework for biotechnology products. The EU biosafety framework was introduced in 1990 and underwent major amendments. In 2001 and 2003 the Directive 2001/18/EC and Regulation (EC) No. 1829/2003 on GM food and feed were introduced. In and 2013 and 2015 the Implementing Regulation (EU) No 513/2013 on requirements for the authorization of genetically modified (GM) food and feed and Directive 2015/412/EU providing EU Member States with the possibility to implement restricting measures on the cultivation of GMOs in their territories were adopted [2]. The decision of the ECJ was a major step in the long and heated debate in Europe concerning the regulation of organisms developed by novel genomic techniques such as genome editing (GE), but did not resolve all uncertainties regarding the regulation of such applications [3]. First, the ruling does not apply to all types of NGTs, which cover a diverse range of methods including cisgenesis, transgrafting and epigenetic engineering by methods of RNA-directed DNA methylation alongside GE [4]. Secondly, it was argued that the ruling does not resolve all pending questions regarding the practical implementation of the EU regulatory framework for GE organisms [5]. Subsequently to the ECJ ruling, the European Commission conducted a stakeholder survey in the framework of a study regarding NGTs including GE to address some of these issues. The recently published study, however, does not provide concrete policy recommendations for further discussion [6].

GE is mostly done through introducing DNA single- or double-strand breaks at specific loci of a target genome by a range of site-directed nucleases (SDN), with CRISPR-Cas-type nucleases being them most prominent among them [7]. Mutations are then introduced at these genomic sites by cellular DNA repair systems. The outcome of the genetic modification may be directed by template DNA sequences supplied in trans or by modifications of the used SDN [8]. SDN-based GE has quickly become a standard tool in molecular biology for a variety of uses, including fast–track plant breeding [9]. The discovery of the CRISPR-Cas system as a genome editing tool was awarded the 2020 Nobel Prize in Chemistry [10]. Due to its simplicity and accessibility, GE has been used at an increasing pace and scale for the development of genetically modified plants in recent years [11]. GE is believed to be of high importance for future plant breeding by certain stakeholders [12,13]. The regulatory uncertainties surrounding GE organisms, particularly the question of whether GE organisms are GMOs according to many existing biosafety frameworks, led to policy considerations and debates in most countries of the world and at the level of international organizations. The increasing use of GE in plant breeding at the global level made this debate more urgent [14–17]. Against the background of the different national systems for the regulation of GMOs, some countries, including a number of Latin American countries, have already introduced supplementary legislation to facilitate the determination of the regulatory status of individual GE applications with regard to the existing biosafety laws [18]. Some countries, such as Australia, have decided to exclude some types of GE applications from their regulatory framework for GMOs [19]. Other legislations such as the EU and New Zealand have sought decisions of their supreme courts to decide whether GE organisms are subject to their existing regulatory system for GMOs. In both cases, the court rulings have positively answered this question [15]. Canada is operating a regulatory system that is based on the novelty of the newly developed traits and the plausibility of hazards that may be associated with the use of modified plants as regulatory triggers. Canadian regulations for plants with novel traits accommodate GMOs as well as plants with novel traits established by GE or conventional breeding within the existing regulatory framework [14,15].

In all countries, the decision to regulate GE plants according to the existing GMO regulations is crucially relevant for the level of regulatory oversight for GE plants. These decisions are thus highly important for the particular risk assessment requirements applied for GE plants [15]. Thus, the current debate in the EU as well as in other countries focuses on two issues: the practical applicability of the current regulatory system for products of novel genomic techniques such as GE and the development of appropriate approaches for the assessment of food safety and the environmental risk assessment (ERA) of organisms developed by GE. This review is focusing on the latter question. Specifically, we discuss considerations regarding an appropriate risk assessment of the traits developed by GE approaches as well as any unintended effects of GE plants. We suggest that further specific guidance for the ERA and monitoring of GE plants should be developed. We note that considerations regarding the risk assessment for GE plants will inform the debate on options for further regulation [20].

2. Recent Considerations for the ERA of GE Plants at the EU Level

In their explanatory note addressing new techniques in agricultural biotechnology [7], the High Level Group of Scientific Advisors to the European Commission concluded that a highly diverse range of applications and possible products of GE and other novel genomic techniques need to be considered in the debate on regulatory approaches and the ERA. As a general conclusion, they suggested an appropriate ERA needs to address the following aspects in a case specific manner:

- Effects due to intended changes present in the modified plant;
- Effects due to unintended changes present in the modified plant;
- Effects due to the characteristics of the modified plant species and its interaction with the receiving environment;
- Effects due to the intended use of the modified plant.

Such considerations apply to the ERA, which is currently conducted for GMOs in accordance with Directive 2001/18/EC and related EU legislation, e.g., Regulation (EC) No 1829/2003 on GM food and feed. The scientific risk assessment for GMOs is based on guidance developed by the EFSA. Such guidance is available for (1) molecular characterization; (2) comparative assessment including agronomic, phenotypic and compositional characterization; (3) food and feed safety assessment; and (4) environmental risk assessment [13]. EFSA published a general guidance document for the ERA of GM plants in 2010 [21]. Furthermore, notifications for authorization of GM products in the EU need to conform to the information requirements as set forth in Implementing Regulation (EU) No 513/2013. This regulation implements elements of the existing guidance document on risk assessment of GM food and feed [22] in a legally binding form.

In 2012, EFSA delivered an opinion addressing the risk assessment of GE plants which contain site specific insertions of exogenous sequences (so called SDN-3 applications) [23]. Against the background of the ruling of the ECJ in case C-528/16, the European Commission tasked EFSA in 2019 with several mandates for opinions concerning emerging novel genomic techniques. A recently published review provides a brief overview on the mandates relevant to the risk assessment of organisms developed by GE [13]. In particular, two opinions and the related documents on the results of the consultation processes conducted for the respective draft opinions are pertinent to the discussion of an appropriate ERA approach for GE plants:

- The opinion on the applicability of the previous EFSA Opinion from 2012 on SDN-3 for the assessment of plants developed using SDN-1, SDN-2 and oligonucleotide directed mutagenesis (ODM), i.e., GE methods to typically generate small-sized random (SDN-1) or template directed (SDN-2) mutations at predefined genomic loci [24,25].
- The opinion on the evaluation of existing guidelines for their adequacy for the molecular characterization and ERA of genetically modified plants obtained through synthetic biology [26,27].

The second opinion discusses a wider range of applications than GE. It, however, addresses a low-gluten wheat plant produced by targeted mutations of multiple alpha-gliadin genes using CRISPR-Cas9 genome editing as one of the three case studies discussed in the opinion.

Due to limitations by the terms of reference, EFSA did not produce a new, stand-alone guidance document for the case-specific risk assessment of GE plants. Rather, the GMO panel stated whether the previous conclusions of the 2012 opinion on SDN-3 applications were applicable for any SDN-1, SDN-2 and ODM applications [13]. The 2020 opinion therefore recurred on the 2012 opinion on SDN-3 applications, which in turn recurred on the general guidance document on ERA. The opinions concluded that the general approach and the principles developed for the assessment of GMOs are relevant and applicable for GE plants. The opinions further stress the necessity of a case specific assessment and indicate that the existing assessment approaches need to be adapted with a view to the characteristics of the individual GE applications. However, no further (case-) specific guidance was provided in the EFSA opinions. This was noted by several comments during consultations, which called for further work to provide more detailed guidance [24]. The recent EFSA opinions also did not address the limitations and shortcomings of the existing assessment and monitoring approach for GMOs, which should also be considered for GE plants [28]. As highlighted in this review, some aspects of the current system may particularly affect the robustness of the assessment of GE plants: (1) the specific focus on newly expressed transgenic proteins, (2) difficulties concerning the choice of appropriate test organisms to assess any adverse effects of modified plants on the receiving environment(s) and (3) the testing of chronic effects, indirect effects and interaction effects focusing on individual new compounds rather than on the entire modified plant. The current limitations regarding the post-marketing environmental monitoring (PMEM) should also be considered with a view of GE plants [28].

3. Generic versus Case-Specific Considerations for the Assessment of GE Plants

The precautionary principle requires a case-by-case evaluation of the risks associated with GMOs. However, the current discussion concerning regulatory approaches regarding GE organisms and specifically regarding GE plants typically focuses on trying to establish classes to categorize GE organisms based on the GE technique used and the type of modification introduced [29]. Some countries used such an approach to specify GE applications which should be further regulated and thus be subject to a risk assessment according to the respective biosafety laws [14,18,19]. A crucial question, however, is whether general denominators of risk/safety are available which would allow for a conclusion on the safety of whole groups of applications instead of applying case-specific considerations for all individual GE applications.

In the following, we discuss some generic considerations with a view to their suitability for such classification, in particular:

- Considerations regarding the type of GE method (SDN-1; SDN-2/ODM; SDN-3);
- Considerations regarding the size of the introduced genetic changes;
- Considerations regarding the precision of the editing process;
- Considerations regarding the complexity of the introduced changes (i.e., the depth of intervention);
- Considerations regarding the novelty of the developed traits;
- Considerations regarding the speed of the development.

3.1. Considerations Regarding the Type of GE Application

The trigger to determine the status of their regulation in some countries, such as Argentina, Brazil, Chile, Colombia, Australia and more recently the USA, is based on considerations regarding the type of GE method which is used to create GE plants [14,15,18,19]. The underlying consideration is that only some GE applications-such as SDN-3 applications result in the integration of longer exogenous sequences into the genome of the modified plants [13]. Rostocks [13] argues that modifications introduced by SDN-1, SDN-2 and ODM in general would resemble mutations which may also be introduced by classical mutation breeding.

However, this does not take into account that the scale, scope and location of mutations which can be introduced by GE may differ quite significantly from those mutations which may arise spontaneously during conventional breeding. A recent review [30] shows that GE facilitates introduction of multiple mutations, such as the simultaneous editing of several genes/alleles (multiplex editing) or the editing of gene alleles that are inaccessible to conventional breeding.

Furthermore, the theoretical comparison of spontaneous mutations with modifications introduced by GE does not consider the specific hazards that may be associated with a particular mutational change. The occurrence of hazards thus would not be correlated in all cases with an exogenous origin of the introduced DNA sequences.

Thus, case-specific considerations seem to be more appropriate than considerations based solely on the type of GE applications.

3.2. Considerations Regarding the Size of the Introduced Genetic Changes

Another general consideration regarding genetic modifications via GE is that the mutations introduced by SDN-1, SDN-2 and ODM applications typically are of small size. In some cases, only minimal sequence changes called single nucleotide variants (SNVs) are introduced [31]. As discussed in Section 3.1, some regulatory frameworks exempt such GE applications, in particular SDN-1 applications, from the scope of their biosafety regulations.

The respective regulations, however, are not consistent upon comparison. In the USA, only GE plants with SNVs are exempt from oversight by USDA APHIS. Organisms with two or more base pair changes do not qualify for automatic exemption [14]. Decision criteria for regulatory exclusion of individual modified organisms from the biosafety laws in Argentina, Brazil, Chile and Colombia exclude small sized SDN-1, SDN-2 and ODM modifications (SNVs and small insertions/deletions). Australia only excludes SDN-1 applications, while regulating all GE applications using repair template sequences, including SDN-2 and ODM applications. A major reason for introducing the specific regulations, particularly in Australia, was to create a simple and enforceable system for determination of the regulatory status of individual GE applications by developers and/or authorities [15,19].

However, **the size of the modification cannot be regarded as a reliable denominator of risk/safety of the specific modifications present in individual GE plants**. On the contrary, it is well known that even small DNA sequence changes can significantly impact the function and effects of the modified genes within the context of the GE plant. Thus, the High Level Group of Science Advisors concluded that the risk associated with particular sequence changes can only be assessed case-by-case [7,32].

Considerations regarding the size of the sequence modifications introduced by GE are more relevant to the question of whether the respective GE plants can be identified as a specific product, i.e., unanimously distinguished from other plant varieties by state-of-the-art detection methods [33]. However, GE plants with multiple small modifications or larger modifications may be identified by such methods [34]. The possibility to analytically identify a specific GE product is less relevant for the ERA than the ability to determine the environmental exposure to certain GE plants during PMEM and other enforcement requirements.

3.3. Considerations Regarding the Precision of the Editing Process

GE methods promise to introduce genetic modifications at specific genomic locations with a much higher precision than other methods for mutagenesis [13]. However, **the specificity of the used GE systems is not absolute. All GE methods are known to have the potential to also introduce off-target modifications [11,20,35].** As acknowledged by Rostoks [13], some off-target activity must be expected with GE. He also indicates that the methods to predict such activity in silico are not absolutely reliable. Furthermore, integration of extraneous DNA elements at DNA-breakpoints such as off-target cleavage sites may occur [13].

The precision of GE, i.e., the specificity for GE to happen only at intended target sites, is therefore a relevant denominator for the potential occurrence of unintended modifications. Such modifications might be associated with adverse effects, thus the identification and characterization of off-target modifications in the final plant product is relevant for the assessment of unintended effects [36,37].

3.4. Considerations Regarding the Complexity of the Introduced Changes

GE plants described in the scientific literature contain a range of different modifications to address different breeding objectives [11]. Only some GE plants contain single or few modifications that result in single, specific phenotypic changes. A significant number of GE plants were modified to facilitate complex physiological or phenotypic changes [20]. In particular, the modification of genes, which facilitate multiple different (pleiotropic) effects or which target genes involved in regulatory responses in the parental plants, may give rise to complex phenotypical changes that may be challenging to identify or assess. Another category of GE applications, which facilitate a higher depth of intervention, are multiplexed GE applications to create complex physiological, developmental or morphological changes. A number of such applications were described in recent reviews [13,20]. Examples include GE wheat with modifications in six homeoalleles of a gene (*TaMLO*) to increase resistance against powdery mildew, GE wheat edited in multiple alpha-gliadin genes resulting in a low gluten content and GE wild tomato modified in several genes for de novo domestication. The latter is a novel approach for the rapid development of tomato varieties that combine desired traits found in wild tomato plants, such as resistance toward pathogens or salt tolerance, with agriculturally favorable traits occurring in domesticated tomato varieties [38].

A high depth of intervention and/or complexity of the introduced changes may serve as an unspecific general indicator that a robust, comprehensive ERA is required. With regard to a respective case study (a low-gluten GE wheat), EFSA concluded that such applications go far beyond any GM plants previously assessed. However, EFSA also concluded that the existing requirements according to the current ERA approach for GMOs are adequate and sufficient for such types of GE plants [27].

3.5. Considerations Regarding the Novelty of the Developed Traits

A wide range of different traits have been developed by GE in different plant species. Some of these traits are related to traits already occurring in crops produced by conventional breeding or in wild relatives which could be crossbred. Other traits described in the scientific literature are similar to ones established in GM plants, e.g., herbicide or disease resistance [20]. However, a significant number of traits were not previously established by conventional breeding or other biotechnological methods, such as classic GM technology or the silencing of endogenous genes through RNAi methods. The latter category thus contains plants with novel traits. Less knowledge is usually available for plants with novel and untried traits than for GE plants that are comparable to conventionally bred plants or already assessed GM plants [20]. In particular, knowledge from practical experience in agricultural production, from observation of related wild plants and/or from previous risk assessments may be lacking. The Plants with Novel Trait (PNT) regulation implemented by Canada mandates a case-specific risk assessment of PNTs.

The available level of knowledge and/or history of safe use needs to be considered for the assessment of the intended modifications and the resulting intended traits with comparable traits in similar or related crop or plant species. However, such information does not relate to any unintended effects due to the modification process by GE. **Familiarity thus cannot serve as a general denominator of overall safety**. Novelty of the trait indicates the need for new data to assess risk issues relevant for the particular GE plant.

3.6. Considerations Regarding the Speed of the Development

GE is expected to reduce development time considerably, particularly for plants harboring multiple independent modifications [39]. It is estimated that the development time for GE plants is substantially shortened compared with classical GM plants and conventionally bred plants. Development time for GE plants is estimated to be 4–6 years in comparison with 8–12 years for GM or conventional plants [9]. **When fewer backcross generations are necessary to develop elite varieties from GE plants, the possibility that unintended modifications are removed during subsequent crossbreeding steps is decreased**. This is particularly important for applications facilitating the direct editing of elite lines, the editing of agricultural plants that are predominantly propagated vegetatively and for GE perennial plants with long generation times such as trees [20]. The speed of the development process may be considered an unspecific and indirect indicator of risk/safety, since a shorter development time of GE plants is constraining the time for the assessment of any unintended and unexpected effects.

3.7. Conclusions Regarding the Appropriate Approach for Risk Assessment

Based on the discussion of the suitability of general denominators for risk/safety, we argue that **a case-specific risk assessment within the current regulatory frameworks for GMOs should be conducted. This is considered a better option than to exclude certain classes of GE application from GMO regulation and from the established systems for risk assessment under these regulations**.

However, some generic considerations can provide relevant input on how to focus the ERA on relevant risk areas (assessment of intended traits or assessment of unintended effects) and on specific risk issues according to the existing guidance [21].

4. Considerations for the Case Specific Assessment of GE Plants

When designing a case-specific assessment, the following characteristics of GE applications need to be considered:

- The different GE techniques (SDN-techniques, ODM) and the various approaches for application that are available or in development and used to modify plant species (SDN-1, SDN-2, SDN-3, base editing, prime editing, epigenetic engineering). An overview on these approaches, their different characteristics as well as recent developments is given, e.g., by Adli [40], Anzalone and coworkers [41] and in a recent study by the Joint Research Centers of the European Commission (JRC) [29].
- The specific characteristics of such GE approaches with regard to their target specificity [20] and their ability to modify genomic locations that are not accessible to conventional breeding [30].
- The wide range of plant species that can be modified by GE approaches. This range includes a multitude of plants used in agriculture and forestry, as well as a range of non-crop plants [20,42].
- The broad range of traits that is under development [9,11]. Some of these GE plants are already marketed in certain countries or may be placed on the market in the near future [12]. A number of these traits are novel, some are highly complex.
- The interactions of the individual GE plants with the respective receiving environments, taking into account the specific conditions of their use and the possibilities for unintended introduction into non-managed habitats.

In addition to the principles applied to the ERA of GMOs according to Directive 2001/18/EC, the ERA conducted for GE plants should also be based on the characteristics presented above. For the design of a case-specific ERA, two sets of considerations need to be taken into account, regarding GE plant x environment interactions:

- Trait-related considerations to assess the effects of the intended trait(s).
- Method-related considerations to assess the unintended effects.

4.1. Trait-Related Considerations

The level of risk associated with a GE plant depends significantly on the effects of the developed trait(s) on the overall characteristics of the modified plant species [32]. Thus, a case-specific ERA must specifically consider the introduced trait(s) as well as the plant species that are modified. Recently, some systematic reviews of the scientific literature on GE plants have been published [9,11,20]. These reviews indicate that:

- **A wide range of plant species is used for GE**, either as model organisms for scientific research and method development, such as *Arabidopsis thaliana*, tobacco and rice, or plants that might be used as ornamental plants or in agriculture, forestry and industrial production. Examples for the latter groups include apple, barley, camelina, cassava, cotton, cucumber, flax, grapefruit, grapevine, legumes (soybean and barrelclover), maize, oilseed rape, opium poppy, poplar, potato, rice, rubber dandelion, red sage, tobacco, tomato, watermelon and wheat (bread wheat and durum wheat) [20].
- The GE applications in such plants are at different stages of development. Most reports in the literature are accounts of early development including proof of concept studies [20]. **A rising number of GE plants are currently developed for marketing. However, only a few are commercialized [12,43]**. The latter groups are particularly interesting for regulators to keep track of since they may be presented for regulatory assessment in the near future.
- **A broad range of traits are considered for development**. The systematic review conducted by Modrzejewski and coworkers [11] listed 101 GE applications that might be relevant for the use in agriculture in the near future. A recent analysis of these applications indicates the following [44]. One major focus is on the development of traits that increase the agronomic value of crop plants (increased yield, improved storage quality, enhanced crop development; 38% of applications), or alter the composition of the plants (e.g., reduced lignin content, altered fatty acid composition; 28% of the applications). Sixteen percent of applications concern different approaches to increase the resistance to biotic stress (particularly for resistance to fungal or bacterial pathogens) and 8% are for modified content for industrial purposes (improved starch quality, altered oil composition). Another 8% are for plants with resistance to broad-band herbicides (e.g., herbicides containing glyphosate or ALS-inhibitors) and 5% of the applications are for enhanced abiotic stress tolerance (e.g., tolerance to drought or salt stress).
- **Most of the applications are aimed at knocking out the expression of plant genes** involved in the above-mentioned processes via SDN-1. Fewer applications are for functional modification of genes (SDN-1, SDN-2, ODM applications). Other applications of agronomic importance, e.g., applications to develop herbicide resistant plants, are based on SDN-3 approaches [20].
- **A majority of the current developments are applications to modify a single target gene**, or all alleles of such genes present in the target plant. However, there is a significant and increasing number of applications for multiplexing. Examples for such developments are provided, e.g., in Kawall et al. [44] and Eckerstorfer et al. [20]. Applications with a higher depth of intervention are developed for different purposes, including altered composition, increased yield and developmental and morphological alterations beneficial for agricultural use.
- **A significant number of the traits developed by GE need to be considered novel.** Some of these developments are not feasible by conventional breeding approaches [30].

We conclude that the assessment of some of these traits will be challenging. EFSA came to the same conclusion in their case study of a complex modified low-gluten wheat plant modified in multiple genes by a CRISPR/Cas-based method [27]. Such applications differ significantly from any plants which were assessed previously and would require a comprehensive approach for risk assessment including ERA and food/feed safety assessment. Similar conclusions are drawn in a recently published study on a GE *Camelina* plant with altered fat composition [45]. A focused but robust ERA also needs to be provided for GE plants with traits that enhance their biological fitness or alter their reproductive properties. In addition, applications which provide a fast-track development of crops from non-domesticated wild forms [38] should be considered novel crops and should undergo a comprehensive risk assessment [20]. In contrast to other GE applications, no history of safe use and possibly only limited scientific data will be available for most of the above-mentioned complex GE applications.

Existing experience ("familiarity") with similar plant x trait combinations should be considered when a similar use of the corresponding GE plant is intended. In some cases, familiarity may be available with a specific trait, which was already used in conventionally bred crops employed in agricultural production for some time, particularly with respect to food and feed safety. The availability of a history of safe use regarding environmental effects is less likely, considering the complex nature of plant x trait x environment interactions. In some cases, however, such as GE herbicide resistant plants, conventional counterparts exist and the respective experiences with the environmental effects of such conventional herbicide resistant plants and its management should be considered in the ERA [46].

However, it needs to be emphasized that the concept of familiarity should be used as a tool to strengthen the case-specific approach to risk assessment. Like EFSA concluded for the concept of substantial equivalence [21], it may be used as a starting point to determine risk assessment needs and the requirement for newly established data rather than as an endpoint of the assessment.

4.2. Method-Related Considerations

Method-related considerations should be applied to facilitate the assessment of unintended effects. As suggested previously, the overall process of modification should be considered, including the steps to introduce GE tools for modification into the target plant cells or tissues. Duensing and coworkers [32] indicate that, in most cases, transgenic constructs are introduced into plant cells transiently or integrated into the genome of the recipient cells to express the required GE tools. While such integrated constructs are typically removed in breeding steps subsequent to GE, **the absence of exogenous constructs or secondary modifications (spurious insertions) need to be confirmed [44,47]**. Lema [47] recommends that routine approaches using Southern hybridization methods should be used to assess spurious insertions. Alternatively, the absence of exogenous sequences can be assessed by whole genome sequencing (WGS) data and bioinformatics analysis [47].

One well known aspect of GE applications is that the used nucleases do not recognize the targeted genome loci with absolute precision, resulting in some level of off-target activity [35–37]. A recent report from the JRC provides a detailed discussion of the available knowledge regarding off-target activities associated with the different GE methods and tools [29]. The report highlights that **the presence of off-target modifications has not been well-studied for a number of GE applications**, in particular for GE applications of recently developed methods or for methods which are only used in a limited number of applications. Thus, the general notion that GE methods are inducing off-target modifications with a low probability is based on a limited amount of reported data [29]. The JRC report also highlights that off-target activity is not only found with SDN introducing DNA double strand breaks, but essentially with all existing GE methods. For example, recent publications address the off-target activity of base-editing enzymes [48] and SDNs that are modified for epigenetic engineering [49].

EFSA also discussed off-target-activity of SDNs [13,25]. As an overall conclusion, they considered the level of off-target activity lower than the mutation rate due to classical mutagenesis [13]. Furthermore, they referred to the availability of strategies to increase the precision of editing and to remove off-target modifications in subsequent crossbreeding steps [13]. Based on such general considerations, EFSA considered the overall risk low and recommended no detailed risk assessment approach in their recently published opinion [25].

However, not all GE approaches can be designed to minimize the occurrence of off-target modifications. In cases aimed at simultaneously modifying a number of genomic loci with slightly different target sequences in a quite simple way, a high level of specificity for all single targets is not feasible. In such applications, genome editing tools with a lower level of specificity (i.e., precision) are employed, which recognize all the slightly different target sequences with appropriate efficiency. Such intentionally "dirty" approaches are a straightforward approach to simultaneously modify different genomic targets sites, which are not perfectly homologous, e.g., different members of a gene family [45]. DNA breaks introduced by off-target activity may facilitate the insertion of extraneous DNA sequences, which in turn may lead to unintended effects [44,47].

Additionally, the introduced off-target modifications may not be readily removed in all cases. This is particularly true for approaches which require fewer backcrossing steps than conventional breeding schemes or are designed to avoid such backcrossing steps altogether, i.e., approaches for "quick" breeding schemes. Also, secondary modifications introduced by GE systems in the vicinity of the intended genomic target site should be appropriately assessed. Such modifications are tightly linked to the intended traits and are not easily lost during subsequent breeding [20,44,47]. Therefore, **we suggest drafting further guidance for the assessment of unintended effects of GE modifications.**

A number of methods, including WGS, are available for a targeted and untargeted analysis of unintended modifications and should be considered for a case-by-case evaluation [20]. Specifically, such tools should be applied if the characteristics of the used GE approach suggest a higher probability for off-target modifications to occur in a GE plant. In particular, "quick and dirty" GE approaches, i.e., GE approaches with a higher level of off-target activity and fewer subsequent breeding steps to remove secondary modifications, should be thoroughly assessed for unintended off-target modifications and associated adverse effects. The previously proposed 10 step approach to assess unintended effects described by Eckerstorfer and coworkers [20] is considered a good starting point for a focused assessment of unintended effects. In addition, recommendations by the French Haut Conseil des Biotechnologies [50], Kawall and coworkers [44] as well as by Lema [47] concerning the assessment of off-target modifications and spurious insertions should be considered to develop appropriate guidance.

5. Implications for Regulatory Approaches for GE Plants

As outlined in the above chapters, the emerging GE applications present a number of challenges for regulators, risk assessors and policy makers. For the policy makers and regulators, one challenge is to ensure a legislation based on regulatory triggers that are simple to use, unambiguous and easily enforceable, yet flexible enough to cope with emerging techniques such as GE. From a risk assessment point of view, the main challenge is that such a legislation should ensure an adequate assessment of the diverse combinations of plants and traits obtained by GE. Such an approach must take into account the associated risks in accordance with the objectives of established biosafety legislation, i.e., a high level of protection of human and animal health and the environment. However, the regulatory solutions developed by policy makers do not necessarily resolve the challenges regarding the ERA and environmental monitoring of biotechnology applications. As discussed in the previous sections, the risks associated with GE plants is correlated with the newly developed traits and/or unintended effects resulting from characteristics of the specific GE approach used to establish a particular GE plant rather than with a certain type of GE approach per se (e.g., SDN-1, SDN-2/ODM, SDN-3). Certain approaches that are complex and/or fast and/or dirty may be associated with a higher risk.

This results in challenges to develop a regulatory framework that is broad enough to include all types of GE applications, while providing enough flexibility to focus the attention and resources of risk assessors on the characteristics that are particularly relevant for the GE plant in question.

In general, we consider the principles and the case-specific approach provided by the current framework for GMOs to be appropriate for the emerging GE applications. This is in accordance with the recent EFSA opinions [25,27].

However, **we consider the exclusion of whole classes of GE applications from the existing regulatory frameworks for biotechnology applications, e.g., the current EU framework for GMO regulation, a poor option from a biosafety perspective**. As discussed previously [15], other applicable regulation is insufficient to address biosafety issues. In fact, the European seed legislation, food and feed law as well as the plant protection law and plant variety protection law are neither individually nor collectively able to ensure an assessment and control of possible negative environmental impacts of NGTs [51]. Such regulations that apply to all agricultural plants, genome edited or not, are thus not well suited to provide an appropriate framework for case-specific risk assessment according to the high safety standards implemented in the respective GMO legislation.

6. Conclusions

Our review indicates the challenges faced by policy makers, regulators and risk assessors to provide an appropriate framework for the risk assessment of GE plants. The risk associated with individual GE applications will be highly variable. While the effects of some GE applications may be well known from conventional varieties with similar traits, other GE applications could be associated with plausible risk issues and may be more challenging to assess and monitor. The latter group will likely be comprised of GE plants with complex and novel modifications as indicated by EFSA [27] and other authors [20,44].

Considering the wide ranges of plant species and the GE methods and traits that need to be considered, there is no safety by default for whole groups of GE applications encompassing different individual GE organisms. Biosafety considerations should instead be based on an appropriate ERA prior to the release of GE plants into the environment.

The case-specific approach incorporated in the EU regulatory framework is a viable way forward provided that further guidance for the risk assessment of GE applications is developed. The existing guidance developed by EFSA and their initial work on GE applications is not sufficient to address these challenges, but rather a starting point for further efforts. In this review, **we argue that general considerations concerning risk/safety of all GE applications or of different classes of GE applications are insufficient to address the challenges at hands. Instead, we suggest that a focused case-specific approach is followed to provide a robust risk assessment of individual GE plants.** This ERA approach should focus on risks that may plausibly manifest themselves in the phenotype or the interaction with the environment of a particular GE plant. To this end, we suggest that two sets of considerations are considered: (1) trait related-considerations to assess the effects associated with the newly developed trait(s); and (2) method-related considerations to assess unintended changes associated with the intended trait(s) or with other modifications in the GE plant. Important aspects concerning both sets of considerations are outlined in Box 1.

Based on these considerations, further guidance should be developed to ensure the high safety standards provided by the current regulatory framework for GMOs in the EU for GE plants in an adequate and efficient way, taking into account the existing knowledge and experience in a case-specific manner. This guidance should thus strengthen the case-specific approach that is recommended by numerous EU and Member States institutions. The precautionary approach of the existing EU GMO regulations should not be weakened by excluding whole groups of GE applications from their scope without having regard to the characteristics of the individual GE plants.

Box 1: Crucial aspects for a two-pronged assessment strategy to address trait-related effects and method-related modifications, respectively.

(1) The assessment of effects associated with the newly developed trait(s) in GE plants should consider, among others:
- The level of knowledge and familiarity with the particular crop and trait combination needs to be considered. As indicated in Section 4.1, only limited scientific knowledge is available for some GE applications.
- Some applications may lead to changes in agricultural management; possible indirect effects resulting from their use need to be addressed during the ERA.
- Complex GE modifications should be thoroughly scrutinized regarding adverse environmental effects resulting from these changes. A robust assessment should be provided for physiological effects of multiple simultaneous changes (multiplexed GE) and for regulatory effects of the introduced modifications on morphology, development and reproduction of the GE plant.
- The ERA conducted for GE plants should also address secondary effects associated with the intended trait(s). This should encompass pleiotropic effects of the intended trait(s).

(2) The assessment of method-related unintended changes associated with the intended trait(s) or with other modifications in the GE plant should take into account the following aspects:
- The available body of evidence with regard to off-target-effects, their occurrence and their identification as indicated in Section 4.2.
- The likelihood that off-target modifications are still present in the final breeding product. This likelihood may be higher with fast-tracked breeding applications, i.e., aimed at modification of elite lines, modification of vegetatively propagated crops, and modification of plant species with longer generation cycles such as trees.
- The available information on unintended secondary modifications introduced by GE systems in the vicinity of the intended genomic target site. Such modifications are tightly linked to the intended traits and are not easily lost during subsequent breeding steps.
- The available recommendations on how an assessment of unintended and off-target effects may be conducted and which kind of aspects should be considered in the framework of the assessment.

Author Contributions: Conceptualization, research and writing—original draft preparation, M.F.E.; writing—review and editing, M.F.E., C.L., A.H., M.G., M.L., M.D., M.E. and S.S. All authors have read and agreed to the published version of the manuscript.

Funding: This research was funded by Federal Office for the Environment (FOEN), Section Biotechnology, Soil and Biotechnology Division; BAFU, CH-3003 Bern, Switzerland, grant number 110011894/8T10/00.5005.PZ/0027.

Institutional Review Board Statement: Not applicable.

Informed Consent Statement: Not applicable.

Acknowledgments: The valuable discussions on the topic in the interest group on risk assessment and monitoring of GMOs of the EPA and ENCA network are kindly acknowledged. We also acknowledge editorial support from the expert management unit at EAA.

Conflicts of Interest: The authors declare no conflict of interest. The authors of this article are members of the interest group on risk assessment and monitoring of GMOs (IG GMO). The IG GMO is jointly organized by the European Nature Conservation Agency Heads Network (ENCA) and the Network of the Heads of Environmental Protection Agencies (EPA) and chaired by the Swiss Federal Office for the Environment (FOEN/BAFU). A draft of this publication was discussed in the IG GMO. However, the authors contributed to the publication as members of their affiliated agencies and in their personal capacity. More information on the IG GMO can be found here: https://www.encanetwork.eu/interest-groups/gmo.

References

1. Spranger, T. Case C-528/16: Questions Raised by the ECJ's Judgement on Gene Editing Technology. *Int. Chem. Regul. Law Rev.* **2018**, *1*, 173–176. [CrossRef]
2. Schuler, L.; Zust, D.; Vybiral, D.; Hau, P. GM Food Regulations in the EU. In *Reference Module in Food Science*; Smithers, G.W., Ed.; Elsevier: Amsterdam, The Netherlands, 2019; ISBN 978-0-08-100596-5.
3. Purnhagen, K.P.; Kok, E.; Kleter, G.; Schebesta, H.; Visser, R.G.F.; Wesseler, J. EU court casts new plant breeding techniques into regulatory limbo. *Nat. Biotechnol.* **2018**, *36*, 799–800. [CrossRef] [PubMed]
4. European Commission; Joint Research Centre; Institute for Health and Consumer Protection; Institute for Prospective Technological Studies. *New Plant Breeding Techniques: State of the Art and Prospects for Commercial Development*; Publications Office: Luxembourg, 2011.
5. Schulman, A.H.; Oksman-Caldentey, K.-M.; Teeri, T.H. European Court of Justice delivers no justice to Europe on genome-edited crops. *Plant Biotechnol. J.* **2020**, *18*, 8–10. [CrossRef]
6. European Commission. *Study on the Status of New Genomic Techniques under Union Law and in Light of the Court of Justice Ruling in Case C-528/16*; Commission Staff Working Document SWD (2021) 92 Final; European Commission: Brussels, Belgium, 2021; Available online: https://ec.europa.eu/food/plant/gmo/modern_biotech/new-genomic-techniques_en (accessed on 10 May 2021).
7. European Commission; Directorate General for Research and Innovation; European Commission's Group of Chief Scientific Advisors. *New Techniques in Agricultural Biotechnology*; Publications Office of the EU: Luxembourg, 2017; ISBN 978-92-79-66222-5. [CrossRef]
8. Pickar-Oliver, A.; Gersbach, C.A. The next generation of CRISPR-Cas technologies and applications. *Nat. Rev. Mol. Cell Biol.* **2019**, *20*, 490–507. [CrossRef] [PubMed]
9. Chen, K.; Wang, Y.; Zhang, R.; Zhang, H.; Gao, C. CRISPR/Cas Genome Editing and Precision Plant Breeding in Agriculture. *Annu. Rev. Plant Biol.* **2019**, *70*, 667–697. [CrossRef]
10. Strzyz, P. CRISPR-Cas9 wins Nobel. *Nat. Rev. Mol. Cell Biol.* **2020**, *21*, 714. [CrossRef]
11. Modrzejewski, D.; Hartung, F.; Sprink, T.; Krause, D.; Kohl, C.; Wilhelm, R. What is the available evidence for the range of applications of genome-editing as a new tool for plant trait modification and the potential occurrence of associated off-target effects: A systematic map. *Environ. Evid.* **2019**, *8*, 27. [CrossRef]
12. Menz, J.; Modrzejewski, D.; Hartung, F.; Wilhelm, R.; Sprink, T. Genome Edited Crops Touch the Market: A View on the Global Development and Regulatory Environment. *Front. Plant Sci.* **2020**, *11*. [CrossRef]
13. Rostoks, N. Implications of the EFSA Scientific Opinion on Site Directed Nucleases 1 and 2 for Risk Assessment of Genome-Edited Plants in the EU. *Agronomy* **2021**, *11*, 572. [CrossRef]
14. Turnbull, C.; Lillemo, M.; Hvoslef-Eide, T.A.K. Global Regulation of Genetically Modified Crops Amid the Gene Edited Crop Boom—A Review. *Front. Plant Sci.* **2021**, *12*. [CrossRef]
15. Eckerstorfer, M.F.; Engelhard, M.; Heissenberger, A.; Simon, S.; Teichmann, H. Plants Developed by New Genetic Modification Techniques-Comparison of Existing Regulatory Frameworks in the EU and Non-EU Countries. *Front. Bioeng. Biotechnol.* **2019**, *7*, 26. [CrossRef]
16. Friedrichs, S.; Takasu, Y.; Kearns, P.; Dagallier, B.; Oshima, R.; Schofield, J.; Moreddu, C. Policy Considerations Regarding Genome Editing. *Trends Biotechnol.* **2019**, *37*, 1029–1032. [CrossRef]
17. Friedrichs, S.; Takasu, Y.; Kearns, P.; Dagallier, B.; Oshima, R.; Schofield, J.; Moreddu, C. An overview of regulatory approaches to genome editing in agriculture. *Biotechnol. Res. Innov.* **2019**, *3*, 208–220. [CrossRef]
18. Lema, M.A. Regulatory aspects of gene editing in Argentina. *Transgenic Res.* **2019**, *28*, 147–150. [CrossRef]
19. Thygesen, P. Clarifying the regulation of genome editing in Australia: Situation for genetically modified organisms. *Transgenic Res.* **2019**, *28*, 151–159. [CrossRef]
20. Eckerstorfer, M.F.; Dolezel, M.; Heissenberger, A.; Miklau, M.; Reichenbecher, W.; Steinbrecher, R.A.; Waßmann, F. An EU Perspective on Biosafety Considerations for Plants Developed by Genome Editing and Other New Genetic Modification Techniques (nGMs). *Front. Bioeng. Biotechnol.* **2019**, *7*, 31. [CrossRef]
21. European Food Safety Authority-EFSA GMO panel. Guidance on the environmental risk assessment of genetically modified plants. *EFSA J.* **2010**, *8*, 1879. [CrossRef]
22. European Food Safety Authority-EFSA GMO panel. Guidance for risk assessment of food and feed from genetically modified plants. *EFSA J.* **2011**, *9*, 2150. [CrossRef]
23. European Food Safety Authority-EFSA GMO panel. Scientific opinion addressing the safety assessment of plants developed using Zinc Finger Nuclease 3 and other Site-Directed Nucleases with similar function. *EFSA J.* **2012**, *10*, 2943. [CrossRef]
24. Raffaello, T.; Casacuberta, J.; Dalmay, T.; Guerche, P.; Hejatko, J.; Nogué, F.; Serrano, J.J.S.; Gennaro, A.; Paraskevopoulos, K.; Rostoks, N. Outcome of the public consultation on the draft Scientific Opinion on the applicability of the EFSA Opinion on site-directed nucleases type 3 for the safety assessment of plants developed using site-directed nucleases type 1 and 2 and oligonucleotide-directed mutagenesis. *EFSA J.* **2020**, *17*. [CrossRef]
25. Naegeli, H.; Bresson, J.-L.; Dalmay, T.; Dewhurst, I.C.; Epstein, M.M.; Firbank, L.G.; Guerche, P.; Hejatko, J.; Moreno, F.J.; Mullins, E.; et al. Applicability of the EFSA Opinion on site-directed nucleases type 3 for the safety assessment of plants developed using site-directed nucleases type 1 and 2 and oligonucleotide-directed mutagenesis. *EFSA J.* **2020**, *18*, e06299. [CrossRef] [PubMed]

26. European Food Safety Authority. Outcome of the public consultation on the draft Scientific Opinion on the evaluation of existing guidelines for their adequacy for the molecular characterisation and environmental risk assessment of genetically modified plants obtained through synthetic biology. *EFSA J.* **2021**, *18*. [CrossRef]
27. Naegeli, H.; Bresson, J.-L.; Dalmay, T.; Dewhurst, I.C.; Epstein, M.M.; Firbank, L.G.; Guerche, P.; Hejatko, J.; Moreno, F.J.; Nogue, F.; et al. Evaluation of existing guidelines for their adequacy for the molecular characterisation and environmental risk assessment of genetically modified plants obtained through synthetic biology. *EFSA J.* **2021**, *19*, e06301. [CrossRef] [PubMed]
28. Agapito-Tenfen, S.Z.; Okoli, A.S.; Bernstein, M.J.; Wikmark, O.-G.; Myhr, A.I. Revisiting Risk Governance of GM Plants: The Need to Consider New and Emerging Gene-Editing Techniques. *Front. Plant Sci.* **2018**, *9*, 1874. [CrossRef]
29. European Commission; Joint Research Centre. *New Genomic Techniques: State of the Art Review*; JRC121847; Publications Office of the European Union: Luxembourg, 2021; ISBN 978-92-76-24696-1. [CrossRef]
30. Kawall, K. New Possibilities on the Horizon: Genome Editing Makes the Whole Genome Accessible for Changes. *Front. Plant Sci.* **2019**, *10*, 525. [CrossRef]
31. Ribarits, A.; Narendja, F.; Stepanek, W.; Hochegger, R. Detection Methods Fit-for-Purpose in Enforcement Control of Genetically Modified Plants Produced with Novel Genomic Techniques (NGTs). *Agronomy* **2021**, *11*, 61. [CrossRef]
32. Duensing, N.; Sprink, T.; Parrott, W.A.; Fedorova, M.; Lema, M.A.; Wolt, J.D.; Bartsch, D. Novel Features and Considerations for ERA and Regulation of Crops Produced by Genome Editing. *Front. Bioeng. Biotechnol.* **2018**, *6*, 79. [CrossRef]
33. Grohmann, L.; Keilwagen, J.; Duensing, N.; Dagand, E.; Hartung, F.; Wilhelm, R.; Bendiek, J.; Sprink, T. Detection and Identification of Genome Editing in Plants: Challenges and Opportunities. *Front. Plant Sci.* **2019**, *10*, 236. [CrossRef]
34. Ribarits, A.; Eckerstorfer, M.; Simon, S.; Stepanek, W. Genome-Edited Plants: Opportunities and Challenges for an Anticipatory Detection and Identification Framework. *Foods* **2021**, *10*, 430. [CrossRef]
35. Yee, J.-K. Off-target effects of engineered nucleases. *FEBS J.* **2016**, *283*, 3239–3248. [CrossRef]
36. Troadec, M.-B.; Pagès, J.-C. Where are we with unintended effects in genome editing applications from DNA to phenotype: Focus on plant applications. *Transgenic Res.* **2019**, *28*, 125–133. [CrossRef]
37. Zhao, H.; Wolt, J.D. Risk associated with off-target plant genome editing and methods for its limitation. *Emerg. Top. Life Sci.* **2017**, *1*, 231–240. [CrossRef]
38. Fernie, A.R.; Yan, J. De Novo Domestication: An Alternative Route toward New Crops for the Future. *Mol. Plant* **2019**, *12*, 615–631. [CrossRef]
39. Wolter, F.; Schindele, P.; Puchta, H. Plant breeding at the speed of light: The power of CRISPR/Cas to generate directed genetic diversity at multiple sites. *BMC Plant Biol.* **2019**, *19*, 176. [CrossRef]
40. Adli, M. The CRISPR tool kit for genome editing and beyond. *Nat. Commun.* **2018**, *9*, 1911. [CrossRef]
41. Anzalone, A.V.; Koblan, L.W.; Liu, D.R. Genome editing with CRISPR-Cas nucleases, base editors, transposases and prime editors. *Nat. Biotechnol.* **2020**, *38*, 824–844. [CrossRef]
42. Metje-Sprink, J.; Sprink, T.; Hartung, F. Genome-edited plants in the field. *Curr. Opin. Biotechnol.* **2020**, *61*, 1–6. [CrossRef]
43. European Commission; Joint Research Centre. *Current and Future Market Applications of New Genomic Techniques*; EUR 30589 EN; JRC123830; Publications Office of the European Union: Luxembourg, 2021; ISBN 978-92-76-30206-3. [CrossRef]
44. Kawall, K.; Cotter, J.; Then, C. Broadening the GMO risk assessment in the EU for genome editing technologies in agriculture. *Environ. Sci. Eur.* **2020**, *32*. [CrossRef]
45. Kawall, K. Genome-edited Camelina sativa with a unique fatty acid content and its potential impact on ecosystems. *Environ. Sci. Eur.* **2021**, *33*. [CrossRef]
46. Schütte, G.; Eckerstorfer, M.; Rastelli, V.; Reichenbecher, W.; Restrepo-Vassalli, S.; Ruohonen-Lehto, M.; Saucy, A.-G.W.; Mertens, M. Herbicide resistance and biodiversity: Agronomic and environmental aspects of genetically modified herbicide-resistant plants. *Environ. Sci. Eur.* **2017**, *29*, 5. [CrossRef]
47. Lema, M. Regulatory Assessment of Off-Target Changes and Spurious DNA Insertions in Gene-Edited Organisms for Agri-Food Use. *J. Regul. Sci.* **2021**, *9*, 1. [CrossRef]
48. Tang, L. Base editors beware. *Nat. Methods* **2020**, *17*, 21. [CrossRef]
49. Galonska, C.; Charlton, J.; Mattei, A.L.; Donaghey, J.; Clement, K.; Gu, H.; Mohammad, A.W.; Stamenova, E.K.; Cacchiarelli, D.; Klages, S.; et al. Genome-wide tracking of dCas9-methyltransferase footprints. *Nat. Commun.* **2018**, *9*, 597. [CrossRef]
50. Haut Conseil des Biotechnologies. Scientific Opinion on New Plant Breeding Techniques. Available online: http://www.hautconseildesbiotechnologies.fr/en/avis/avis-sur-nouvelles-techniques-dobtention-plantes-new-plant-breeding-techniques-npbt (accessed on 10 May 2021).
51. Spranger, T.M. *In-Depth Analysis of Various European Directives and Regulations with Regard to Their Potential to Regulate Environmental Effects of New Technologies besides Genetic Engineering Law*; Rheinische Friedrich-Wilhelms-University: Bonn, Germany, 2017; Available online: https://www.bfn.de/fileadmin/BfN/recht/Dokumente/NT_Auffangrechte_RGutachten_Spranger_en.pdf (accessed on 10 May 2021).

BioTech

MDPI

Article

Ethical Challenges in Organoid Use

Vasiliki Mollaki

Hellenic National Bioethics Commission, PC 10674 Athens, Greece; v.mollaki@bioethics.gr

Abstract: Organoids hold great promises for numerous applications in biomedicine and biotechnology. Despite its potential in science, organoid technology poses complex ethical challenges that may hinder any future benefits for patients and society. This study aims to analyze the multifaceted ethical issues raised by organoids and recommend measures that must be taken at various levels to ensure the ethical use and application of this technology. Organoid technology raises several serious ethics issues related to the source of stem cells for organoid creation, informed consent and privacy of cell donors, the moral and legal status of organoids, the potential acquisition of human "characteristics or qualities", use of gene editing, creation of chimeras, organoid transplantation, commercialization and patentability, issues of equity in the resulting treatments, potential misuse and dual use issues and long-term storage in biobanks. Existing guidelines and regulatory frameworks that are applicable to organoids are also discussed. It is concluded that despite the serious ethical challenges posed by organoid use and biobanking, we have a moral obligation to support organoid research and ensure that we do not lose any of the potential benefits that organoids offer. In this direction, a four-step approach is recommended, which includes existing regulations and guidelines, special regulatory provisions that may be needed, public engagement and continuous monitoring of the rapid advancements in the field. This approach may help maximize the biomedical and social benefits of organoid technology and contribute to future governance models in organoid technology.

Keywords: organoids; biobanking; ethics; bioethics; regulation

Citation: Mollaki, V. Ethical Challenges in Organoid Use. *BioTech* **2021**, *10*, 12. https://doi.org/10.3390/biotech10030012

Academic Editor: Maestri Enrico

Received: 13 April 2021
Accepted: 23 June 2021
Published: 28 June 2021

1. Introduction

Organoids are mini organs grown as 3D cell structures in the lab that display architectures and functionalities similar to in vivo organs, derived from Embryonic Stem Cells (ESCs), induced Pluripotent Stem Cells (iPSCs), adult stem cells and tissue-specific progenitors [1]. They have the ability to self-organize, they are multicellular and can be grown indefinitely. Multiple organoid systems have already been developed from both mouse and human stem cells, including taste bud organoids, salivary gland, esophagus, stomach, intestine, colon, liver, pancreatic, prostate, lung, retina, inner ear, kidney, heart, thyroid, skeletal muscle, bone, skin and brain organoids [2,3]. They can exhibit close resemblance to real organs, in terms of architecture and function, and therefore hold substantial opportunities for the investigation of complex human diseases, drug development, regenerative and precision medicine, as well as transplantation.

Despite the promises for science, the technology of organoids poses complex ethical challenges because it involves use of human tissues, production of sensitive personal data, long-term storage in biobanks, as well as the potential for some organoids to obtain human characteristics. Although to date there are no specific guidelines or regulations for organoid use and biobanking, there are several instances where organoids are already being used at the stage of clinical trials [4], demonstrating the quick pace at which this technology moves. As a result, considering the unique near-physiological characteristics of human organoids, a more thorough consideration of the ethical issues posed by organoids is necessary to achieve ethical use and societal acceptance of organoid technology.

This study aims to analyze the multifaceted ethical issues posed by organoids and to identify potential measures that need to be taken at various levels to ensure the ethical use and application of this technology. It is concluded that despite the multifaceted ethical challenges posed by organoid use and biobanking, we have a moral obligation to support and pursue organoid research, in order to make sure that we do not lose any of the potential benefits that organoids offer. A stepwise approach is recommended, which may help maximize the biomedical and social benefits of organoids and contribute to future governance models in organoid technology.

2. The Promises of Organoid Technology

One cannot deny that there are still certain limitations in organoid development and function than we need to overcome. For example, the lack of vascularization and maturation in the developing organoids, the lack of standardization in organoid establishment and quality control, the variability of phenotypes produced and the lack of inter-organ communication are remaining challenges [5]. However, organoid technology holds great potential in clinical translational research.

2.1. Alternatives for Drug Testing in Animals

First, organoids provide complementary approaches to the use of laboratory animals for scientific purposes. In vivo studies screening for novel drug compounds, testing efficacy and toxicity are necessary for drug approval by the competent authorities. Following proper validation as pre-screening systems for novel drugs, in vitro studies in organoids can substantially reduce the number of animals used [6]. Moreover, organoids provide greater experimental flexibility and accessibility compared to vertebrate animal models, allowing for extensive research at a lower cost.

2.2. Disease Modelling

Second, the ability of organoids to mimic human pathologies at the organ level will counteract the lack of appropriate animal disease models, particularly for chronic, infectious or complex diseases, and will facilitate the study of disease mechanisms. Even in cases where appropriate animal models exist, they cannot entirely reflect human physiology. Organoids can bridge this gap in research between animals and humans. They can be used in disease modelling aiming to develop advanced therapies for various human diseases. To name a few, they have already been used as models of genetic conditions such as cystic fibrosis [7], polycystic kidney disease [8] and Zika virus infection [9]. Brain organoids, in particular, have huge potential for modelling neurodevelopmental disorders, such as microcephaly [10], which are either impossible to model in animals or existing animal models are not appropriate.

2.3. Living Biobanks

Third, small tissue biopsies from humans can be used to develop human organoids which can be grown indefinitely. Derived either from healthy volunteers or patients, these organoids can be stored and serve as living biobanks for the study of different pathologies in translational research. Such biobanks do not only provide a source of biological material, but can also provide information on organ physiology and function.

2.4. Precision Medicine

Fourth, human genetic variation may influence the disease onset, symptoms, severity, progression and drug response. Patient-derived organoids provide the means to develop personalized approaches and lead to precision medicine. They can be used to select for appropriate drugs in patients with genetic diseases or cancer, to predict response to drugs and choose better therapeutic options for each individual or groups of individuals. In other words, organoid biobanking can be a valuable resource to identify effective drugs against a broad spectrum of disease phenotypes. If these biobanks manage to cover the range of genetic variance in populations worldwide, they will eventually facilitate the design of powerful drug screening platforms, which will be effective for targeted groups of patients [11].

2.5. Regenerative Medicine

Fifth, organoids derived from healthy individuals can provide the basis for advanced therapies. Organoids comprise an exceptional source of stem cells for cell therapies and tissue engineering products with potential applications in numerous human diseases. A characteristic example is the transplantation of human embryonic stem cell-derived retinal tissue in two primate models of retinal degeneration [12]. Patient-derived organoids can even be combined with in vitro genome modification technologies, such as CRISPR (Clustered Regularly Interspaced Short Palindromic Repeats), to edit genetic mutations causing disease and replace existing pathological tissues. The study by Schwank et al. provided the proof-of-concept by using the CRISPR/Cas9 genome editing system to correct the Cystic Fibrosis Transmembrane Conductor Receptor (*CFTR*) locus by homologous recombination in cultured intestinal stem cells of cystic fibrosis patients, and the corrected allele is expressed and fully functional as measured in clonally expanded organoids [13].

2.6. Models of Organ Development

Sixth, the ability of organoids to self-organize and self-assemble makes these structures an excellent tool to model organ development, a process that cannot be studied in animal models due to interspecies differences [3].

2.7. Transplantation

Finally, organoids could provide an alternative source of organs for transplantation in humans. Although this application may seem remote and less realistic, at least for now, human organoids could potentially play a role in autologous, whole-organ replacement without having to face the challenges of immunocompetency and rejection. For example, the successful reconstitution of 3D nephric tubules and glomeruli, the two main components for kidney functions, from mouse and human PSCs provides insight on how organoid technology could be used in renal replacement strategies [14]. Again, transplantation applications of organoids could be combined with genome editing technologies to provide "healthy", autologous organoids. For instance, the use of the CRISPR/Cas9 system in organoids to correct mutations in the *CFTR* gene causing cystic fibrosis, has also demonstrated that it is possible to use a similar strategy to generate autologous organoids for transplantation in patients [13].

3. Ethical Challenges in Organoid Use

Overall, organoids present with enormous potential for drug screening, disease modelling and therapeutic applications. However, their derivation and their current or future applications, raise a number of ethical issues that are discussed below. Some of the ethical dilemmas posed by organoids are similar to the ones raised by debatable issues existing for decades, such as research in human embryos and use of ESCs or informed consent and privacy of donors whose materials, e.g., cells, are used in existing technologies. Nevertheless, the use and storage of organoids pose additional, novel ethical challenges related to the potential acquisition of human "characteristics or qualities", to their moral and legal status, to the level of acceptable organ maturation for certain applications, whether their creation constitutes life or whether they deserve special protection.

3.1. Source of Stem Cells

Organoids derive from fetal or adult tissues, from ESCs or iPSCs. ESCs are PSCs, possessing a nearly unlimited self-renewal capacity and developmental potential to differentiate into any cell type of the human body. This property allows ESC-derived organoids to serve as outstanding in vitro models for developmental biology. ESCs are isolated from the inner cell mass of in vitro fertilized blastocysts. Nonetheless, their isolation from human embryos, which deals with early forms of human life, creates significant ethical concerns over their use in research, including organoid research. Controversial beliefs can attribute a moral status to the human embryo ranging from that of human organs or tissues to that of a human being [15]. Consequently, the use of ESCs in organoid technology raises major ethical concerns on the value of human life and respect to human dignity.

Of course, this has also legal ramifications, as the human embryo is subject to stringent regulation in most jurisdictions. Under the "gradualist approach" adopted by several jurisdictions, the moral status of the embryo increases during its development as we move from fertilization, to implantation, to primitive streak and nervous system formation (the 14-day limit) and to subsequent developmental stages. Therefore, research on human embryos and consequent use of ESCs in organoids can be ethically acceptable depending on the developmental stage of the embryo, but always under strict conditions of informed consent and appropriate licensing. For example, research in embryos and human ESCs is prohibited in Italy and Germany, whereas the regulatory framework in Greece and Portugal allows for research in surplus embryos only until the 14th day of in vitro development, after informed consent of gamete donors and approval by the competent authorities. In only a few countries, such as the UK and more recently the Netherlands, the in vitro creation of embryos for research purposes is allowed after licensing [16].

Nevertheless, ESC use raises additional concerns over whether there is appropriate informed consent provided by the gamete donors or whether there is potential inducement. An informed consent for research purposes, which may include research for in vitro fertilization and infertility, ESC use, creation of ESC lines or use of ESCs for commercial purposes, may be considered too generic unless it is explicit enough to define the area of research and the potential uses of embryonic tissues. Therefore, a valid informed consent must be explicit enough to define the area of research and the potential uses of embryonic tissues. In the case where embryos are primarily created for research purposes, there are further issues that must be considered. These include health and safety risks for egg donors, as well as the compensation for egg donation, which remains a controversial issue, particularly because it entails the commodification of human body parts.

The development of iPSCs provided a revolutionary alternative approach to the use of ESCs. Through the reprogramming of adult somatic cells, iPSCs exhibit pluripotency comparable to ESCs. Essentially, organoid technology was fired by studies showing that PSCs have the capacity to self-organize into the complex structure of an optic cup [17] and that intestinal organoids can be derived from single adult iPSCs [18]. Subsequent studies continued to demonstrate that adult stem cells can be propagated in various organoids, mimicking real organs.

Although iPSCs may not be a complete alternative of ESCs in organoid technology, they can certainly help avoid the major ethical and legal challenges posed by the use of ESCs. iPSCs can circumvent the destruction of embryos, and set aside the significant issues of potential health risks and compensation for egg donors. They can be collected with minimally invasive or even non-invasive techniques, posing limited health risks to the donors, and most frequently, they are used for personal treatments of the donors themselves. In that sense, whenever science allows it, iPSCs may be preferable to ESCs in organoid technology.

3.2. *Informed Consent of Cell Donors*

The use of iPSCs in organoid technology raises less complex concerns compared to the use of ESCs, which relate mainly to the informed consent of tissue donors. Ethically, informed consent is the ultimate manifestation of respect of an individual's autonomy. Legally, informed consent safeguards individuals' or patients' rights to autonomy and self-determination with diverse legal consequences in different jurisdictions. Nevertheless, whether donors are healthy individuals or patients, the purpose of donating cells for organoid creation can sometimes be unclear. Do they consent to the development of standard therapy? This presupposes that the end product (the therapy) has been previously validated and approved by competent authorities for this specific use. Do they consent to the development of an advanced therapy? This may include unproven therapies, for which limited or no proof on their safety and efficacy has been produced. Do they consent to research in organoid technology? If yes, do they consent to the development of disease models or novel therapies? This encompasses a systematic study which will lead to the documentation and establishment of results. Such questions are very difficult even for researchers to answer and the cell donors find it difficult to process all these possibilities and related information. In any case, a vague purpose of iPSC use for the development of organoids is not acceptable for a real and proper informed consent. The issue of informed consent is further discussed below in the context of organoid biobanking, which can include consent in both clinical and research settings.

3.3. Issues Specific to Embryoids

Studying the early phases of human development is of particular importance for birth defects and teratogenesis, as well as for prevention of implantation failure, pregnancy loss, infertility treatment and assisted reproduction. The main body of knowledge of embryonic development is derived from animal models, which, however, exhibit limitations due to morphological and genetic differences to humans. In vitro fertilization has enabled the study of human embryos, but this is restricted by the 14-day limit post-fertilization and poses serious concerns on the moral status of the embryo, as discussed above for the use of ESCs. Advances in stem cell biology and the use of embryonic and extraembryonic stem cells, including those derived from embryos, have made it feasible to study embryogenesis and embryo development in embryo-like structures called embryoids [19]. Unlike organoids that mimic a specific organ, embryoids model integrated development of the entire conceptus or a part of it, and may in the future have the potential of a full organism. Despite their differences, both organoids and embryoids show properties of self-organization and can be derived from pluripotent or differentiated cells [20]. In addition, they both show resemblance to their in vivo counterparts. Human embryoids exhibit similar morphological and gene expression features to real human embryos, which makes them the only resource to study embryo development beyond the limit of two weeks post-fertilization. In this context, embryoids are examined herein as distinct but similar 3D structures to organoids, which serve as models to investigate human biological processes or developmental diseases.

Although the use of human embryoids may help avoid the concerns of using human embryos, they provoke significant ethical controversy, mainly because some individuals may consider them a form of human life. The matter whether human embryoids could be considered as embryos holds implications for both research and policy. The moral status of these structures is debatable. They are derived from ESCs or iPSCs and they do not constitute zygotes derived from the fertilization of an egg with sperm. As a result, the narrow definition of a human being "from the moment of conception" that some individuals use may not be applicable here. Accordingly, the days post-fertilization cannot be defined and the 14-day limit may not be relevant, either. Hence, the question that arises is whether the 14-day rule could be breached, at least for embryoids derived from iPSCs.

As a consequence, the legal status of these structures is also questionable. To date, there is little explicit regulation of human embryoid research. Depending on the definition of embryos in various jurisdictions, on the occasions that such a definition exists in the national laws, the use of embryoids in research can fall under existing provisions [21]. Hyun et al. make a distinction of different embryo models, depending on whether they attempt to model the integrated development of the entire conceptus, i.e., whether they have the potential to form a full organism or not, which may prove to be useful in future regulation of embryo models [22].

Another important issue to be considered here is that human embryoids derived from iPSCs could be considered by some as cloned embryos, as they are genetically identical to the cell donors, which could be subsequently used for therapeutic or reproductive applications. This will certainly complicate the regulation of embryoid use taking into consideration that worldwide policies on human cloning vary significantly, from permissive to restrictive or a complete lack of a specific policy. This is another reason why it is extremely important to provide a definition of an embryo and distinguish embryo models based on whether they have the potential to form a full organism or not. An equally important issue that is worth consideration is that of human cloning combined with eugenics. In pursuit of "perfection", cloned human embryoids derived from iPSCs genetically modified to carry desired characteristics (physical or cognitive) may be considered by some as morally objectionable, leading to fundamental social inequalities and loss of inter-individual variability.

As technology progresses, cell culture methodologies will be refined and the development of embryoids will better resemble the morphology and development of their in vivo counterparts. At the same time, this will elevate ethical concerns over the conduct of research in embryoids having the full potential to form an organism, and special legal oversight will be necessary. The degree of maturation is particularly relevant for embryoids. To which extend should human embryoids be allowed to mature? The answer to this question will have significant implications on their moral status, the degree of protection that they deserve and the "rights" of embryoids. The more they mature, the more closely they resemble human embryos and this implies that more research restrictions may be applicable. Rules, such as the 14-day limit or the appearance of a primitive streak, may also be applied in the case of such embryoids. The transfer of human embryoids to the uterus (either human or other mammalian) raises even more ethical concerns and may violate existing recommendations to ban human cloning.

3.4. Issues Specific to Brain Organoids

Human brain development and diseases affecting the brain are difficult to study in animal models, mainly due to differences in complexity, physiology and mechanisms between human and other species. In addition, based on moral grounds, the study of human brain in fetuses remains controversial. For the above-mentioned reasons, cerebral or brain organoids are extremely useful to investigate the complex processes of the brain. Various cerebral organoids have already been developed including forebrain, midbrain, hypothalamic and whole-brain organoids [10] exhibiting variable resemblance to their in vivo counterparts.

The main concerns on brain organoids revolve around the fact that these miniature organs constitute neural entities of human origin and whether they could obtain human characteristics, cognitive abilities or be sentient. Although researchers working on brain organoids may not directly aim to develop sentient organoids or organoids with cognitive abilities, this could be a consequence of their original aim to investigate human diseases and develop therapies. Thus, a key question that arises is whether they can exhibit consciousness, feel pain, respond to stimuli or even gain experiences in any way. The possibility that human brain organoids may develop consciousness has major complications. Of course, considering the lack of consensus on what constitutes consciousness, the lack of knowledge and the technical challenges on how to detect consciousness or investigate whether organoids can feel pain, it becomes evident that these issues are difficult to address. Some argue that the evaluation of the possible state of consciousness in brain organoids depends on the theory of consciousness that is adopted [23], while others support that existing tests to assess consciousness in brain-injured non-communicating patients may provide methods to assess consciousness in brain organoids [24]. In any case, the ability of brain organoids to host consciousness or feel pain depends on the degree of development and the maturity at different developmental states.

A portion of researchers argue that scientific knowledge in brain organoids has not yet enabled organoids to interact and respond to stimuli or gain experience, and perhaps such concerns seem premature at present. Nonetheless, future advancements in methodology may allow brain organoids to develop cognitive functions, comparable to the human brain. Already, Muotri and colleagues have developed human cortical organoids, a brain region that controls cognition and interprets sensory information. These cortical organoids exhibited electrical activity, similar to the ones observed in premature babies born at 25–39 weeks post-conception [25]. Although brain organoids may not be mature enough to closely resemble the adult brain, their potential to host cognitive abilities demands strict ethical scrutiny before the technology progresses up to that point.

To date, the degree of maturity that can be eventually reached by a brain organoid remains unknown and this has major implications on the informed consent provided by the cell donors. Uncertainties about the state of consciousness in brain organoids and whether they are able to feel can dispute that informed consent is really true and informed. To stretch this point, could there be any kind of connection between the cell donor and the brain organoid? How could such an issue be reflected in an informed consent?

Whether and to what degree brain organoids can exhibit human characteristics has major implications on the moral status attributed to brain organoids. In the case that brain organoids are eventually found to exhibit even a minimal state of consciousness or found to be the least sentient, they may require special protection. This implies that limitations should be introduced to regulate the relevant research, including their storage, manipulation and destruction. For instance, if in the future it is demonstrated that brain organoids feel pain, then the comparison to animal studies is inevitable, and it will be necessary to impose rules equivalent to the principles of Replacement, Reduction and Refinement (3Rs).

3.5. Issues Specific to Gonadal Organoids

Establishing and characterizing testis and ovarian organoids from human iPSCs is a promising tool in male and female reproductive biology, pathology and toxicology. Indeed, studies have generated testis-like cells [26] and ovaries [27] with the ability to be cultured as an organoid from human iPSCs. Gonadal organoids offer an alternative to experiments that cannot be performed in humans due to ethical or regulatory issues, but their development and use certainly raise novel ethical concerns.

As with other types of organoids, gonadal organoids can serve as a source of cells which could be likely used for in vitro fertilization (IVF). This includes cases where no viable oocytes can be extracted for IVF or cases of cancer where prepubescent girls undergo chemotherapy treatments destroying their oocytes. Although more research is necessary to reach the point that iPSCs can be used to develop gonadal organoids that could provide viable oocytes or sperm, progress in this field may open up new possibilities for infertility in the future. Indeed, this could help overcome the ethical issue of maternity and paternity in cases where infertile people use donated gametes that are genetically different from them. Even so, more complex ethical concerns are raised by the use of gonadal organoids in fertilization. In theory, a gonadal organoid developed by male iPSCs may be used to generate oocytes and vice versa, totally challenging the established religious beliefs or social standards that human reproduction requires a male and a female partner or donor.

The potential of gonadal organoids to be used for reproductive purposes also requires the explicit consent of tissue donors. In analogy to posthumous gamete and embryo use for reproductive purposes, which in many jurisdictions is permitted when written documentation from the deceased allowing the procedure is available, the use of gonadal organoids could be ethically acceptable only in the case that the cell donor has consented to this specific purpose. This issue is extremely sensitive considering that the original consent for the development of the organoid may have been obtained for other purposes, such as research or treatment, not explicitly for reproductive purposes. Informed consent by the cell donor in this case is a moral and legal recognition of the person's autonomy and will certainly require regulatory oversight.

In any case, a consensus should be reached at an international level on whether gonadal organoids could be used for reproductive purposes or whether this should be prohibited. It is important however, to define the scope of such a prohibition. The use of gametes originating form gonadal organoids may be banned for clinical use, i.e., transfer to the uterus after fertilization, but it could be allowed for research purposes to investigate infertility.

3.6. Issues Specific to Multi-Organoid Complexes

The field of organoid research is undeniably advancing, and although not completely mature, scientific and technological developments may allow for connection of multiple human organoids to create multi-organoid complexes. With the advantage of the organ-on-a-chip technology and the use of microfluidics, assembling different organoids to multi-organoid complexes has already been demonstrated. For instance, merging organoid and organ-on-a-chip technology successfully generated complex multi-layer tissue models in a human retina-on-a-chip platform [28]. Skardal et al. also described a three-tissue organ-on-a-chip system, comprised of liver, heart and lung using bioengineered tissue organoids and tissue constructs that are integrated in a closed circulatory perfusion system [29]. Even more importantly, Xiang and colleagues recently established the fusion of two distinct region-specific organoids representing the developing thalamus or cortex, which are critically involved in sensory-motor processing, attention and arousal, and exhibited the feasibility of fusion of disparate regionally specific human brain organoids [30].

Although multi-organoid complexes broaden the horizons for drug testing, drug discovery and personalized medicine [31], these humanized models raise additional concerns and demand moral consideration. As Munsie et al. argue, "the degree of integrated biological functioning in multi-organoid complexes might trigger moral reactions on the appropriateness of creating and experimenting with such familiar, biologically humanized entities" [32]. As demonstrated by Xiang et al., this is of particular importance in cases where a brain organoid is connected with other nerve tissues or in cases where a brain organoid is connected with other organoids [30].

The potentiality of such human organoid complexes to accept and respond to stimuli or to exhibit some kind of autonomous behavior may provoke strong opinions on their human-like moral status, demanding special protection from harm. Consequently, the comparison between using multi-organoid complexes and animals is inevitable here. Multi-organoid complexes that include brain organoids would demand the obligation of researchers to seek alternative methods of experimentation. At least, they would demand the imposition of strict rules for pain minimization, manipulation refinement and appropriate methods of destruction or "sacrifice", just as in animal studies, which would be assessed through in-depth ethics review processes by Research Ethics Committees.

3.7. Gene Editing

Human organoid technology can be used in combination with genome (or gene) editing technologies to either study human diseases or develop novel therapies. Gene editing techniques can be applied to edit genes in ESCs, iPSCs, germ cells, somatic cells or even human embryos and hold great therapeutic potential. The CRISPR system has gained more interest compared to other technologies such as transcription activator-like effector nucleases (TALENs) and zinc-finger nucleases (ZFNs), because it is simpler, more flexible and has a low cost. The proof-of-concept study demonstrated that the CRISPR/Cas9 genome editing system can be used to correct a mutation in the *CFTR* gene in cultured intestinal stem cells of cystic fibrosis patients, and the corrected allele is expressed and fully functional as measured in clonally expanded organoids [13]. This study demonstrated the potential of CRISPR technology combined with patient-derived organoids and their utility as platforms for in vitro research and diagnostics. Since then, new applications of the CRISPR technology in organoids have appeared. CRISPR has been utilized in gut organoids to model cancer and hereditary diseases, in liver, pancreatic or mammary organoids to model cancer and in kidney organoids to model polycystic kidney disease (reviewed in [33,34]).

Furthermore, genome editing technologies offer a significant advantage in representing rare genotypes in organoid development. Donors exhibiting unique or rare genotypes may be extremely valuable in organoid technology, but this creates an enormous ethical pressure for them to donate their cells [35]. Gene-edited organoids with established rare genotypes can help avoid the ethical issue that arises in such cases.

CRISPR-edited patient-derived organoids hold great promise for personalized cell treatments and the replacement of impaired tissue in patients. However, CRISPR/Cas9 is known to be prone to off-target effects, which was also the case in the proof-of-concept study in organoids [13]. Off-target effects can mediate unexpected mutations at different loci, raising concerns on the safety of this genome editing technology, mainly due to its oncogenic potential. This concern is particularly relevant when organoids or cells derived from organoids are intended to be used for in vivo therapeutic applications, where genomic integrity is threatened, generating serious ethical implications. Nevertheless, continuous research has showed that off-target effects can be predicted and protocols can be refined to increase specificity of the CRISPR technology. Additionally, other Cas9 variants or other CRISPR-associated nucleases (Cpf1 and C2c1) have been shown to be highly specific and reduce off-target effects, suggesting that off-target effects will be eventually minimized. Thereupon, what is the level of safety that should be reached to allow the use of gene-edited organoids for clinical use in patients? A suggestion here is to use the existing ethical and legal framework for gene therapy clinical trials. When CRISPR is proved to achieve a safety level analogous to that of gene therapies reaching the clinical trial stage, the next step would be to study gene-edited organoids as potential therapies, in the setting of a robust, first-in-human clinical trial producing accurate evidence on safety.

However, even in the case that an optimum level of safety has been reached for genome editing technologies, it may not be ethically acceptable to alter the human genome. Some argue that editing the human genome in cells subsequently transplanted into humans could mark the beginning of a slippery slope, which will eventually lead to other applications, being gene editing in germ cells and human embryos, human cloning or the creation of human–animal chimeras, and such applications fail to protect the fundamental value of human dignity.

Yet again, we should consider essential differences for certain types of organoids. The special moral status attributed to embryoids and cerebral organoids and the potential use of gonadal organoids in reproduction perhaps allow their genetic manipulation and subsequent use for research purposes but not for clinical applications. A consensus should be reached between researchers on whether the use of CRISPR-edited embryoids, brain and gonadal organoids must be prohibited at the clinical level.

3.8. Creation of Chimeras

Transplantation of human cells in animal models and the subsequent creation of human-animal chimeras has been widely used in certain research fields. For instance, humanized mouse models are being extensively studied in cancer research, without generating massive arguments. In principle, human stem cell transplantation into animals is not distinct from transplanting human organoids into animals, but the latter may create major ethical concerns, mostly due to the fact that the transplanted human mini organs closely resemble their in vivo counterparts.

Before all else, a key question that should be addressed in chimeric research is whether crossing species boundaries is ethically acceptable. For some, this is a violation of human dignity and human nature. Animals have a different moral and legal status from that of human beings, and are consequently treated differently. Animals are neither considered as "things" nor "persons" and do not have rights (at least yet) merely because they cannot fulfill any obligations. Quite the reverse, humans do have an obligation to protect animals and this is inherently recognized by permitting animal experimentation for scientific purposes to obtain new knowledge for the benefit of mankind, but with respect to certain principles for animal welfare, under specific legislation and under strict conditions of licensing by the competent authorities [36]. Accordingly, a primary ethical issue in chimeric research concerns animal welfare and the effects of organoid engraftment in the health of animals. In this respect, depending on the chimeric model and the human organoid used, the extent of maturation is critical and it is crucial to restrict the development of chimeric organisms, e.g., into early life instead of allowing them to reach an advanced age.

As organoid technology progresses, however, the ethical concerns grow to include particularly the use of human brain and gonadal organoids in chimeric research. When human brain organoids are transplanted in animals, this may change the cognitive capabilities of the resulting chimera [37,38]. Considering also the possibility of human brain organoids developing sentience or consciousness (as discussed earlier), such human-animal chimeras are ethically highly problematic. When human gonadal organoids are used in animals, this raises the additional possibility of cross-species fertilization. Following these possibilities for brain and gonadal organoids, the confusion as to the moral status of the chimeric organism and whether it should be treated as a human or an animal is apparent and justifiable. This is of greater concern when larger animal models than mice are used, such as non-human primates, at least due to their morphological similarity to humans.

The use of human organoids in animals probably does not require new legislation, as it falls under existing regulatory frameworks of chimeric research and animal welfare. Many European countries including Greece, Cyprus, Italy and Germany prohibit the creation of human–animal chimeras by law, mainly due to ethical issues that arise by chimeric research and the lack of ability to predict the potential outcomes of such experiments. Such prohibitions are included in existing regulations for medically assisted reproduction and in vitro fertilization.

On the other hand, the creation of human–animal chimeras and even the development of cytoplasmic hybrid embryos for research purposes are permitted in the UK. As organoid technology progresses, legislations in the USA and Europe may need to be revised regarding chimeric research in order to avoid lagging behind in research compared to countries such as China and the UK that allow it. In any case, however, ethical scrutiny is required by the competent Research Ethics Committees reviewing the relevant protocols of organoid transplantation into animals, especially when the resulting chimeric organisms are expected to create confusion over their human or animal nature. Research protocols of human–animal chimeras involving use of human whole organoids should be reviewed on a case-by-case basis, because the potential benefits and risks and the ethical concerns which vary according to the type of organoid must be taken into consideration in each case. It is also important that research involving transplantation of human organoids into animals should be conducted gradually, closely monitoring any changes in the body and behavior of the resulting chimeric organisms at every step.

3.9. Organoid Transplantation

It has been proposed that organoid technology may serve as a source of organs for transplantation, even though most researchers believe this goal is a long way off. Moving from bench to bedside, human organoids could serve an unmet worldwide need: the shortage of grafts for transplantation for replacing damaged tissues or whole organs. Of course, for clinical translation of organoids, certain standards of size, degree of maturity, organoid functionality and safety need to be achieved first. With ongoing research and continuous improvement of organoid technology, some of these obstacles are expected to fade. In a very recent example, Liu et al. managed to scale up mini-organs by using Multi-Organoid Patterning and Fusion, a robust organoid engineering approach to assemble individual airway organoids of different sizes into upscaled, scaffold-free airway tubes with predefined shapes [39], demonstrating that the size of organoids may not be a problem for transplantations in the future.

Hence, before moving from bench to bedside, there is a need to analyze and consider the ethical issues of a first-in-human organoid transplantation trial. Such issues are not new, in the sense that they are common for all first-in-human trials involving a novel therapeutic approach. A first-in-human organoid transplantation trial would pre-require extensive preclinical research in human–animal chimeras showing sufficient evidence for organ engraftment, organ functionality and safety of the transplantation should include a full assessment of potential benefits and risks, a favorable risk–benefit balance that justifies the intervention, selection of participants and appropriate informed consent procedures. A distinction in a first-in-human organoid transplantation trial is the fact that it would require the participation of vulnerable patients in Phase I, who are at late stage of disease and urgently require organ transplantation. Therefore, it contains the risk of the so-called "therapeutic misconception", a phenomenon during which the study participants have no other available therapeutic options and believe that they will be personally benefited therapeutically by the clinical trial rather than they will help to generate knowledge and advance the science for certain diseases [40]. In view of that, the risk of therapeutic misconception must be taken into consideration during the informed consent procedure and ensure that participants in the trial fully understand the true benefits of research.

Some scientists have even raised the question about whether it is ethically acceptable to include children in a first-in-human organoid transplantation clinical trial and under which conditions. Of course, these would be children who suffer from severe conditions that predominantly affect children, such as metabolic diseases [41]. In such cases, additional ethical concerns should be considered including the principle of subsidiarity, which demands that clinical research involving children is only permissible if the clinical study cannot be performed in adults. Such first-in-children clinical trial for liver organoid transplantation could be ethically justified provided that certain guidelines are followed and various safeguards are met [41].

Finally, it is worth noting that organoid transplantation may offer an alternative to xenotransplantation [42]. Xenotransplantation is the transplantation, implantation or infusion of living cells, tissues or whole organs from animals to humans and has been examined as a possible solution to the scarcity of human organ donors, to the illegal trade of organs from living donors and the use of condemned prisoners as donors, which is permitted in some countries. It involves genetic modification of animals (e.g., pigs and non-human primates) so that their organs cause a reduced immune response when transplanted into humans, raising arguments on the welfare of the donor animals. In addition, xenotransplantation encompasses serious safety issues, because of the possibility to transmit infectious agents from animals to human recipients threatening the recipient's health but also public health. Perhaps more importantly, transplanting animal organs into humans raises concerns over whether this changes the human nature of the recipient and whether it violates the integrity of the human species. These issues result in reduced societal acceptability of xenotransplantation. Could organoid transplantation offer a substitute approach that can diminish such ethical concerns? Indeed, organoids are derived from humans, and therefore cannot change our human nature. They can even be derived from the recipient's cells, vanishing the risk of transmitting (animal) diseases and minimizing the risk of organ rejection by the recipient's immune system.

3.10. Commercialization of Organoids

Human tissues and cells hold great commercial significance beyond transplantation and transfusion, and this is well exhibited through their use in organoid technology and its numerous applications in disease modelling and regenerative and precision medicine. Nevertheless, commercialization of human body parts and tissues poses ethical and legal challenges arising from the main question of whether it is possible to have property rights in biological materials extracted from the human body and consequently, whether we can sell them and have a financial gain. Opponents of human body commercialization are in favor of donation in research or therapy as an act of altruism of the donors and solidarity with those in need. In this context, it should be examined whether it is ethically acceptable to commercialize organoids derived from human tissues. On the one hand, if it is not allowed to commercialize organoids, even independently of the tissue donor's will, then the risk of halting or placing obstacles in biomedical research is apparent. On the other hand, if organoids can be "traded" as commodities, then the interests of third parties ultimately have more value that the rights of tissue donors. Of course, property and commercialization concerns do not have a basis in the case of autologous use of human organoids, where the donor and the recipient are the same person who will potentially benefit from such a procedure.

An approach to address this difficult issue is to classify human bodily material as either subject or object, but this may not reflect their true moral value. As discussed earlier, certain types of organoids may deserve special protection due to their "special" moral status. Depending on their maturation, embryoids may closely resemble human embryos, brain organoids may exhibit even a minimal state of consciousness, or multi-organoid complexes may respond to stimuli or exhibit autonomous behavior, and therefore, their moral value is certainly higher compared to, say, kidney or intestine organoids. Accordingly, embryoids, brain organoids and multi-organoid complexes may be considered closer to "subjects" than "objects", but as with animals which are neither considered as "things" nor "persons", human organoids could be something between "subjects" and "objects".

Boers et al. proposed that instead of categorizing human bodily material as either subject or object, organoids should be recognized as hybrids, which are neither human nor non-human, by considering that organoids exhibit: (i) subject-like values since they can relate to the bodily integrity of donors and recipients, to the personal identity and values of donors, to the privacy of donors and they can impact the well-being of donors, and (ii) object-like values, since they constitute biotechnological artefacts, they are a technology and they can serve as instruments to achieve scientific, clinical or commercial aims. They further described a process of legitimizing the commercialization of organoids by a detachment of the instrumental and commercial value of organoids from their associations with persons and their bodies [43]. Indeed, such an approach respects both the moral value of organoids, which stems from their connection to the cell donors and the advantages for science.

According to normative national or European documents and guidelines, the human bodily parts (including not only whole organs but also human tissues) shall not give rise to financial gain. Nevertheless, current practices in Europe and an analysis of normative documents shows that the ban on commercialization of bodily material is not as strict as it may appear at first sight. Some countries have not ratified the relevant conventions or certain European directives and that leaves room for the commercial practice of tissue procurement and transfer [44]. Looking into the future, organoid technology with its enormous potential deserves and should have a clearer regulatory framework on whether the commercialization of human organoids is legitimate or whether it should be prohibited.

3.11. Patentability of Organoids

A relevant point to the commercialization of organoids is whether they should be patentable. Both dilemmas derive from the demand of property or ownership of the produced organoids. Patenting is a system of intellectual property protection designed to reward inventors. Organoids derived from human cells, either embryonic or adult stem cells, are biotechnology products resulting from the application of cell and molecular biology methods to manipulate biological processes, and thus can be deemed as patentable interventions. Indeed, a number of patents have been granted for various organoids or methods to develop organoids in the USA and Japan [45].

On the one hand, a robust patent system is desirable to ensure funding and progress in organoid technology, to encourage research in such beneficial areas that hold great promises in disease modelling and personalized treatments. On the other hand, in some cases, patent protection for biotechnological inventions can be limited for ethical reasons. It can be argued that the principles of beneficence and justice are not served by patent systems because patents lead to increased costs for patients and National Health Systems. At least in the European patent system, certain methods or products may be prohibited if they are contrary to "ordre public" or morality.

Particularly for organoids, once more, the type of organoid produced could play a significant role on whether it is eligible for a patent or not. Due to their special moral value, embryoids and brain organoids could be excluded from patents based on the notion of morality. Brain organoids with their potential to obtain human characteristics, cognitive abilities or to develop sentience may not be patent eligible based on the general prohibition against the patenting of immoral inventions. Likewise, the patentability of embryoids can be challenged due to their potential, particularly for the European patent system. For instance, the decision of the Courts of Justice of the European Union on the case of Oliver Brüstle v Greenpeace, related to neural precursor cells and the processes for their production from embryonic stem cells and their use for therapeutic purposes [46], illustrated that patenting of interventions that require prior destruction of human embryos or their use as base material can be problematic. The Courts of Justice of the European Union subsequently considered that the patent prohibition applies to anything functionally equivalent to an embryo with the "inherent capacity of developing into a human being", and determined that parthenotes which are produced from an unfertilized ovum do not possess that capacity and so are patent eligible [47]. This latest decision may also have implications for the patenting of human embryoids, but considering the progress in this field and that the degree of maturity in various embryoids varies, it is difficult to assess whether embryoids have the "capacity of developing into a human being". As a result, definitions are of major importance here, too, with implications on whether organoids will be patent eligible or not.

3.12. The Cost of Treatments and Issues of Equity

Commercialization and patentability of organoids have major implications on the final cost of the produced treatments. Existing examples of advanced therapies have shown that stem cell therapies may be expensive [48,49], which raises serious ethical concerns over the unequal distribution of effective therapies based on wealth and socioeconomic status. Increased cost means that not all patients in need will have access to expensive personalized treatments, despite the fact that they may be life-saving. On the other hand, iPSCs are relatively easy to obtain, which means that in the future, organoids derived from iPSCs may indeed provide a more affordable option for treatment. Thus, equity is a primary concern since the potential benefits of organoid technology should be distributed evenly.

3.13. Misuse and Dual Use Issues of Organoids

As with most biotechnologies, organoid technology could also be used for malevolent purposes. Rinaldi and Colotti argue that organoids can be used for harmful purposes and bioterrorism. For instance, lung and brain organoids could be used to test the toxicity of new chemical weapons, toxic chemicals or toxins, or to assess the infectivity of biological agents [50]. More than other in vitro cell systems, the knowledge gained through the use of organoids can also be used for military applications. Biobots combining robots and human tissues, such as organoids, are typical examples of items raising dual-use concerns. This is particularly possible for brain organoids connected to a body, such as a robot, not necessarily a human-like robot. Small insect- or amphibian-like robots can provide a "vector" for military applications with even autonomous or semi-autonomous properties.

Such malevolent and dual use applications must be considered at an early stage because, as the technology progresses, certain characteristics or "abilities" of organoids evolve. Raising these ethical issues among researchers is a necessary first step to prevent such applications. Although researchers have benign intentions when they develop and experiment on organoid technology and its applications, this does not mean that the technology or the knowledge gained by it cannot fall in the wrong hands. Special regulations may not be necessary for dual and malevolent use of organoids, but current legislations and ethics standards covering the potential misuse or dual use of biotechnologies can be applicable in organoids, too.

3.14. Organoid Biobanking

Organoid biobanking is extremely important for translational research. Organoid biobanks constitute living biobanks storing viable cells, tissues or even whole mini organs that can play a double role in research (e.g., alternatives for drug testing in animals, disease modeling, models of organ development) and clinical settings (e.g., precision medicine, regenerative medicine, transplantation). Large collections of different types of organoids representing the genetic heterogeneity of healthy individuals or patients with various diseases offer tremendous advantages for the study of human diseases and the development of treatments.

Small or larger collections of patient-derived organoids have already been established, mainly for cancer studies. These biobanks store patient-derived tumor and matching healthy organoids including colorectal cancer, pancreatic ductal adenocarcinoma, breast cancer, prostate cancer and liver cancer organoids, mainly used to test drug sensitivity (reviewed in [51]). Recently, the first pediatric cancer organoid biobank containing tumor and matching normal kidney organoids was also set up, aiming to capture the heterogeneity of pediatric kidney tumors [52]. The potential advantages of organoid technologies have led large, international initiatives, such as the Human Cancer Models Initiative (HCMI) [53], to join forces and generate large biobanks of organoids available for the research community.

Nevertheless, organoid biobanking has ethical implications. Some concerns are old but new ethical issues arise due to the very nature of organoids. At the current stage of organoid biobanking, there are no binding rules, principles or legal norms defining the rights and duties of donors and biobankers. Notably, the ambiguous moral and legal status of organoids further complicates the issue of who owns the cell-derived organoids. Organoids are biological entities that do not clearly fall into the categories of cells, gametes, tissues or organs which are legally regulated under relevant laws. Defining the legal status of organoids, including certain types such as brain organoids, gonadal organoids and embryoids, is the cornerstone for the consent of cell donors and the subsequent uses of organoids (e.g., research, clinical, not-for profit, for-profit). Ultimately, defining the legal status of organoids is a central element in the governance of organoid biobanks.

Commercialization of organoid biobanks raises the issue of fairness and can affect the donors' trust and their willingness to provide their samples [54]. Anonymization of the samples would practically make organoids ownerless but this approach does not allow donors to maintain their right to withdraw consent. The ownership status of organoids becomes even more ambiguous if organoids are modified through gene editing, which means that the final organoid has been produced by means of a technical process, allowing room for patenting. To overcome the issue of ownership, many existing biobanks that store and use human biological materials have agreed to be custodians or trustees. A similar strategy can also be applicable to organoids biobanks. Custodians can act as the organization that actually holds the assets and trustees can act as managers of the assets for the beneficiaries of a trust or other party. The literature also suggests that the idea of treating participants more like "partners" rather than passive tissue "donors" makes biobank governance more ethically responsible and fair, particularly in the context of living organoids derived from stem cells of donors [54].

Organoid biobanking demands proper informed consent strategies for both research and clinical purposes. Similarly to biobanking of human cells and tissues, different consent approaches can be followed in organoid biobanking: (a) a blanket consent without any limitations, (b) a broad consent with some restrictions, (c) a tiered consent for certain areas (e.g., cancer), or for specific diseases (e.g., breast cancer), or (d) a continuous consent, which requires re-consent for new uses or purposes. There is no consensus on the most suitable type of consent for organoid biobanking. As in many other cases, a continuous consent would be impractical and requires an investment of time and resources that impedes the accomplishment of biobanks' aims. On the one hand, the more specific a consent is, the more control is given to donors over their donation. On the other hand, in order to prevent losing potential social benefits from the use of organoids, a broad consent may be a better option in organoid biobanking, as long as donors are provided with sufficient information to make a reasonably informed decision.

However, donors may have specific concerns, as in the case that the biobank is commercial or for-profit. Therefore, a significant point which must not be missed in the informed consent is whether the cell donor is informed about the prospect of commercialization of organoids, and whether he/she agrees to it. Objections may also arise based on the type of organoid that is biobanked. For brain organoids or embryoids, donors may feel more attached to them compared to other organoids. Opt-out options should be available in such cases, providing donors the opportunity to object to certain uses or purposes (e.g., object to use after the donor's death, non-therapeutic uses, commercial purposes), according to their personal values and beliefs. In any case, the consent procedure is and should remain central in the governance of organoids biobanks, to ensure voluntary and well-informed donation of samples.

In biobanking, donors provide their consent (whether broad or specific) based on the condition that their privacy and personal data are protected by de-identification of the samples. Perhaps one of the major harm risks in biobanking is associated with breaking privacy of donors. One approach to de-identification is anonymization of samples. This may be applicable for organoid biobanks for research purposes only, in which case the return of results to donors may not be necessary. Nevertheless, one should not overlook the skepticism that true anonymization of genetic data may not be feasible, due to their very nature. Some believe that the availability of DNA sequencing technology can make it difficult to maintain anonymization without previous agreements to not pursue identification via next-generation sequencing.

However, for evident reasons, anonymization is unsuitable for biobanks that eventually use organoids for clinical applications, such as personalized treatments, precision medicine and transplantation, as none of these therapeutic approaches are feasible without knowing the donor's identity. The decision of patients to donate their stem cells for organoid biobanking partly depends on the possibility of them being cured from severe diseases for which no other effective treatments exist. Thus, anonymization is not deemed appropriate in this case.

What we also need to take into consideration is the fact that organoids are accompanied by genetic data, which are sensitive personal data and demand robust measures of data protection, particularly for organoids stored long-term and used many years after the original stem cell donation. Again, this issue must be addressed during the informed consent procedure. At the same time, bankers and investigators are legally and ethically obligated to protect sensitive data of donors. They are required to take appropriate measures to minimize the risk of unauthorized third parties obtaining access to health and genetic data. Finally, the unclear legal status of organoids and the ambiguous ownership status also have implications on the ownership of the genotypic or phenotypic data produced in organoid studies, and this deserves close consideration.

When some of these organoid applications move from research to clinical uses, e.g., the production of personalized treatments, further considerations must be taken into account. The clinical validation of organoids must precede and subsequently, possible risks and benefits of the treatment, of alternative treatments and of refusing the treatment must also be considered. As a matter of fact, every research activity or clinical application does involve a certain level of risk for participants or patients. As with human cell and tissue biobanking, a key issue is that the potential risks to cells donors are disproportionate to the overall benefits of organoids biobanking. Obviously, this does not lift the obligation of bankers and researchers to take every possible measure to protect donors from such risks. In any case, the long-term storage and use of "live" organoids demands meticulous, continuous ethics review and oversight by independent ethics bodies. Members of these Ethics Bodies should have a high level of expertise in ethics, law, organoid technology and biobanking, and of course, representatives of donors or patients should also participate.

Finally, let us not forget the lessons learnt from the past regarding human biological material biobanks. What will the fate of organoids be upon unexpected or planned closure of a biobank? In this respect, a strategy must be in place in each biobank to handle the organoids according to the relevant legislation but also according to the donor's informed consent. This, of course, requires that the possibility of closure of the biobank has been taken into consideration during the informed consent procedure. Instead of losing the benefits from previous work on organoids, perhaps the best plan in case of closure is to ensure that stored organoids are preserved by transferring the biobank's resources to another entity [55]. In addition, the organization level of organoid biobanks will play a key role in their sustainability, but also in the quality of services provided. To protect and ensure a high quality of research and services, organoid biobanks should implement standard operating procedures, quality assurance and quality control programs. In order to achieve consistency in their practices, organoid biobanks should also obtain accreditation, which requires previous dedication of staff and resources. This is particularly important as organoid biobanking is expected to increase in the near to mid-term future.

4. Concluding Remarks

Organoid technology holds great promises as alternatives for animal experiments, disease modeling, regenerative medicine, precision medicine and transplantation. However, this technology raises complex ethical issues related to the moral and legal status of organoids, informed consent and privacy of donors, property rights and governance of biobanks, in both research and clinical settings. A special moral status can be attributed to certain types of organoids, such as brain and gonadal organoids, creating debates amongst scientists and members of society on whether they demand special protection compared to other organoids. In the present manuscript, the ethical challenges posed by organoid technology have been analyzed and specific recommendations on ethical and regulatory oversight have been offered.

In view of the fact that up to this moment, there are no specific regulations or guidelines for organoid use in research and clinical care, a general combined approach should be followed to achieve ethical use of organoid technology. The first step would be to examine if existing ethics review processes, guidelines and regulatory frameworks are also applicable to organoids. To the degree that organoids show similarities with hESCs or iPSCs, their use can be examined through existing guidelines of the International Society for Stem Cell Research (ISSCR) for both stem cell research and clinical translation [56], which could be adapted if necessary. For organoids used for the development of novel therapies, the standard approaches to ethics oversight in gene therapy and the relevant legislation may also be applicable. Likewise, for long term storage of organoids in biobanks, existing oversight mechanisms in human biological material and DNA biobanking could be extended to ensure ethically sound strategies for organoid biobanking.

Even so, some of the ethical challenges posed by organoids are not specifically addressed. Therefore, a second step is required to ensure ethical use of organoids. This is to examine whether specific types of organoids or specific applications demand special regulatory provisions. This certainly includes the case of brain organoids and embryoids, which may have an increased moral status. For instance, existing legislations in various jurisdictions regulating in vitro fertilization and embryo research may not be appropriate for embryoids that are not a product of egg fertilization. In such cases, specific regulatory frameworks will promote and support ethical organoid research or applications in clinical care.

A third complementary step would be essential to ensure societal acceptance of organoid use and participation in relevant research. This is to engage the public and promote a dialogue between science and civil society on the ethical issues around organoids including informed consent and privacy, and experimenting with human brain tissues and embryo-like tissues. Public engagement will also help minimize public confusion and misinterpretations of using "mini-organs in a dish" and at the same time will avoid promises of organoid technology that cannot be confirmed. Of course, this needs to be combined with appropriate public (media) communication to avoid hyperboles and excessive expectations of organoid use.

A final, equally important step to ensure ethical oversight and ethical use of organoids would be to continuously monitor the rapid advancements of this technology. This is particularly important as organoid research moves into clinical trials to ensure that any new ethics issues or any changes in the complexity of existing issues will be taken into consideration.

This four-step approach will help maximize the biomedical and social benefits of organoid technology. Despite the multifaceted and complex ethical challenges posed by organoid use and biobanking, we have a moral obligation to make sure that we do not lose any of the potential benefits through careful considerations, ethical and legal oversight.

Funding: This research received no external funding.

Institutional Review Board Statement: Not applicable.

Informed Consent Statement: Not applicable.

Conflicts of Interest: The author declares no conflict of interest.

References

1. Bartfeld, S.; Clevers, H. Stem cell-derived organoids and their application for medical research and patient treatment. *J. Mol. Med.* **2017**, *95*, 729–738. [CrossRef] [PubMed]
2. Fatehullah, A.; Tan, S.H.; Barker, N. Organoids as an in vitro model of human development and disease. *Nat. Cell Biol.* **2016**, *18*, 246–254. [CrossRef]
3. Lancaster, M.A.; Juergen, A.; Knoblich, J.A. Organogenesis in a dish: Modeling development and disease using organoid technologies. *Science* **2014**, *345*, 1247125. [CrossRef]
4. ClinicalTrials.gov. Available online: https://clinicaltrials.gov/ct2/results?cond=&term=organoid&cntry=&state=&city=&dist (accessed on 27 January 2021).
5. Kim, J.; Koo, B.-K.; Knoblich, J.A. Human organoids: Model systems for human biology and medicine. *Nat. Rev. Mol. Cell Biol.* **2020**, *21*, 571–584. [CrossRef] [PubMed]
6. Marx, U.; Akabane, T.; Andersson, T.B.; Baker, E.; Beilmann, M.; Beken, S.; Brendler-Schwaab, S.; Cirit, M.; David, R.; Dehne, E.M.; et al. Biology-inspired microphysiological systems to advance patient benefit and animal welfare in drug development. *ALTEX* **2020**, *37*, 365–394.
7. Dekkers, J.F.; Wiegerinck, C.L.; De Jonge, H.R.; Bronsveld, I.; Janssens, H.M.; Groot, K.M.D.W.-D.; Brandsma, A.M.; de Jong, N.; Bijvelds, M.J.C.; Scholte, B.J.; et al. A functional CFTR assay using primary cystic fibrosis intestinal organoids. *Nat. Med.* **2013**, *19*, 939–945. [CrossRef]
8. Xia, Y.; Nivet, E.; Sancho-Martinez, I.; Gallegos, T.F.; Suzuki, K.; Okamura, D.; Wu, M.-Z.; Dubova, I.; Esteban, C.R.; Montserrat, N.; et al. Directed differentiation of human pluripotent cells to ureteric bud kidney progenitor-like cells. *Nat. Cell Biol.* **2013**, *15*, 1507–1515. [CrossRef]
9. Dang, J.; Tiwari, S.K.; Lichinchi, G.; Qin, Y.; Patil, V.S.; Eroshkin, A.M.; Rana, T.M. Zika Virus Depletes Neural Progenitors in Human Cerebral Organoids through Activation of the Innate Immune Receptor TLR3. *Cell Stem Cell* **2016**, *19*, 258–265. [CrossRef]
10. Lancaster, M.A.; Renner, M.; Martin, C.A.; Wenzel, D.; Bicknell, L.S.; Hurles, M.E.; Homfray, T.; Penninger, J.M.; Jackson, A.P.; Knoblich, J.A. Cerebral organoids model human brain development and microcephaly. *Nature* **2013**, *501*, 373–379. [CrossRef]
11. Rossi, G.; Manfrin, A.; Lutolf, M.P. Progress and potential in organoid research. *Nat. Rev. Genet.* **2018**, *19*, 671–687. [CrossRef] [PubMed]
12. Shirai, H.; Mandai, M.; Matsushita, K.; Kuwahara, A.; Yonemura, S.; Nakano, T.; Assawachananont, J.; Kimura, T.; Saito, K.; Terasaki, H.; et al. Transplantation of human embryonic stem cell-derived retinal tissue in two primate models of retinal degeneration. *Proc. Natl. Acad. Sci. USA* **2016**, *113*, E81–E90. [CrossRef]
13. Schwank, G.; Koo, B.-K.; Sasselli, V.; Dekkers, J.F.; Heo, I.; Demircan, T.; Sasaki, N.; Boymans, S.; Cuppen, E.; van der Ent, C.K.; et al. Functional Repair of CFTR by CRISPR/Cas9 in Intestinal Stem Cell Organoids of Cystic Fibrosis Patients. *Cell Stem Cell* **2013**, *13*, 653–658. [CrossRef]
14. Taguchi, A.; Kaku, Y.; Ohmori, T.; Sharmin, S.; Ogawa, M.; Sasaki, H.; Nishinakamura, R. Redefining the In Vivo Origin of Metanephric Nephron Progenitors Enables Generation of Complex Kidney Structures from Pluripotent Stem Cells. *Cell Stem Cell* **2014**, *14*, 53–67. [CrossRef]
15. Brown, M.T. The Moral Status of the Human Embryo. *J. Med. Philos.* **2018**, *43*, 132–158. [CrossRef] [PubMed]
16. Matthews, K.R.; Moralí, D. National human embryo and embryoid research policies: A survey of 22 top research-intensive countries. *Regen. Med.* **2020**, *15*, 1905–1917. [CrossRef]

17. Eiraku, M.; Takata, N.; Ishibashi, H.; Kawada, M.; Sakakura, E.; Okuda, S.; Sekiguchi, K.; Adachi, T.; Sasai, Y. Self-organizing optic-cup morphogenesis in three-dimensional culture. *Nature* **2011**, *472*, 51–56. [CrossRef]
18. Sato, T.; Vries, R.G.; Snippert, H.J.; Van De Wetering, M.; Barker, N.; Stange, D.E.; Van Es, J.H.; Abo, A.; Kujala, P.; Peters, P.J.; et al. Single Lgr5 stem cells build crypt-villus structures in vitro without a mesenchymal niche. *Nature* **2009**, *459*, 262–265. [CrossRef]
19. Denker, H.-W. Self-Organization of Stem Cell Colonies and of Early Mammalian Embryos: Recent Experiments Shed New Light on the Role of Autonomy vs. External Instructions in Basic Body Plan Development. *Cells* **2016**, *5*, 39. [CrossRef]
20. Simunovic, M.; Brivanlou, A.H. Embryoids, organoids and gastruloids: New approaches to understanding embryogenesis. *Development* **2017**, *144*, 976–985. [CrossRef] [PubMed]
21. Pera, M.F.; De Wert, G.; Dondorp, W.; Lovell-Badge, R.; Mummery, C.; Munsie, M.; Tam, P.P. What if stem cells turn into embryos in a dish? *Nat. Methods* **2015**, *12*, 917–919. [CrossRef] [PubMed]
22. Hyun, I.; Munsie, M.; Pera, M.F.; Rivron, N.C.; Rossant, J. Toward Guidelines for Research on Human Embryo Models Formed from Stem Cells. *Stem Cell Rep.* **2020**, *14*, 169–174. [CrossRef] [PubMed]
23. Lavazza, A. Human cerebral organoids and consciousness: A double-edged sword. *Monash Bioeth. Rev.* **2020**, *38*, 105–128. [CrossRef] [PubMed]
24. Lavazza, A.; Massimini, M. Cerebral organoids: Ethical issues and consciousness assessment. *J. Med. Ethic* **2018**, *44*, 606–610. [CrossRef]
25. Trujillo, C.A.; Gao, R.; Negraes, P.D.; Gu, J.; Buchanan, J.; Preissl, S.; Wang, A.; Wu, W.; Haddad, G.G.; Chaim, I.A.; et al. Complex Oscillatory Waves Emerging from Cortical Organoids Model Early Human Brain Network Development. *Cell Stem Cell* **2019**, *25*, 558–569.e7. [CrossRef] [PubMed]
26. Sakib, S.; Voigt, A.; Goldsmith, T.; Dobrinski, I. Three-dimensional testicular organoids as novel in vitro models of testicular biology and toxicology. *Environ. Epigenet.* **2019**, *5*, dvz011. [CrossRef]
27. Heidari-Khoei, H.; Esfandiari, F.; Hajari, M.A.; Ghorbaninejad, Z.; Piryaei, A.; Baharvand, H. Organoid technology in female reproductive biomedicine. *Reprod. Biol. Endocrinol.* **2020**, *18*, 64. [CrossRef]
28. Achberger, K.; Probst, C.; Haderspeck, J.; Bolz, S.; Rogal, J.; Chuchuy, J.; Nikolova, M.; Cora, V.; Antkowiak, L.; Haq, W.; et al. Merging organoid and organ-on-a-chip technology to generate complex multi-layer tissue models in a human retina-on-a-chip platform. *eLife* **2019**, *8*, e46188. [CrossRef]
29. Skardal, A.; Murphy, S.V.; Devarasetty, M.; Mead, I.; Kang, H.-W.; Seol, Y.-J.; Zhang, Y.S.; Shin, S.-R.; Zhao, L.; Aleman, J.; et al. Multi-tissue interactions in an integrated three-tissue organ-on-a-chip platform. *Sci. Rep.* **2017**, *7*, 8837. [CrossRef]
30. Xiang, Y.; Tanaka, Y.; Cakir, B.; Patterson, B.; Kim, K.-Y.; Sun, P.; Kang, Y.-J.; Zhong, M.; Liu, X.; Patra, P.; et al. hESC-Derived Thalamic Organoids Form Reciprocal Projections When Fused with Cortical Organoids. *Cell Stem Cell* **2019**, *24*, 487–497.e7. [CrossRef]
31. Miranda, C.C.; Fernandes, T.G.; Diogo, M.M.; Cabral, J.M.S. Towards Multi-Organoid Systems for Drug Screening Applications. *Bioeineering* **2018**, *5*, 49. [CrossRef]
32. Munsie, M.; Hyun, I.; Sugarman, J. Ethical issues in human organoid and gastruloid research. *Development* **2017**, *144*, 942–945. [CrossRef]
33. Driehuis, E.; Clevers, H. CRISPR/Cas 9 genome editing and its applications in organoids. *Am. J. Physiol. Liver Physiol.* **2017**, *312*, G257–G265. [CrossRef] [PubMed]
34. Hendriks, D.; Clevers, H.; Artegiani, B. CRISPR-Cas Tools and Their Application in Genetic Engineering of Human Stem Cells and Organoids. *Cell Stem Cell* **2020**, *27*, 705–731. [CrossRef]
35. Lavazza, A. What (or sometimes who) are organoids? And whose are they? *J. Med. Ethic* **2018**, *45*, 144–145. [CrossRef]
36. The European Parliament and the Council of the European Union. Directive 2010/63/EU of the European Parliament and of the Council of 22 September 2010 on the Protection of Animals Used for Scientific Purposes. *Off. J. Eur. Union* **2010**, *276*, 33–79. Available online: https://eur-lex.europa.eu/LexUriServ/LexUriServ.do?uri=OJ:L:2010:276:0033:0079:EN:PDF (accessed on 8 April 2021).
37. Mansour, A.A.; Gonçalves, J.T.; Bloyd, C.W.; Li, H.; Fernandes, S.; Quang, D.; Johnston, S.; Parylak, S.L.; Jin, X.; Gage, F.H. An in vivo model of functional and vascularized human brain organoids. *Nat. Biotechnol.* **2018**, *36*, 432–441. [CrossRef] [PubMed]
38. Han, X.; Chen, M.; Wang, F.; Windrem, M.; Wang, S.; Shanz, S.; Xu, Q.; Oberheim, N.A.; Bekar, L.; Betstadt, S.; et al. Forebrain Engraftment by Human Glial Progenitor Cells Enhances Synaptic Plasticity and Learning in Adult Mice. *Cell Stem Cell* **2013**, *12*, 342–353. [CrossRef]
39. Liu, Y.; Dabrowska, C.; Mavousian, A.; Strauss, B.; Meng, F.; Mazzaglia, C.; Ouaras, K.; Macintosh, C.; Terentjev, E.; Lee, J.; et al. Bio-assembling Macro-Scale, Lumenized Airway Tubes of Defined Shape via Multi-Organoid Patterning and Fusion. *Adv. Sci.* **2021**, *8*, 2003332. [CrossRef]
40. E Henderson, G.; Churchill, L.R.; Davis, A.M.; Easter, M.M.; Grady, C.; Joffe, S.; Kass, N.; King, N.M.P.; Lidz, C.W.; Miller, F.G.; et al. Clinical Trials and Medical Care: Defining the Therapeutic Misconception. *PLoS Med.* **2007**, *4*, e324. [CrossRef] [PubMed]
41. Schneemann, S.A.; Boers, S.N.; Van Delden, J.J.M.; Nieuwenhuis, E.E.S.; Fuchs, S.A.; Bredenoord, A.L. Ethical challenges for pediatric liver organoid transplantation. *Sci. Transl. Med.* **2020**, *12*, eaau8471. [CrossRef]
42. Loike, J.D.; Pollack, R. Develop Organoids; Not Chimeras; for Transplantation. *The Scientist*. Available online: https://www.the-scientist.com/news-opinion/opinion--develop-organoids--not-chimeras--for-transplantation-66339 (accessed on 18 March 2021).

43. Boers, S.N.; Van Delden, J.J.M.; Bredenoord, A.L. Organoids as hybrids: Ethical implications for the exchange of human tissues. *J. Med. Ethic* **2019**, *45*, 131–139. [CrossRef]
44. Lenk, C.; Beier, K. Is the commercialisation of human tissue and body material forbidden in the countries of the European Union? *J. Med. Ethic* **2012**, *38*, 342–346. [CrossRef] [PubMed]
45. Smadar, C.; Dvir-Ginzberg, M. Recent patents in organoids. *Nat. Biotechnol.* **2016**, *34*, 619. [CrossRef]
46. CURIA, Judgment of the Court (Grand Chamber) of 18 October 2011. Oliver Brüstle v Greenpeace eV. The Courts of Justice of the European Union. Available online: https://curia.europa.eu/juris/liste.jsf?language=en&num=C-34/10 (accessed on 24 March 2021).
47. CURIA, Judgment of the Court (Grand Chamber) of 18 December 2014. The Courts of Justice of the European Union. Available online: https://curia.europa.eu/juris/document/document.jsf?docid=160936&text=&dir=&doclang=EN&part=1&occ=first&mode=lst&pageIndex=0&cid=176842 (accessed on 24 March 2021).
48. Gonçalves, E. Advanced therapy medicinal products: Value judgement and ethical evaluation in health technology assessment. *Eur. J. Health Econ.* **2020**, *21*, 311–320. [CrossRef] [PubMed]
49. Huang, C.-Y.; Liu, C.-L.; Ting, C.-Y.; Chiu, Y.-T.; Cheng, Y.-C.; Nicholson, M.W.; Hsieh, P.C.H. Human iPSC banking: Barriers and opportunities. *J. Biomed. Sci.* **2019**, *26*, 87. [CrossRef]
50. Rinaldi, T.; Colotti, G. Use of organoids in medicinal chemistry: Challenges on ethics and biosecurity. *Future Med. Chem.* **2019**, *11*, 1087–1090. [CrossRef] [PubMed]
51. Drost, J.; Clevers, H. Organoids in cancer research. *Nat. Rev. Cancer* **2018**, *18*, 407–418. [CrossRef]
52. Calandrini, C.; Schutgens, F.; Oka, R.; Margaritis, T.; Candelli, T.; Mathijsen, L.; Ammerlaan, C.; Van Ineveld, R.L.; Derakhshan, S.; De Haan, S.; et al. An organoid biobank for childhood kidney cancers that captures disease and tissue heterogeneity. *Nat. Commun.* **2020**, *11*, 1310. [CrossRef]
53. Human Cancer Models Initiative. Available online: https://ocg.cancer.gov/programs/HCMI (accessed on 29 March 2021).
54. Lensink, M.A.; Boers, S.N.; Jongsma, K.R.; Carter, S.E.; van der Ent, C.K.; Bredenoord, A.L. Organoids for personalized treatment of Cystic Fibrosis: Professional perspectives on the ethics and governance of organoid biobanking. *J. Cyst. Fibros.* **2021**, *20*, 443–451. [CrossRef]
55. Organisation for Economic Co-Operation and Development. Guidelines on Human Biobanks and Genetic Research Database 2009. Available online: http://www.oecd.org/sti/emerging-tech/guidelines-for-human-biobanks-and-genetic-research-databases.htm (accessed on 8 April 2021).
56. Daley, G.Q.; Hyun, I.; Apperley, J.F.; Barker, R.A.; Benvenisty, N.; Bredenoord, A.L.; Breuer, C.K.; Caulfield, T.; Cedars, M.I.; Frey-Vasconcells, J.; et al. Setting Global Standards for Stem Cell Research and Clinical Translation: The 2016 ISSCR Guidelines. *Stem Cell Rep.* **2016**, *6*, 787–797. [CrossRef]

BioTech

Article

Public Perceptions Regarding Genomic Technologies Applied to Breeding Farm Animals: A Qualitative Study

Francis Z. Naab [1], David Coles [1,2], Ellen Goddard [3] and Lynn J. Frewer [1,*]

1 School of Natural and Environmental Sciences, Newcastle University, Newcastle upon Tyne NE1 7RU, UK; francis.naab@bristol.ac.uk (F.Z.N.); david.coles@hazyrays.com (D.C.)
2 Enhance International, The Bacchus, Elsdon, Newcastle upon Tyne NE19 1AA, UK
3 Agricultural Marketing and Business, Faculty of Agricultural, Life and Environmental Sciences, 515 General Services Building, University of Alberta, Edmonton, AB T6G 2H1, Canada; egoddard@ualberta.ca
* Correspondence: lynn.frewer@newcastle.ac.uk; Tel.: +44-(0)7553152743

Abstract: The societal acceptability of different applications of genomic technologies to animal production systems will determine whether their innovation trajectories will reach the commercialisation stage. Importantly, technological implementation and commercialisation trajectories, regulation, and policy development need to take account of public priorities and attitudes. More effective co-production practices will ensure the application of genomic technologies to animals aligns with public priorities and are acceptable to society. Consumer rejection of, and limited demand for, animal products developed using novel genomic technologies will determine whether they are integration into the food system. However, little is known about whether genomic technologies that accelerate breeding but do not introduce cross-species genetic changes are more acceptable to consumers than those that do. Five focus groups, held in the north east of England, were used to explore the perceptions of, and attitudes towards, the use of genomic technologies in breeding farm animals for the human food supply chain. Overall, study participants were more positive towards genomic technologies applied to promote animal welfare (e.g., improved disease resistance), environmental sustainability, and human health. Animal "disenhancement" was viewed negatively and increased food production alone was not perceived as a potential benefit. In comparison to gene editing, research participants were most negative about genetic modification and the application of gene drives, independent of the benefits delivered.

Keywords: breeding; ethics; farm animals; focus groups; genomics; public attitudes

Citation: Naab, F.Z.; Coles, D.; Goddard, E.; Frewer, L.J. Public Perceptions Regarding Genomic Technologies Applied to Breeding Farm Animals: A Qualitative Study. *BioTech* **2021**, *10*, 28. https://doi.org/10.3390/biotech10040028

Academic Editor: Maestri Enrico

Received: 8 April 2021
Accepted: 1 December 2021
Published: 3 December 2021

1. Introduction

Much of the world population is still dependent on animals as a source of protein [1]. Increasing demand is a consequence of increased populations, incomes, and urbanisation in both low- and high-resource countries [2]. At the same time, there is increasing societal concern about ethical issues associated with animal welfare standards [3], such as, for example, intensive production systems [4] and the application of novel technologies to enhance animal production [5]. As a result, there has been a considerable focus within scientific and policy communities on the application of novel genomic technologies to improve animal production systems and disease resistance in livestock [6], including *inter alia* genetic modification [5], gene editing, such as CRISPR-Cas9 [7], and the prospective application of synthetic biology [8]. At the same time, there is a body of evidence to suggest that public acceptance of the application of genomic technologies to animal production systems is nuanced by the type of genomic technology being applied (e.g., genetic modification versus gene editing), the intended outcome of the modification (e.g., improved animal welfare or increased profitability), and the target organisms used in the modification (e.g., mammals, birds, or fish) [9]. Differences in public attitudes toward applying gene editing to agricultural crops have been observed when compared to genetic modification, and conventional breeding technologies are applied to meet the same objectives. Kato-Nitta et al. [10] report that participants in their survey tended to have more favourable attitudes toward gene editing than toward genetic modification when applied to crops. Attitudes toward the use of gene editing in plant breeding appear less firmly entrenched than for genetic modification [11,12]. It is notable that some applications of gene editing are more acceptable than others. Yunes et al. [13] report, in a quantitative study of gene editing applied to cattle, low public acceptance overall. In cases where support was given, it was highly dependent on the type and purpose of the application proposed. Similarly, Busch et al. [14] indicate that their participants evaluated the application of gene editing to promote disease resistance in humans most positively, followed by disease resistance in plants, and then in animals, but considered changes in product quality and quantity in cattle as the most negative outcome of gene editing.

The aim of the research presented here is to understand public perceptions of the use of different genomic technologies in breeding farm animals used in food production, including ethical concerns linked to different technological outcomes. An extensive body of literature regarding public perceptions and other socio-economic aspects of genetically modified animals or other genomic technologies such as cloning applied to food production and other areas of application is available (see, inter alia [15–17]), although less research has been conducted in relation to gene-edited animals. It has been established that the way people perceive new (food) technologies, for example, in relation to potential risks and benefits, determines whether they accept the development and implementation [18]. Risk perception refers to people's subjective judgments about the likelihood of negative occurrences, such as negative impacts on animal health or the environment, and is important in health and risk communication because it determines which hazards people care about and how they deal with them [19]. This includes communication about buying products produced using genomic technologies [20]. Risk perception is important to policy makers as the public may reject technologies that they perceive to be risky or unethical, independent of technical risk assessments provided by experts. It is important to note that research into risk perception reflects an objective analysis of public or consumer attitudes (Nuffield Council of Bioethics (2021) Genome editing and farmed animal breeding: social and ethical issues. NCOB, London, UK).

Advances in biotechnology have given rise to novel approaches to breeding farmed animals for human consumption. This includes, for example, breeding disease-resistant, healthier, and more productive animals (e.g., the case of CRISPR-Cas9 in pigs [21–23]), animal production systems with reduced environmental impacts, for example, in relation to greenhouse gas emissions [24], and producing animals more amenable to being managed in existing animal husbandry systems [25]. It is important to understand how citizens perceive the application of different genomic technologies in animal production systems, as they are unlikely to be adopted if there is societal opposition to their application, which is frequently underpinned by moral concerns [26]. Public acceptance may be linked to both the acceptability of the specific biotechnological process applied in the process of modification [9] and the developers' reason for applying it. For example, public concerns about the acceptability of animal products have focused on different issues, such as animal welfare [27,28] and environmental and human health concerns [29,30].

The evolving legislative framework, the potential impact of public perceptions of risk, benefit, and ethical concern on this framework [31], and the extent to which consumer perceptions have contributed to the European Union's regulations regarding genetic modification within animal production systems clearly indicate [20] that consumer acceptability has to be taken into account.

However, differences in perceptions and attitudes need to be assessed in relation to different types of genomic application. Variations in legislative frameworks between diverse regions also exist. For example, within Europe, CRISPR-Cas9 technology is regulated in the same way as genetic modification (GM) [32], whereas in the US the resultant product is not considered GM. Hence, there exists a fundamental difference in approach where the US focus is on the ultimate "product", while the EU focus is on the "process" [33].

Perceptions of, and Attitudes towards, Genomic Technologies Applied to Agriculture

While there is an extensive body of literature on public perceptions of and attitudes towards the genetic modification of plants, and to some extent to animals and micro-organisms, other areas of genomic science applied to food production, for example, using animals, have not been so extensively researched. However, there is some evidence that public attitudes to gene drives used in agriculture are, as for genetic modification, nuanced by moral concerns and associated attitudes [34]. Similar findings have been reported for agricultural applications of gene editing [35]. Generally, the focus of this body of research has tended to be on understanding public attitudes to biotechnological methods applied to plants. There is little research conducted in relation to some comparator technologies, for example, accelerated animal breeding, although there is some evidence that the public associate the latter with genetic modification [36].

The focus groups methodology was applied in order to (1) explore the attitudes of UK citizens towards some genomic technologies; (2) discuss and consider ethical dilemmas that may occur as a result of the use of genomic technologies in animal production systems.

2. Materials and Methods

Following ethical approval for the research (Newcastle University Ethics Committee, approval number 7235/2018), focus group discussions were used to initiate discourses between participants, allowing the researcher to decipher and moderate the divergent opinions [37]. Five (5) focus group discussions were organised, with 6–12 individuals in each group discussion. In total, 38 respondents participated, and the discussions took place between November and December 2018. Four focus group discussions were conducted in the city of Newcastle, and the fifth in a village in rural Northumberland. Each focus group discussion lasted between 50 and 70 min and was moderated by a trained researcher and an assistant. Saturation was reached during the fifth focus group discussion, with no further information being obtained.

2.1. Recruiting Participants

Initially, posters and flyers advertised for potential recruits on public notice boards. Respondents who expressed interest in taking part in the discussions were sent further information regarding the study's purpose and informed that if they were selected to take part, they would receive a GBP 10.00 shopping voucher. Interested respondents were sent a brief socio-demographic questionnaire to complete (age, occupation, gender, educational background, nationality, and dietary preferences). People below the age of 18 years were excluded, and participants with different socio-demographic characteristics were randomly allocated across the four urban and rural groups (Table 1). The results of the initial pilot group were included in the main analysis as no changes were made following the pilot.

Four of the discussions were held within Newcastle University and the fifth focus group discussion was held in Elsdon, a rural village 40 km north of Newcastle.

2.2. Structure and Approach to Focus Group Discussions

Participants were briefed on the discussions and asked to sign consent forms. They were subsequently randomly allocated numbers with which they were identified in the discussion in order to anonymise responses. They were from that point only referred to by their gender, random number, and the focus group in which they participated (e.g., a female that received the random number 3, in focus group 1, would be identified only as (F3, FG1). All focus groups followed the same protocols, developed by the authors of this paper. Each focus group discussion was preceded by a PowerPoint presentation where the moderator presented an overview of the technological issues discussed in the focus groups in relation to biotechnology.

Table 1. Summary demographics of focus group discussion participants.

VARIABLE	NUMBER (%)
Gender	
Male (M)	22 (58)
Female (F)	16 (42)
Age groups	
18–30	18 (47.4)
31–43	9 (23.7)
44–56	4 (10.5)
>57	7 (18.4)
Mean (age)	37.6
Nationality	
United Kingdom	23 (60.5)
European	3 (8)
Asian	4 (10.5)
African	7 (18.4)
Caribbean	1 (2.6)
Employment status	
Unemployed	1 (2.6)
Paid employment	15 (39.5)
Student	18 (47.4)
Retired	4 (10.5)
Self-stated dietary preferences	
Asian	1 (2.6)
None	27 (71)
Halal	3 (8)
Lacto-ovo free	1 (2.6)
Vegan	2 (5.2)
Vegetarian	3 (8)
Non-Vegetarian Hindu	1 (2.6)

2.2.1. Part I—Attitude to Different Genomic Technologies Applied to Animal Production Systems

Participants were provided with descriptions of various genomic technologies applied to animals used in food production systems. As a "warm -up" exercise, participants were asked to rate how ethically acceptable they viewed each type of genomic technology listed on a scale of 0–5, with 0 being unacceptable and 5 being entirely acceptable. The genomic technologies considered here were genetic modification (GM), structural genomics, functional genomics, conservation genomics, proteomics, and gene drive (see Table 2). Participants were asked to describe why they assigned the score given to that particular genomic technology, which then led to a group discussion of the various technologies about why the various technologies were or were not ethically acceptable. The aggregated results were provided as feedback to frame the discussion, but will not be considered further here because small sample sizes mean that statistical analysis is not appropriate.

Table 2. Areas of genomic technology discussed.

Type of Genomic Technology	Brief Description of Technology	Examples of Application to Animal Production Systems for Food Use
Genetic Modification	Changing the genetic makeup of cells, including the transfer of genes within and across species boundaries, to correct defects or produce improved and/or novel organisms.	Insertion into pigs of spinach gene to change body composition for better food production. Insertion of a modified gene to create animals resistant to heat stress.
Structural Genomics	DNA sequencing, sequence assembly, sequence organisation, and management and determination of the structure of every protein encoded by the genome.	Identifying animals with "desirable" genes, e.g., greater productive yield, better disease resistance.
Functional Genomics	Reconstruction of genome sequences to discover the functions of the genes together.	Identifying how genes interact to produce desirable traits, e.g., animal behaviour, health, and increase in productivity.
Conservation genomics	Use of genomic sequencing to better evaluate genetic factors key to species conservation.	Establishment of the size and health of a gene pool or genetic diversity of a population including preserving at-risk genotypes.
Proteomics	The large-scale study of the structure of proteins and what their function is and how they interact in animals.	Understanding of the function and regulation of genes, and how these participate in complex networks producing proteins and other biological agents controlling the phenotypic characteristics of a trait.
Gene Drive	Natural or genetically engineering the characteristics of a particular trait so that it dominates other traits and can propagate throughout a whole population or species.	Gene drives can be used to counter animal-borne diseases and can either arise naturally or be genetically engineered, e.g., using CRISPR (gene editing) technology.

2.2.2. Part II—Relative Importance of Genomic Technologies Applied to Animal Production Systems

This section was designed to understand what participants thought about the different genomic technologies under consideration in relation to their potential impacts within society. Information was provided to participants linking some claimed potential benefits of the use of genomic technologies to breeding farm animals, including pigs and cattle.

2.2.3. Part III—Ethical Dilemmas in the Use of Genomic Technologies

Given that ethical concerns are raised as an important societal barrier to the adoption of GM in animal production systems, this was further explored in relation to each of the gene technologies under consideration. An important ethical question in animal breeding is the consideration of whether the "naturalness" (or "*telos*" (The telos of an animal is defined as "its nature or 'beingness'". Harfeld, J.L., 2013. Telos and the ethics of animal farming. Journal of agricultural and environmental ethics, 26(3), pp.691–709. In the focus groups, this was considered by participants as being linked to "naturalness" and so the two concepts are addressed together in the subsequent analysis and discussion.)) of animals should be preserved. The concept of naturalness was introduced to the groups, which led to their discussing the extent to which the animals themselves might ethically be adapted to their environment in order to promote and improve their welfare and facilitate their management. Both natural and unnatural methods of adaptation were discussed, including cases where some methods may lead to the "disenhancement" (Making an animal less sensitive to and more able to cope with adverse characteristics that may exist in its environment that may prove difficult to that animal species in its natural state, e.g., see Murphy, K.N. and Kabasenche, W.P., 2018. Animal disenhancement in moral context. NanoEthics, 12(3), pp. 225–236) of farm animals, and thus potentially affect their "*telos*". This may reflect a more biocentric perspective, which is, in a political, ecological, and literal sense, an ethical point of view that extends inherent value to all living things (see, inter alia [38,39]).

In order to facilitate and catalyse the discussions, two scenarios were presented to participants. These are provided in Appendix A.

Each scenario was discussed with participants in relation to the acceptability of each of the solutions with regard to animal welfare and the *telos* of the animals and whether applying the different genomic technologies to achieve the same goals would be preferable. Finally, the moderator encouraged the discussions to consider more general attitudes and perceptions of participants towards using genomic technologies in breeding farm animals, focusing on the various ethical considerations.

2.3. Data Recording, Coding, and Analysis

All discussions were recorded and transcribed. Preliminary codes were developed from notes taken during discussions and debriefing sessions. Thematic analysis was subsequently conducted on the transcripts using NVivo, version 20, QSR International, Melbourne, Brevard County, Australia. Thematic analysis is a qualitative data analysis method that involves reading through a dataset (such as transcripts from focus groups) and identifying patterns in meaning across the data [40]. Coding was initially validated using the first focus group transcript and further discussed by researchers. During this process, further codes (and subcodes) emerged. Codes and sub-codes were then organised into themes and sub-themes (Table 3). The remaining transcripts were then coded, and the coding scheme amended if additional themes emerged during the analysis. To maintain the anonymity of participants, the audio records were destroyed once transcription was completed and validated, in line with ethical requirements for participant anonymisation required by General Data Protection Regulation (GDPR) requirements. This may have limited subsequent reanalysis of participants' affective responses, but was appropriate given data protection regulation applied at the time of data collection.

Table 3. Codes and emerging themes from data.

SUPERORDINATE THEME	CODE AND SUBCODE
Attitudes towards the use of different genomic technologies	*Perception of the use of genomic technology* Genetic modification Gene drive Functional genomics Structural genomics Conservation genomics Proteomics Animal health and diseases Animal welfare *General concerns about the use of genomic technologies*
Prioritising the use of genomic technologies	*The relative importance of genomic technologies* Animal health Environmental sustainability Animal welfare Greater productivity Safer human food Efficient feed use Improved human wellbeing and health *Telos*
Ethical dilemmas from the use of genomic technologies	Animal welfare Animal health Free-range Concerns Religious concerns Naturalness *Telos*
Additional concerns	Climate change Organic vs. inorganic production Need for risk communication

The researchers discussed the various themes that emerged from the analysis. The quotes used in the text represent the emerging themes and the divergent opinions held by participants.

3. Results

All focus group discussions were highly interactive, with all participants engaging in the discussion. This reflects the level of interest, understanding, and knowledge of the participants relating to the subject area. In general, participants were open-minded and frequently challenged the views of other participants. Most of the participants agreed that there was a need to conduct genomic research into animal production. However, participants expressed divergent views concerning how the information should be applied. Some participants expressed specific cultural and ethical views about the use of various genomic technologies in animal breeding. In contrast, others were more positive about using genomic technologies if those technologies were appropriately regulated, and if societal preferences and priorities for technological innovation were taken into account. Some participants argued that genomic technologies could improve animal welfare and/or improve environmental sustainability. The overall conclusions of the discussions were broadly consistent across the five groups and reflected in the various themes presented in this research.

3.1. Attitudes towards to the Use of Genomic Technology in Animal Production Systems

The first part of the discussions involved participants assigning scores to six genomic technologies and then discussing their results with the rest of the group. The means of the scores were then calculated and used to complement the discussions that followed. Participants tended to agree about the acceptability of proteomics, conservation genomics, structural genomics, and functional genomics (see Table 2).

Participants were less positive about applying genetic modification and gene drives in breeding new traits in farm animals for human food production. Proteomics was rarely mentioned in the discussions, and participants were more confident in discussing conservation genomics and structural genomics. Participants associated structural genomics with traditional selective breeding.

> *... It's like selective breeding except you have more revision and knowledge to see what are actually selectively breeding towards ... if you are looking at the actual genes you know what you are aiming for, you don't have those mistaken ones, you have the good ones ...* (M, FG2).

However, a few participants, after clarifying the meaning of both structural and functional genomics, were negative towards these applications and/or the use of information from them.

> *We've always done it for years, but we've just modernised it to an advanced state that now threatens our very existence* (M, FG1).

Some participants indicated that natural selection is a natural process, but that this was not the case for all applications of genomic technologies. This line of reasoning represented a common thread through subsequent discussions. Participants held that understanding genomic structures and using that information for selective breeding of farm animals would benefit farmers. However, a majority of the participants expressed the view that such breeding processes should be "natural", for instance, by identifying, through genomic analysis, and then selecting pigs with a desirable trait to produce pigs with traits "useful" for supply chain requirements. Most participants expressed more negative opinions about genomic technologies perceived as "artificial" (especially GM and gene drives), especially for the development of animals with characteristics that could have unintended negative effects, with potentially severe consequences for human health and wellbeing as well as for the animal species concerned.

I just think it could be dangerous, like getting rid of a gene or modifying it. Like what they did to mosquitoes, that's good, but if you start doing to the animals we eat, it's hard to model interactions as in the rest of the ecosystem, so it might result in something negative (F, FG2).

3.2. Imposing a Global Control System

Some participants expressed the view that there are potential benefits from the application of *all* the genomic technologies discussed if the route to application was cautious, precautionary, and appropriately regulated. However, they also recognised the difficulty of establishing an appropriate and consistent regulatory framework.

At first I indicated we should use these technologies with moderation, but how can we moderate their use, on a global scale, it has become increasingly difficult (F, FG 3).

So where do you draw the line when you start doing that? (F1, FG4).

Some participants did not believe that individual and country-level controls were adequate to moderate potentially extreme or maleficent use of genomic technologies:

…… there should be a global thing, …… there should be a global kind of system of policing, and you know the sort of ethical side (F1 and M2, FG5).

Participants expressed the need for industry and national regulation to introduce a system of governance that includes regulations based on ethical considerations as well as risk issues.

……. that code of conduct, that code of ethics, so there should be some mechanism by which they [industry and national governments] have to be held to accountable to (F1, FG5).

This was linked to the need to apply universal governance:

I think the most important part is to give the universal limits, I think that's the reason why the government exists, to set limits for some of these things (F3, FG4).

3.3. Applications for Health Versus Food

Participants agreed that there was a need to conduct research in these areas using animal genomic technologies. Many participants indicated that they thought there was the need to use genomics for fundamental research, particularly functional genomics, structural genomics, conservation genomics, and proteomics, in order to understand the nature of organisms.

I feel like there's a line between the research and the product … I find important to do research because I feel that is the only way we would be able to understand anything after (M, FG 1).

The development and application of genomic technologies and their potential benefits were also regarded as important by some participants. While participants held generally negative views in relation to applying the genomic techniques to animals for food production purposes, participants were more positive about the application of genomic technologies for medical and veterinary research and to health care.

If we're all scared of manipulation, I'm not sure we would have gotten treatment for some of the diseases we have" (F3, FG3).

… we already know about the CRISPR/Cas9 technology and it's currently used in cancer technology and the treatment of cancer (F4, FG4).

*… I think its uses in disease control, for example if this became an alternative to badger culling …… * (M, FG2).

Some study participants expressed reservations about the use of genomics and genomic technologies in this context, particularly if they involved the insertion of human genes in animals for the purposes of xenotransplantation. This view was sometimes expressed through the lens of religion.

> *I think that these [genomic] technologies in general] would be more suited for sustaining food production ... but I don't agree too much with applying to human health, I feel like the human health, I think it's worse, and for me my religion doesn't permit that"* (M, FG 1).

3.3.1. Fear of the Unknown, Novel or Unanticipated Outcomes in Animal Production Systems

The fear of the "unknown", which underpinned some participant concerns about using genomic technologies applied to animals for food production, was mainly linked to discussions on genetic modification and gene drives. This may be related to concerns about cross-species genomic technologies or perceptions of uncontrollability.

> *Mixing species is just mind blowing, it frightens me just the thought of mixing genes from different species* (F1, FG5).

> *... it can propagate through the population-what if you were wrong, then you screwed it up basically* (F1, FG3).

Many participants expressed a preference for the application of genomic technologies to conserve animal species compared to other potential benefits that could be generated from the use of such technologies. This was not particularly related to farm animals but related more generally to both domestic animals and those living in the wild. This is also consistent with views from discussions which suggest that participants were more open to the study and analysis of the genomes of animals and plants, which, in most cases, can be achieved through conservation genomics, proteomics, structural genomics, and functional genomics, but were highly sceptical about genetic modification and gene drives. However, many participants displayed some concerns about how knowledge gathered from the study of animal genomes might be applied in the future.

3.3.2. Perceptions of Benefits Associated with the Use of Genomic Technologies Applied to Animal Production Systems

For most participants, the beneficial aspects of genomic technologies linked to outcomes that would improve the lives of animals were considered to be the most important, for example, in relation to conservation genetics. These included:

3.3.3. Animal Health and Welfare

Discussion about animal health and welfare was an important topic for most participants and was closely linked to the concept that animal welfare equates to animal health and disease control.

> *... animal health ... control of animal welfare* (F1, FG3).

> *... improved animal health which I think it probably crosses over to animal welfare, that idea of any common diseases, approach as many as you can sort of help identify you breed out diseases* (M3, FG5).

While some participants perceived animal health as being distinct from animal welfare, the majority viewed animal health as part of animal welfare. Thus, genomic technologies were viewed to be helpful and important if they could be used to improve animal health and welfare. The majority of participants viewed animal welfare as an important consideration when using genomic technologies. Following the presentation of the case studies, some participants disliked the idea of using genomic technology to cause changes in animals. One participant described it as an "obvious violation" (F, FG1) of the rights of these animals and, to another, "absolutely unacceptable," (M2, FG2) or "inhumane".

However, a few participants disagreed, reasoning that:

> *... all animals were created in the perfect form, heat, drought, water resistant etc. ... you can find each animal is created in its form and place"* (M5, FG2).

For some participants, genomic technologies were seen as advantageous to animal welfare and hence production.

I don't think breeding to make them gentler and less aggressive is slightly less unethical [laughter] (M, FG4).

Some participants indicated that they felt that animal welfare was only used as a justification for genomic research insofar as this was a scientific bridge to improving human health.

... lot of the things we are talking about we're saying it's better for animals, they are not necessarily better for animals, they are better for us to get something out of the animals and I'm not sure if I am totally comfortable with that (F1, FG3).

Other participants indicated that, independent of the reasons why farmers might use genomic technologies (for example, to lower costs of production, increase productivity, and to improve environmental sustainably to mitigate the impacts of not using optimum animal husbandry practices), the welfare of animals should always be considered and given a high priority. Participants who held this view suggested that seeking the best welfare conditions for animals ultimately will lead to all other benefits that farmers may seek.

When the animal is feeling better, when the animal is feeling natural, when their wellbeing is enhanced then they will be more productive in the end, if they lived in a natural environment the food would be safer, they would feel more motivated and healthy (F1, FG4).

But basically you have got to link your low cost with your animal welfare, the two have got to come together (M5, FG5).

Some participants expressed the view that animal welfare problems were a consequence of human actions and that the conditions associated with animal husbandry should be changed to accommodate animal welfare needs, rather than developing new technological approaches to addressing animal welfare within these systems.

"If people want to continue eating meat, then surely they should change the environment that these animals are supposed to live in and not genetically modifying the animals to endure the conditions" (F2, FG2).

3.3.4. Safer Human Food and Health

Some participants emphasised the importance of the application of genomic technologies to improve human food security. In this context, some participants expressed concern about which genomic technologies should be applied to food production and the need to prioritise improved food safety over other beneficial impacts.

... Safer human food should be first [most important] because if you want for example a lot of the health problems we encounter nowadays can be traced to the food we eat ... having a safe diet can help cut the risk of certain diseases like cancer (F3, FG4).

3.3.5. Environmental Sustainability

Participants indicated that environmental and ecological problems and factors linked to climate change could justify the application of many genomic technologies if their application mitigated these. For some participants, environmental sustainability was viewed as the most important potential impact of genomic technologies, leading to greater productivity, safer human food, improved animal health and welfare, and the preservation of ecosystems. However, one participant considered that the motives driving investment in genomic technologies were driven only by the financial interests of corporations and individuals.

The main thing and my fear is the money culture, you have separate ambitions and rules, and it can be an issue. I think it's disgusting to try to genetically modify the horrible life of an animal just for money, and it's nothing to do with global warming (F2, FG2).

3.3.6. Low Cost and Greater Productivity

The use of genomic technologies to improve productivity was viewed as a "game changer". Lower production costs and increased productivity associated with genomic technologies were viewed as important by some discussants, particularly in relation to global population growth.

> *I think with technology, we can produce more at very low cost to feed the increasing human population* (M1, FG5).

Not all participants, however, held this view. Some associated the use of genomic technology with financial incentivisation on the part of industry stakeholders. The view was expressed that there is enough food to feed the world population, but food insecurity is driven by inequitable food distribution of food and food waste in supply chains.

> *... For me, I don't think there is scarce food in the world, there is abundance of food, it is a problem of the distribution of the food that is causing all the food insecurity in the world"* (M, FG1).

> *"The whole thing that screams at me ... it says it's all to do with lower cost and greater productivity ... meanwhile the only reasons is to financially drive us to where and what we don't need* (M1, FG5).

3.3.7. Naturalness and Temperament

Participants were generally not in favour of applying any genomic breeding techniques that resulted in the modification of the temperament or *telos* of animals. There was some difference of opinion amongst participants as to whether animal "naturalness" or animal temperament were more important in this regard.

> *Naturalness, that's highly important ... the animals should be living their natural lives in a as close to it as possible ...* (M, FG1).

> *Temperament is slightly more important than naturalness, because by the time you have been domesticating animals for ten thousand years a lot of the naturalness [is lost]* (M2, FG2).

4. Ethical Concerns

The specific ethical scenarios considered during the discussions focused to a considerable extent on participant opinion on the use of genetic modification. The common themes that were consistent across the focus groups included animal rights and welfare, *telos*, access to more extensive conditions in which animals could be reared, and due consideration of alternatives to the use of genomic technologies.

4.1. Telos (Naturalness)

Many participants discussed the importance of maintaining the "naturalness" or *telos* of farm animals. The use of genomic technologies that completely change the natural characteristics, or attributes perceived to be natural, of farm animals was unacceptable. The view was expressed that the phenotypical features of animals were integral to the nature of the animal and existed for a reason.

> *... While chickens use their eyes to see and beaks to feed, pigs wag their curly tails as a result of emotional expression* (M, FG1).

> *it's disgusting to .... remove beaks, eyes or tails of animals or do anything that will make them look less animals* (F2, FG2)

Any changes in the phenotype of animals, unless it was for welfare and animal health which ultimately led to better productivity, were viewed to be unethical. Breeding to change the temperament of animals was seen by the majority as a violation of their fundamental nature and "natural rights", and thus was not considered welfare-driven.

> *In terms of naturalness, the aggression might be useful to the pig, it might be their nature to be aggressive* (M, FG1).

Participants who expressed concerns about genomic technologies in animal welfare also indicated that these concerns also had an ethical basis. Alternative futures that did not involve genomic technologies were described.

Reduced Meat Consumption

Some participants emphasised the need to reduce meat consumption. Other participants expressed the view that they were in favour of reduced meat production while giving livestock appropriate space to enjoy their natural habitats. These discussants claimed that increased societal demand for meat is driven by increasing meat supply, which makes the meat very cheap. This, in turn, triggers the need for the introduction of genomic technological innovations.

> *I think people are going to have to get used to the fact they have to pay more for their meat, it's too cheap ...*
>
> *... In an ideal world we would all eat less meat, and we would have much higher welfare chickens* (F1, FG3).

4.2. *Overall Concerns about the Use of Genomic Technologies in Animal Production Systems*

4.2.1. Use of Genomic Information and Technology

While there was a general agreement that the study of the structure and functions of the animal genomes was important, some participants had concerns about the ways in which the resulting information might be used, and that genetic information should only be used to promote animal health and welfare.

> *... I have no problem with that, it's just doing DNA analysis and obtaining information, it's what you do with that information that is potentially disturbing* (F, FG 3).
>
> *Any technology that doesn't seek to improve animal health, helping prevent diseases, or identify and cure ailments in animals and lead to higher animal welfare ... in my opinion is not good to us ...* (M2, FG4).

Other participants viewed genomic technologies as a way of improving productivity to meet the food security requirements of our ever-increasing global population, while to others, these technologies offered ways of protecting the environment and ensuring the existence of endangered species.

4.2.2. Motivation by Financial Interests

Participants expressed concerns about the motives of industry actors that drive the use of genomic technologies. Some participants believed that farmers and producers are motivated by profit alone. Others were concerned about the role of patent rights that have been generated from the use of genomic information and technology.

> *... It is just the huge businesses which will take over and then becomes another capitalist kind, you know where that transition occurs* (F2, FG5).
>
> *... my fears of the money culture [referring to financial interests of corporations] ...* (F, FG2).

5. Discussion

The research results indicated that, although additional information and clarification had been provided throughout the focus groups, there remained a general lack of participant differentiation between the different genomic technologies applied to farm animals. Participants expressed a preference for "non-invasive" technologies where no genetic modification or editing was applied, but where technological innovation was directed instead towards mapping existing animal genomes and used to selectively breed for desirable traits. Ethical concerns were frequently expressed about the technological processes being applied, particularly in relation to the extent to which such processes were perceived to be different from "natural" breeding techniques, and also in relation to the objective of the application, such as animal health and welfare or environmental protection, which tended to be viewed as more ethical than applications that increased yield or economic value within supply chains. However, exceptions to this increased ethical acceptability were those genomic applications that increased animals' tolerance of intensive production systems or lower welfare standards. This does not align with the argumentation proposed by Thompson [41], where it is proposed that genomic disenhancement, which changes the *telos* of animals so as to enhance animal welfare in intensive animal production systems, is acceptable. The results appear to reflect Thompson's perspective that there are moral intuitions that militate against animal enhancement in the absence of strong philosophical arguments against it. Some ethicists argue that disenhancement may be a temporary measure to relieve animal suffering in environments that humans have created for them [42], although it has, in turn, been argued that it is better to address the conditions that give rise to poor welfare [43] (an issue also raised in the focus group discussions), or indeed rethink the concept of telos to address what "is important" to an animal [44]. Further research to understand differences between the ethical reasoning of experts and public representations of and beliefs about the same issues is required.

When provided with further information about the different technological innovations applied to animals, participants expressed the view that gene editing (where the cell's genome can be cut at a desired location, allowing existing genes to be removed and/or new ones added, representing the precise and targeted alteration of a DNA sequence in a living cell) was preferred over and above genetic modification (involving the transfer of genetic material from another species) and the use of gene drives (which propagates a particular suite of genes throughout a population by altering the probability that a specific allele will be transmitted to offspring). The latter were associated with perceptions of unnaturalness and uncontrollability, as well as being perceived to increase risks to human and animal health, as well as the environment. The observation was that the focus group participants were more accepting of genomic technologies (for example, accelerated breeding) that did not result in "invasive" genetic changes but allowed a more rapid and precise strategy to genetic change based on the "observation" of genes rather than the introduction of artificial genetic changes. This suggests that it is not the concept of genetic change that is of concern to the public, but rather the technological mechanism by which it is achieved, and the extent to which this can be obtained using natural breeding techniques. As has been found in previous research studies, the perceived potential for unintended health and environmental impacts associated with genetic technologies (e.g., see [43,44]), and ineffective or contradictory regulatory mechanisms to control and mitigate these (e.g., see [45,46]), contributed to these concerns.

Participants recognised the transboundary nature of potential risks and ethical issues and suggested that, as well as the need to include and address ethical issues in the construction of regulations associated with genomic technologies applied to animals and their products, there was also a need to include these in transboundary regulatory systems, given that the risks and ethical issues also had transboundary implications. Ethical concern was expressed about the continued use of genomic technologies to further the development of existing intensive animal production systems in their current trajectory (for example, through applying these technologies to disenhance negative animal behavioural responses to such production systems), rather than mitigating the problems by reassessing production system structures and regulation, and so improving animal health and welfare through changing current practices. Notably, many participants perceived that the application of some or all genomic technologies applied to animal production systems was, in fact, unregulated at a global scale. This could be associated with the lack of trust that consumers have in research institutions, governance practices, and industry [5,45]. Financial gain was perceived by many participants to motivate the biotechnology industry to use all genomic technologies in ways that are potentially detrimental to animal health and welfare (see also [46–50]). It was suggested that developing and communicating how governance systems work at local, regional, and international levels might reassure the public that good governance practices are being applied. Increased co-production involving all sectors of society, in the development of regulations, policies, and how these are applied and monitored, may increase societal trust in governance practices. However, it is important to note that many different perceptions and opinions are likely to be associated with different individuals and groups within the public, and understanding these differences is an important issue in relation to the co-production of policies.

The technologies considered in this research were all identified as having at least the potential of being used for breeding farm animals [51]. Those technologies, which were all viewed as a means of studying and accumulating knowledge about the genomes of organisms, were, however, viewed more favourably than those that were associated with structural changes to an animal's DNA. Participants did not really differentiate between different types of genomic technology unless prompted to do so, including in relation to their ethical concerns. There was general acceptance of traditional selective breeding techniques, and from this accelerated breeding technologies were also considered acceptable, assuming established breeding techniques were still used. However, those technologies where some modification of animal genetic structures was involved were considered less acceptable, although this was more pronounced for genetic modification than for gene editing such as the CRISPR-Cas9 technology. This suggests that a different labelling approach may be required for genetically modified, as distinct from gene-edited, animal products, as the latter may be more acceptable to concerned consumers than the former, although such an approach is not accommodated within some legal frameworks. For example, CRISPR-Cas9 technology is currently regulated under the GMO regulations in Europe [52]. The proponents of modern gene editing techniques such as CRISPR-Cas9 argue that such techniques can be used to give additional or more complex types of genetic changes to those that would occur naturally. This should therefore be taken into account in legislative frameworks, for example, in the EU definition [53]. The main question that needs to be addressed is whether products developed using gene editing should be regulated on the basis of the process or the final products' characteristics, or whether a hybrid approach should be taken (https://www.europarl.europa.eu/RegData/etudes/ATAG/2020/641535/EPRS_ATA(2020)641535_EN.pdf, accessed 10 March 2021). It is important that the technologies used to produce foods will be labelled on products in order to promote transparency in food systems and the availability of information for those who would like it.

Finally, the convergence on views of discussants about the use of genomic technologies and information to facilitate human health care and veterinary research could be linked to the increasing role of genomics in health care [52,53]. While noting the relative importance of genomic technologies in health care for both humans and animals, participants also suggested that there were potential unintended consequences of undesirable traits being passed to offspring as a consequence of genetic alteration.

6. Conclusions

This research suggests that the public are more positive about the use of (various) genomic technologies to study and accumulate genetic information about animals, including farm animals, and which inform and accelerate traditional breeding practices, compared to techniques that modify the genome of animals. There was more consensus regarding applications that improved information for conservation, environmental sustainability, health, and animal welfare, with the exception of animal "disenhancement". Maintaining the "*telos*" of animals was important to study participants. The integration of societal preferences into regulations and labelling strategies may increase public trust in science and regulatory institutions, but further research in different cultural contexts and at scale is needed to enable a "co-produced" future regulatory landscape to be developed.

Author Contributions: Conceptualization, L.J.F., E.G. and D.C; methodology, L.J.F.; formal analysis, F.Z.N., D.C.; investigation, D.C., F.Z.N.; resources, E.G.; data curation, L.J.F.; writing—original draft preparation, F.Z.N., L.J.F., D.C., writing—review and editing, L.J.F.; supervision, L.J.F.; project administration, L.J.F., E.G.; funding acquisition, E.G., L.J.F. All authors have read and agreed to the published version of the manuscript.

Funding: The authors would like to acknowledge Genome Canada and Genome Alberta who funded the research. The research was undertaken as part of a Genome Canada LSARP 2015 project "Application of genomics to improve disease resilience and sustainability in pork production" which is registered at the University of Alberta under the number RES0030284 and a Genome Canada LSARP 2015 project ""Increasing feed efficiency and reducing methane emissions through genomics: a new promising goal for the Canadian dairy industry", which is registered at the University of Alberta under the number RES0030198.

Institutional Review Board Statement: The study was conducted according to the guidelines of the Declaration of Helsinki The University Ethics Committee (UEC) is the formal body responsible for developing and implementing ethical policy and procedure. This research was approved by Newcastle University Ethics Committee, approval number 7235/2018).

Informed Consent Statement: Informed consent was obtained from all subjects involved in the study.

Data Availability Statement: Data are available from the corresponding author on request.

Conflicts of Interest: The authors have no conflict of interest.

Appendix A. Scenarios Presented to Participants Regarding "Ethical Dilemmas"a

- Scenario 1 was structured around the practice of tail removal in intensive pig production systems to prevent tail biting. Possible solutions to reducing pig tail biting were identified, which included (1) surgically removing the tails of pigs, (2) using genomic technologies to breed pigs without tails, (3) using genomic technologies to breed pigs that do not bite the tails of other pigs, and (4) reducing the intensity of the production system, so fewer pigs are in close proximity and with larger housing, which would reduce the incidence of tail biting.
- Scenario 2 was structured around the practice of debeaking chickens within intensive production systems to prevent inter-bird aggression. Potential solutions included (1) breeding chickens without beaks that could not, therefore, engage in these behaviours, (2) breeding chickens that are blind and so are not concerned about the proximity of other chickens, which would prevent problems associated with aggressive behaviours, and (3) putting fewer chickens in close proximity to each other and providing larger housing, which would have similar impacts on aggressive behaviours in chickens.

References

1. Nadathur, S.R.; Wanasundara, J.P.D.; Scanlin, L. Proteins in the diet: Challenges in feeding the global population. In *Sustainable Protein Sources*; Academic Press: Cambridge, MA, USA, 2017; pp. 1–19.
2. Boland, M.J.; Rae, A.N.; Vereijken, J.M.; Meuwissen, M.P.; Fischer, A.R.; van Boekel, M.A.; Rutherfurd, S.M.; Gruppen, H.; Moughan, P.J.; Hendriks, W.H. The future supply of animal-derived protein for human consumption. *Trends Food Sci. Technol.* **2013**, *29*, 62–73. [CrossRef]
3. Clark, B.; Stewart, G.B.; Panzone, L.A.; Kyriazakis, I.; Frewer, L.J. A systematic review of public attitudes, perceptions and behaviours towards production diseases associated with farm animal welfare. *J. Agric. Environ. Ethics* **2016**, *29*, 455–478. [CrossRef]
4. Clark, B.; Panzone, L.A.; Stewart, G.B.; Kyriazakis, I.; Niemi, J.K.; Latvala, T.; Tranter, R.; Jones, P.; Frewer, L.J. Consumer attitudes towards production diseases in intensive production systems. *PLoS ONE* **2019**, *14*, e0210432. [CrossRef]
5. Frewer, L.J.; Kleter, G.A.; Brennan, M.; Coles, D.; Fischer, A.R.; Houdebine, L.M.; Mora, C.; Millar, K.; Salter, B. Genetically modified animals from life-science, socio-economic and ethical perspectives: Examining issues in an EU policy context. *New Biotechnol.* **2013**, *30*, 447–460. [CrossRef]
6. Proudfoot, C.; Burkard, C. Genome editing for disease resistance in livestock. *Emerg. Top. Life Sci.* **2017**, *1*, 209–219.
7. Bruce, A. Genome edited animals: Learning from GM crops? *Transgenic Res.* **2017**, *26*, 385–398. [CrossRef]
8. Jin, S.; Clark, B.; Kuznesof, S.; Lin, X.; Frewer, L.J. Synthetic biology applied in the agrifood sector: Public perceptions, attitudes and implications for future studies. *Trends Food Sci. Technol.* **2019**, *91*, 454–466. [CrossRef]
9. Critchley, C.; Nicol, D.; Bruce, G.; Walshe, J.; Treleaven, T.; Tuch, B. Predicting public attitudes toward gene editing of germlines: The impact of moral and hereditary concern in human and animal applications. *Front. Genet.* **2019**, *9*, 704. [CrossRef] [PubMed]
10. Kato-Nitta, N.; Maeda, T.; Inagaki, Y.; Tachikawa, M. Expert and public perceptions of gene-edited crops: Attitude changes in relation to scientific knowledge. *Palgrave Commun.* **2019**, *5*, 1–14. [CrossRef]

11. Yang, Y.; Hobbs, J.E. Supporters or opponents: Will cultural values shape consumer acceptance of gene editing? *J. Food Prod. Mark.* **2000**, *26*, 17–37. [CrossRef]
12. Basinskiene, L.; Seinauskiene, B. Gene Editing Versus Gene Modification: Awareness, Attitudes and Behavioral Intentions of Lithuanian Consumers, Producers, and Farmers. *Chem. Eng. Trans.* **2021**, *87*, 433–438.
13. Yunes, M.C.; Osório-Santos, Z.; von Keyserlingk, M.A.; Hötzel, M.J. Gene Editing for Improved Animal Welfare and Production Traits in Cattle: Will This Technology Be Embraced or Rejected by the Public? *Sustainability* **2021**, *13*, 4966. [CrossRef]
14. Busch, G.; Ryan, E.; von Keyserlingk, M.A.; Weary, D.M. Citizen views on genome editing: Effects of species and purpose. *Agric. Hum. Values* **2021**, *38*, 1–14. [CrossRef]
15. Frewer, L.J.; van der Lans, I.A.; Fischer, A.R.; Reinders, M.J.; Menozzi, D.; Zhang, X.; van den Berg, I.; Zimmermann, K. Public perceptions of agri-food applications of genetic modification–a systematic review and meta-analysis. *Trends Food Sci. Technol.* **2013**, *30*, 142–152. [CrossRef]
16. Rose, K.M.; Brossard, D.; Scheufele, D.A. Of society, nature, and health: How perceptions of specific risks and benefits of genetically engineered foods shape public rejection. *Environ. Commun.* **2020**, *14*, 1017–1031. [CrossRef]
17. Franklin, S. *Dolly Mixtures: The Remaking of Genealogy*; Duke University Press: Durham, NC, USA, 2007. [CrossRef]
18. Raue, M.; Lermer, E.; Streicher, B.; Slovic, P. *Psychological Perspectives on Risk and Risk Analysis*; Springer: Berlin/Heidelberg, Germany, 2018; pp. 2–18.
19. Slovic, P. Understanding perceived risk: 1978–2015. *Environ. Sci. Policy Sustain. Dev.* **2016**, *58*, 25–29. [CrossRef]
20. Hassan, A.E.; Afroz, N. Implications of Risk Governance in Genetically Modified Food: A Comparative Discussion on European and United States Contexts. *Asian Soc. Sci.* **2020**, *16*, 33–42. [CrossRef]
21. Tait-Burkard, C.; Doeschl-Wilson, A.; McGrew, M.J.; Archibald, A.L.; Sang, H.M.; Houston, R.D.; Whitelaw, C.B.; Watson, M. Livestock 2.0–genome editing for fitter, healthier, and more productive farmed animals. *Genome Biol.* **2018**, *19*, 1–11. [CrossRef] [PubMed]
22. Burkard, C.; Lillico, S.G.; Reid, E.; Jackson, B.; Mileham, A.J.; Ait-Ali, T. Precision engineering for PRRSV resistance in pigs: Macrophages from genome edited pigs lacking CD163 SRCR5 domain are fully resistant to both PRRSV genotypes while maintaining biological function. *PLoS Pathog* **2017**, *13*, 1–28. [CrossRef]
23. Menchaca, A.; Dos Santos-Neto, P.C.; Mulet, A.P.; Crispo, M. CRISPR in livestock: From editing to printing. *Theriogenology* **2020**, *150*, 247–254. [CrossRef]
24. Mueller, M.L.; Cole, J.B.; Sonstegard, T.S.; Van Eenennaam, A.L. Comparison of gene editing versus conventional breeding to introgress the POLLED allele into the US dairy cattle population. *J. Dairy Sci.* **2019**, *102*, 4215–4226. [CrossRef]
25. Ufer, D.; Ortega, D.L.; Wolf, C.A. Economic foundations for the use of biotechnology to improve farm animal welfare. *Trends Food Sci. Technol.* **2019**, *91*, 129–138. [CrossRef]
26. Clark, B.; Stewart, G.B.; Panzone, L.A.; Kyriazakis, I.; Frewer, L.J. Citizens, consumers and farm animal welfare: A meta-analysis of willingness-to-pay studies. *Food Policy* **2017**, *68*, 112–127. [CrossRef]
27. European Commission. Attitudes of Europeans towards Animal Welfare European Union: Director Generate for Health and Social. Special Eurobarometer. 2016. Available online: http://ec.europa.eu/COMMFrontOffice/publicopinion/index.cfm/Survey/getSurveyDetail/instruments/SPECIAL/surveyKy/2096 (accessed on 29 March 2021).
28. Spooner, J.M.; Schuppli, C.A.; Fraser, D. Attitudes of Canadian citizens toward farm animal welfare: A qualitative study. *Livestock Science* **2014**, *163*, 150–158. [CrossRef]
29. Verbeke, W.; Pérez-Cueto, F.J.A.; Barcellos, M.D.; Krystallis, A.; Grunert, K.G. European citizen and consumer attitudes and preferences regarding beef and pork. *Meat Sci.* **2010**, *84*, 284–292. [CrossRef] [PubMed]
30. Quinlan, M.M.; Smith, J.; Layton, R.; Keese, P.; Agbagala, M.; Lorelie, U.; Palacpac, M.B.; Ball, L. Experiences in engaging the public on biotechnology advances and regulation. *Front. Bioeng. Biotechnol.* **2010**, *4*, 3. [CrossRef]
31. Costa-Font, M.; Gil, J.M.; Traill, W.B. Consumer acceptance, valuation of and attitudes towards genetically modified food: Review and implications for food policy. *Food Policy* **2008**, *33*, 99–111. [CrossRef]
32. Callaway, E. CRISPR plants now subject to tough GM laws in European Union. *Nature* **2018**, *560*, 16–17. [CrossRef]
33. Friedrichs, S.; Takasu, Y.; Kearns, P.; Dagallier, B.; Oshima, R.; Schofield, J.; Moreddu, C. Policy considerations regarding genome editing. *Trends Biotechnol.* **2019**, *37*, 1029–1032. [CrossRef]
34. Jones, M.S.; Delborne, J.A.; Elsensohn, J.; Mitchell, P.D.; Brown, Z.S. Does the US public support using gene drives in agriculture? And what do they want to know? *Sci. Adv.* **2019**, *5*, 8462. [CrossRef]
35. Calabrese, C.; Featherstone, J.D.; Robbins, M.; Barnett, G.A. Examining the relationship between gene editing knowledge, value predispositions, and general science attitudes among US farmers, scientists, policymakers, and the general public. *J. Sci. Commun.* **2021**, *20*, A02. [CrossRef]
36. Boersma, R.; Poortvliet, P.M.; Gremmen, B. The elephant in the room: How a technology's name affects its interpretation. *Public Underst. Sci.* **2019**, *28*, 218–233. [CrossRef] [PubMed]
37. Hennink, M.M. *Focus Group Discussions*; Oxford University Press: Oxford, UK, 2013.
38. Verhoog, H. Defining positive welfare and animal integrity. In *Diversity of Livestock Systems and Definition of Animal Welfare*; University of Reading: Reading, UK, 2000; pp. 108–119.
39. Noll, S. Balancing Food Security and Ecological Resilience in the Age of the Anthropocene. In *Food, Environment, and Climate Change: Justice at the Intersections*; Rowman & Littlefield: Lanham, MD, USA, 2018; pp. 179–192.

40. Terry, G.; Hayfield, N.; Clarke, V.; Braun, V. Thematic analysis. *SAGE Handb. Qual. Res. Psychol.* **2017**, *2*, 17–37.
41. Thompson, P.B. The opposite of Human Enhancement:Nanotechnology and the blind chicken problem. *Nanoethics* **2008**, *2*, 305–316. [CrossRef]
42. Fischer, B. In defense of neural disenhancement to promote animal welfare. In *Neuroethics and Nonhuman Animals*; Johnson, L., Fenton, A., Shriver, A., Eds.; Springer: Cham, Switzerland, 2020; pp. 135–150.
43. Wawrzyniak, D. Why fitting animals itself is ethically dubious. *Landbauforsch.-J. Sustain. Org. Agric. Syst.* **2020**, *70*, 1–4.
44. Kramer, K.; Meijboom, F.L.B. Using Breeding Technologies to Improve Farm Animal Welfare: What is the Ethical Relevance of Telos? *J. Agric. Environ. Ethics* **2021**, *34*, 1–18. [CrossRef]
45. Vidal, N.; Barbosa, H.; Jacob, S.; Arruda, M. Comparative study of transgenic and non-transgenic maize (*Zea mays*) flours commercialized in Brazil, focussing on proteomic analyses. *Food Chem.* **2015**, *180*, 288–294. [CrossRef]
46. Frewer, L.J.; Bergmann, K.; Brennan, M.; Rene, L.; Meertens, R.; Rowe, G.; Siegrist, M.; Vereijken, C.M.J.L. Consumer response to novel agri-food technologies: Implications for predicting consumer acceptance of emerging food technologies. *Trends Food Sci. Technol.* **2011**, *22*, 442–456. [CrossRef]
47. Pidgeon, W.; Pidgeon, N.F. Trust in risk regulation: Cause or consequence of the acceptability of GM food? *Risk Anal. Int. J.* **2005**, *25*, 199–209. [CrossRef] [PubMed]
48. Fleming, A.; Abdalla, E.A.; Maltecca, C.; Baes, C.F. Invited review: Reproductive and genomic technologies to optimise breeding strategies for genetic progress in dairy cattle. *Arch. Fuer Tierz.* **2018**, *61*, 43. [CrossRef]
49. Onyango, B.; Ferdaus, H.; Hallman, W.; Schilling, B.; Adelajan, A. Public Perceptions of Food Biotechnology: Uncovering Factors Driving Consumer Acceptance of Genetically Modified Food. *J. Food Distrib. Res.* **2003**, *34*, 37–42.
50. Savadori, L.; Savio, S.; Nocotra, E.; Rumiati, R.; Finucane, M.; Slovic, P. Expert and public perception of risk from biotechnology. *Risk Anal.* **2004**, *24*, 1289–1299. [CrossRef] [PubMed]
51. Coles, D.; Frewer, L.J.; Goddard, E. Ethical issues and potential stakeholder priorities associated with the application of genomic technologies applied to animal production systems. *J. Agric. Environ. Ethics* **2015**, *28*, 231–253. [CrossRef]
52. European Court of Justice. Judgement of the Court (Grand Chamber), 25 July 2018 in Case C-528/16. 2018. Available online: http://curia.europa.eu/juris/document/document.jsf?text=&docid=204387&pageIndex=0&doclang=en&mode=req&dir=&occ=first&part=1&cid=133112 (accessed on 29 March 2021).
53. van der Meer, P.; Angenon, G.; Bergmans, H.; Buhk, H.J.; Callebaut, S.; Chamon, M.; Eriksson, D.; Gheysen, G.; Harwood, W.; Hundleby, P.; et al. The status under EU law of organisms developed through novel genomic techniques. *Eur. J. Risk Regul.* **2020**, 1–20. [CrossRef]

BioTech

Article

Synthetic Biology: Old and New Dilemmas—The Case of Artificial Life

Nikolaos Kolisis [1,*] and Fragiskos Kolisis [2]

1 School of Law, National and Kapodistrian University of Athens, Solonos 57, 10679 Athens, Greece
2 Biotechnology Laboratory, School of Chemical Engineering, National Technical University of Athens, Zografou Campus, 9, Iroon Polytechniou str, 15780 Athens, Greece; kolisis@chemeng.ntua.gr
* Correspondence: nkolisis@yahoo.gr; Tel.: +30-698-285-2587

Abstract: This article aims to examine some of the ethical questions emerging from the use of already existing biotechnological tools and the issues which might occur by synthetic biology's potential future possibilities. In the first part, the essence of synthetic biology and its relation to the contemporary biotechnological research is analyzed. In the second part, the article examines whether the new biotechnological inventions pose new or revive old moral questions about the ethics of science, engineering, and technology in general. After briefly addressing some of the various issues which are raised by experts, philosophers, but also the general public, concerning synthetic biology in general, it focuses on the topic of "artificial life creation" and presents moral reasons which may or may not allow it. The topic is approached by referring to consequentialist, deontological, but also, virtue theory arguments for and against it and the possibility of a partial permission of "artificial life" experiments, asking whether the benefits outweigh the risks and moral implications is explored. Finally, it proposes an argument in favor of the future exploration of biological innovation, underlying the need for a more balanced access to its beneficial results.

Keywords: biotechnology; synthetic biology; system biology; bioethics; synthetic life; ethics

Citation: Kolisis, N.; Kolisis, F. Synthetic Biology: Old and New Dilemmas—The Case of Artificial Life. *BioTech* **2021**, *10*, 16. https://doi.org/10.3390/biotech10030016

Academic Editor: Vasiliki Mollaki

Received: 12 April 2021
Accepted: 14 July 2021
Published: 20 July 2021

1. Introduction

Synthetic biology and its aims has been a subject of discussion among scientists, philosophers and the wider public. Its applications influence our lives, and the orientation of its further development is crucial for the progress of humanity in the following years. As expected by such a "scientific revolution", its birth and growth has led to the emergence of moral and empirical issues. In this article we will try to approach the nature of synthetic biology and its relation to novel biotechnological methods and aims. We will subsequently try to present some of the arguments raised by its applications, especially the emerging controversial subject of synthetic life. After addressing some of the most common arguments against life synthesis, we propose a way to continue research on artificial life under specific moral and empirical terms.

2. The Nature of Synthetic Biology

The successful completion of the Human Genome Project triggered an explosive development of contemporary biological research. Based on its findings it was showed that a human has about 25.000 genes, little more than a chimpanzee and far less than a pine tree (about 100.000). It became evident that the function of living organisms could not be addressed satisfactorily by looking at genes and molecules alone, even if all of them were studied [1]. Consequently, at the dawn of the so-called "metagenomics" era of the 21st century, biological research needed to adopt a stochastic approach instead of the, until then, popular deterministic one [2]. The concept of "Systems Biology", in other words the study of living organisms in terms of their underlying network structure rather than simply their individual molecular components, emerged, conceiving as a "system" anything from a gene regulatory network to a cell, a tissue, or an entire organism [3,4]. The growth of biological research influenced the technological evolution and vice versa, as it happens when big scientific breakthroughs occur. Technological innovations supported biological research by providing sophisticated and precise apparatus as well as "high throughput techniques". From that moment, it became obvious that computational approaches are required to handle and interpret the data necessary to understand the complex biological systems. Computational Technology was linked with System Biology [5]. This interconnection with the additional integration of engineering principles gave birth to synthetic biology. Synthetic biology can be considered as a research area in which scientists and engineers try to modify existing organisms by redesigning and synthesizing artificial genes, proteins, and metabolic pathways, as well as complete biological systems [6]. This emerging research field is interdisciplinary and consists of scientific tools and principles taken from biology, chemistry, informatics, engineering, mathematics and computational modeling. Synthetic biology's main aims are first, to improve our understanding of biological systems, of their complexity and of the properties emerging from their interactions, and second, to make possible the use of organisms—cells and their systems—as "factories" for the production, among others, of drugs, biomedical products like vaccines and diagnostics or new tools for biosecurity, and new "smart materials" with specialized properties. The experts of synthetic biology are aiming not only to provide novel biotechnological applications but also to contribute to the advancement of the science of biology in general.

As it happens with many emerging scientific fields, there is not an explicit and universally accepted definition for synthetic biology. Due to its experimental nature, a functional definition could depend on its expected results and applications, or generally on its basic research aims. For instance, some definitions include: "*Synthetic biology aims to design and engineer biologically based parts, novel devices and systems as well as redesigning existing, natural biological systems*" [7], or "*Synthetic biology is the engineering of biology: the deliberate (re)design and construction of novel biological and biologically based parts, devices and systems to perform new functions for useful purposes, that draws on principles elucidated from biology and engineering*" [8]. A definition which seems to represent in a better way the nature of synthetic biology and to clarify that it is not a novel scientific discipline underlines that: "*Synthetic Biology is a further development and new dimension of modern biotechnology that combines science, technology and engineering to facilitate and accelerate the understanding, design, redesign, manufacture and/or modification of genetic materials, living organisms and biological systems*" [9].

One of the fields which attract the interest of many researchers in the development of synthetic biology is the dynamics of the Synthetic Genome. In the Synthetic Genome research projects, scientists can make use of the wealth of information available about genomics as well as the tools that can be used for their manipulation. Amongst them is the oligonucleotide synthesis or genetic modification of the genome towards the creation of new types of genomes, which could lead to new biotechnological applications. Synthetic biologists use two strategic approaches in their studies: the "top-down" and the "bottom-up". In the top-down strategy they attempt to re-design existing organisms (a bacterium or a virus) or gene sequences in order to remove the genetic parts which are not necessary for the role this organism is intended to play. Specific genetic parts of them can also be replaced or added in order to give the organisms in question new characteristics and functions. The final goal is to create a "minimum genome" or a "minimal cell" (as simple as possible for its survival), which can be used as a "chassis", where the new genes will be introduced to change or enrich its biological properties and lead to innovative processes [10]. In this "platform" the addition of synthetic genes, or even a whole synthetic genome, are possible, using genetic codes which could consist of synthetic bases, other than the known four of existing life forms, namely A, T, C and G [5,10].The tools of this strategy are computational and experimental comparative genomics, minimal genomics, synthetic genes, metabolic engineering, new metabolic pathways, genetic circuits, etc.

While top-down synthetic biology in general uses properties from living systems to create something new, in bottom-up synthetic biology, which is significantly more challenging, scientists aim to build living systems from raw materials starting from non-living components. In this approach researchers try to create genetically engineered circuits and switches to turn specific functions "on" and "off" in response to designed stimuli, with an ultimate aim to include them in reconstructed vesicles as protocell- approach and cell-free systems [11,12]. A simple gene circuit comprises of a promoter, a ribosome binding site, the protein coding sequence, and a terminator. The reconstitution of the biological systems is based on the idea of their modularity. Each module—which is considered as the smallest functional entity of a biological system—consists of different building blocks with independent functional bio-parts and bio-devices. In current synthetic biology there is a hierarchy based on (a) the bio-parts, which encode biological functions (e.g., synthetically designed DNA), (b) the bio-devices, which are made from a collection of bio-parts and encode human defined functions (e.g., logic gates), and (c) bio-systems, which perform tasks, such as counting and intracellular control functions. This complex network can be re-designed and reconstructed according to the properties one wants the system under investigation to have [6].

To sum-up, the Systems Biology approach uses quantitative methods and, based on the systems engineering principles and on signal theories, attempts to analyze the biological systems under investigation. From the moment a system can be described in mathematical terms, synthetic biology organizes it into bio-parts or bio-devices and estimates their functionality using the classic reductive method. Following this methodology, complex systems and processes can be synthesized by well characterized, registered, and standardized parts and devices. An ideal objective could be the construction of a synthetic cell—an artificial synthetic life form—which can have various applications, such as the synthesis of products of high added value or can be used as an instrument of high technological specialization in specific applications (for example as biosensors used for the diagnosis of various diseases or in order to control the levels of toxic substances in the environment).

3. Critique of Synthetic Life Experiments

Public, philosophical and scientific scepticism towards biotechnological advancements involves opinions which oppose the "substitution" of God or nature by humanity, fear of the potential emergence of reductionist views about life (which may lead to undermining its value and affect the way humanity conceives itself and the environment) and finally, question the moral status of the artificially created life forms. As we have argued continuous innovation in the field of biology and the contribution of sciences like physics, mathematics and computer science rendered biologists capable of creating their own models and to intervene to life forms rather than just observing them. Thus, the drawbacks mentioned are not considered novel. Yet, since the first steps towards life creation by experiments such as the one conducted in the Craig Venter Institute [13], criticism and concerns have been revived. In this part, we will try to address the "playing God", "undermining life's value", "creating organisms of unknown status" arguments. We will explore different aspects of terms such as "living organism", "artificially created life" and "natural" beings and environment, and will approach according to consequentialist, deontological and virtue theory-based principles the issue of "synthesizing life forms".

3.1. *The "Natural"-"Artificial" Dipole*

The differences between "top-down" and "bottom-up" approaches have already been analyzed. Top-down processes are characterized by the use of already existing cells. Experiments, such as the one conducted at the Craig Venter Institute which resulted to the creation of "Synthia", are substituting natural DNA with an artificial. For this reason this procedure is not considered to be a complete life synthesis, it has been characterized as a copy of an already existing organism. Bottom-up experiments on the other hand are intended to create viable organisms from simple matter. Their approach seems to be closer to what we might call "life synthesis" [14]. Before we proceed to the examination of whether the creation of "artificial life" is morally acceptable or not and, if so, under what terms, we need to make a brief assessment on what can be perceived as a living entity.

The question "what is life" has been central since humanity's first steps in rational thinking. Since the Aristotelian conception of life, there has been significant alteration of the exact meaning of the term. In general, a living being can be defined by its capacity to metabolize, to reproduce and die [15]. An organism can also be conceived as an entity in constant flux. A living being must interact with its environment in order to survive—it needs to get the substances which are essential for its self-preservation. An organism, by interacting with its environment and eventually by dying, becomes a part of the process of evolution [16]. Living organisms are morally important as they have interests; through research and observation one can conceive what is good for them and what makes them flourish and act accordingly. For some thinkers who adopt a bio-centrist approach [17], all living entities matter morally and their interests need to be taken into account when planning our actions. Life synthesis may bring novel moral questions when adding moral agents—organisms with interests—which might be taken under consideration. So far, part of the moral argument in favor of the respectful treatment of organisms, other than human, was our common ancestry through evolution. Synthetic biology might change that by creating artificial life. The question might now be whether artificial beings matter morally.

But where does one draw the line between the "natural" and the "artificial"? The concept of nature and its relationship with humanity—humans in nature—has been the subject of discussion for many thinkers. J.S. Mill has famously approached nature either as: (a) anything that happens in the world or (b) anything that happens without human voluntary causation. Some preservationists aim at conserving the parts of the world which have not been altered definitely by human intervention [18]. A more recent approach, made by K. Soper [19] defines nature in three ways: either as a concept needed for the separation of humanity by its environment; a concept useful for us so that we can think of the distinction between human and non-human, or as the way in which natural sciences interpret and explain what occurs in the world (including human actions). In "lay terms", this means taking as "natural" anything that is not profoundly human made, such as environments other than cities or factories; this may include non-human animals, forests, etc. Following J.S. Mill, we believe that what is considered "natural" cannot be the guide for human behavior, let alone the basis of moral claims. For this reason, in our opinion, arguments criticizing synthetic biology's "unnaturalness" need to focus more on the way the procedure is conducted (how scientists conceive of their role, how the created organisms are treated, how respectful for life is the regulation etc. [20]). Secondly, as we tried to show, synthetic biology is not a novel discipline, rather it combines already used methods in order to achieve its aims so far. For example, we find that the procedures and tools used by synthetic biology have not been criticized as immoral when applied in genomics or systems biology.

For some thinkers, living beings are characterized by the fact that they have an inherent purpose—a "telos" or aim to flourish or to satisfy their interests. According to them, a synthetic organism will have both transcendental and immanent aims or, in some other thinkers' terms, proximate and ultimate interests, thus occupying a position between fully artificial and fully natural beings [21]. Fully artificial beings have no goal separate from that of their user/creator and therefore have only transcendental aims, while fully natural beings—as we believe—have immanent aims naturally emerging through evolution. By immanent or proximate interests, we classify all functions which aim at the conservation or the reproduction of the organism. Therefore, their use by humans must be regulated accordingly [15].

Humans must conceive both their intrinsic and their instrumental value. The lines blur if we consider activities such as animal breeding, which follows a natural process but is human directed; many species would have been completely different had humanity not intervened, shaping them for its own aims. Furthermore humans do create, but they are a part of nature. Humanity is a product of evolution; humans are animals which, by using their evolved capabilities, interacted with the environment in different ways than other animals did in order to achieve self-preservation and conservation of the species. Despite humanity's achievements, it remains part of nature, so whatever humanity produces could, in this way, be considered natural. Humans obey the laws of physics and are part of the evolutionary process just like every other being on Earth. It can also be noted that if any synthetic life form (even organisms that do not exist in nature, such as XNA-organisms) obey to the same laws of physics, biology etc. and are thought of as "living", they can be considered also a part of nature. Other thinkers underline that for many years vocabulary used to describe machines was also employed in order to explain biological processes and functions. In these terms, the blurring of the line between "machine" and "organism" or "artificial" and "natural" might not be so obvious, especially in an age of intervention to and manipulation of the genome of natural organisms. On the other hand, an abstract approach of genetically modified life forms, synthetic life forms and "living machines" may prove to be a very slippery slope and prepare a way of unequal treatment of the beings "created" [22].

3.2. *"Playing God" or "Substituting Nature"*

In our opinion, in order to address the problem of the moral status and the treatment of synthetic organisms, we must first ask whether their creation is inherently wrong. We find that the commonly presented and frequently adopted "playing God" or "substituting Nature" argument must be examined under the perspective of previous and future human actions. It is claimed that humans must not mess with certain aspects of nature: that reaching so far into the secrets of life constitutes a hubris, an immoral attitude, or our species tendency towards domination and control [21,23,24]. As humans are neither omnipotent nor omniscient, the consequences of their actions in this field may be proven disastrous for the planet [25]. We believe that although it is true that humans present a destructive tendency to expand and consume the planet's resources and to mistreat non-human animals, it might be claimed that this tendency is linked to a specific way of organizing our society and developing our economy and not part of our biology. In other words, whether these experiments will end up being another addition in the series of human products is a matter of control and regulation.

As mentioned, humans have always manipulated other life forms in order to ameliorate their own state. Of course, the fact that something has always been this way is not enough to justify anything (the examples of slavery, sex inequality and the current harsh treatment of animals prove so). For this reason, it might be morally sound that humans better abstain from deepening their knowledge in this domain. One could also argue that if there indeed exists a special value in natural organisms and life forms in general, this might be based on the fact that they are products of the evolutionary process—we share with them a common ancestor and we have a genetic proximity. The same cannot be said for organisms that are synthesized in a lab. For this reason, these kind of organisms are different and, as they are manmade, they are inferior.

Contrary to these claims, we find that, the inherent value of a being rests not on the way it is brought to life, but on the properties we choose to attribute to it. As the example of the IVF babies shows, we don't consider IVF babies to be inferior. If indeed there exists a special value in life it must be conserved and shared by all beings we consider "living"—artificial or natural [26,27]. The fact that science needs to advance humanity's knowledge on life's mechanisms and characteristics admits exactly that we are not omniscient and will never be. The way we approach the world around us—the inherent curiosity of mankind—helps us understand and admire its complexity. It is our belief that a push forward towards scientific research expresses exactly this kind of admiration.

3.3. *Is Synthetic Life Leading to Reductionism?*

Another argument which opposes the development of artificial life forms supports that such type of experiments may create a reductionist conception of life and its value [23].

This critique is based on a fear that scientists tend to follow a mechanistic approach of nature and make descriptions of biological phenomena to look like a series of chemical interactions obeying mathematical equations. Yet, the majority of scientists reject the idea that life is just a sum of chemical substances interacting with each other—they do not conceive the whole of a living organism as a sum of its parts. In our opinion, it is quite improbable that this view will change in the future, as the more we discover about life the more we realize that there is more to it than that and we remain ignorant of many of life's mysteries [28].

In sum, we understand that realizing humanity's present capacity to take such a big step towards comprehending and controlling some of the mechanisms of life might inspire sentiments of fear, especially given the history of uses of scientific discoveries and innovations (gunpowder, nuclear weapons), yet it is in our hands to control the way scientific knowledge might be used. In other words, we find that as with every other technological advancement, it is the use that might be immoral, not the technology itself.

3.4. Virtue Ethics and Life Synthesis

Apart from the fear of hubris or disrespect towards God or nature which, for some, makes life synthesis intrinsically bad (a deontological perspective), or a belief that such experiments will lead to dangerous paths, creating new weapons or threatening the environment (a more consequentialist approach), a type of virtue theory ethics also disapproves this kind of research [15]. This view emphasizes the importance of the virtues which must be cultivated, namely humility, gratefulness for the giftedness of life, respect for the laws of nature, and precaution in front of the unknown consequences, which may lead to an abstention from the use of all the technological means humanity has under its disposition. According to the teleological point of view of virtue ethics, the manipulation of life alienates our species from the universal telos of shared existence—it generates a conception of "sheer thinghood" for living beings and separates humanity from the other species, creating an "us and them" [15]. This attitude towards nature neglects the fact that we are part of an ecosystem and tries to bring every aspect of the environment under control for the maximization of utility.

Summarizing, one can find that the arguments opposing the current and future projects of synthetic biology draw from the vocabulary and theoretical basis of all three basic moral theories. We must also acknowledge the existence of an intuition among the wider public against the synthesis of life forms. It has been pointed out that artificial life brings humanity to a new place in its relationship with nature, and that the "living machines" are a new adjustment in the ecosystem in the sum of morally significant entities [29–31]. In the next part we will try to provide an answer to the arguments presented and develop our own approach, promoting the permissibility of the creation of synthetic life under specific terms.

3.5. Difference between Artificial "Copies" and Natural Beings

One of the main sources of concern towards creating life is the fact that the new organism's synthesis out of non-living parts (its artificiality) will constitute a breach with the natural world. We mentioned that part of our connection to the ecosystem is our common ancestry—humans constitute a part of the sum of living beings of planet Earth, they are beings which emerged after millions of years of evolution. For some, when creating living organisms, humanity bypasses natural selection and makes scientific will superior to natural evolution, acting thus in a hubristic way. In order to respond to this argument, we need to distinguish between a potential creation of artificial copies of existing organisms and a synthesis of completely new types of organisms. As far as copies are concerned, one must underline that the existence of an identical—artificially-generated—organism carries no special moral weight. In order to discriminate between the natural organism and its copy one must prove that the different way they came into existence (synthesis or birth) is morally significant. We find that a copy does not constitute a breach in the chain of evolution as it is identical with the natural entity. By copying nature, humanity does not prove its superiority towards it but rather expresses admiration and curiosity for its complexity. We base this argument on the assumption that if one can spot no difference between a "copied" artificial life form and the natural "original", one cannot discriminate between the two [32]. If one would create, for example, a jellyfish identical to a natural one, there is no sufficient moral reason for us to judge that one—the natural—is better than the other. If this were the case, one would tell us that the so-called "copy" is, in reality, a natural jellyfish, and vice versa. In particular, we would have to change the way we value the animal accordingly, something which would be absurd.

There can also be the case of a potential creation of an organism which will externally resemble a natural one but will have different properties, for example, a jellyfish created to be used as a biosensor to detect high levels of pollution by changing color when exposed to a specific substance. In that case, these organisms constitute an almost entirely different type of entity—it will be an organism which must matter morally according to its complexity and not be treated as a mere instrument.

We argue that the potential creation of an organism which resembles a natural one must be regulated taking into account the level of its biological complexity, as one may argue that it does not carry the same moral worth as its "natural" twin.

On the other hand, scientists may be considering the possibility of creating entirely new life forms, as has happened in the past with hybrids, which were generated by humans through breeding. At the time however, human capabilities in animal-crossing were limited due to the knowledge of genetics. In this new era, genetic technology has given scientists the power to create chimeras and make the first steps towards the synthesis of life. Thus, it is crucial to regulate the terms under which potential new life forms may come into existence. For these reasons, we need to consider whether the creation of entirely new organisms is morally significant, if the creation of new species causes negative intuitions, and if so, for what reasons [33].

4. What Kind of Organisms Shall We Create?

In examining this topic, we claim that the thin line between artificial–natural must be conserved in order to better understand the way in which a being comes to life and make the distinction between an organism created from scratch and an organism generated through natural reproduction. However, at the same time, as mentioned, we find that this distinction is morally insignificant as far as the treatment of these organisms is concerned. We have argued that the moral status of an organism remains the same if it is a copy of an existing species, but on what terms does a completely new life form (an XNA organism for example) obtain its status?

We find that organisms complex enough to be considered morally—in other words multicellular conscious beings—would rather not be created. In our opinion, the more complex an organism is, the more difficult it is to ignore its immanent aims and its interests for self-sustainability and pain avoidance. A potential cause of suffering to a sentient being by its scientist/creator may significantly harm these types of organisms' interests and, as we consider them to matter morally, we prefer not to put the creators in the position in which they may harm the new being. For this reason, its creation must be strictly regulated [34] for aims generally judged as superior, such as research for health issues of more complex organisms and environmental sustainability. We are critical of the creation of entirely new complex organisms, not only for reasons of biosafety and security but also for moral reasons. We understand the complexity of the term consciousness, thus we choose a more biological approach in our effort to specify it. We also stress the need for up to date legislation with research concerning levels of consciousness in living beings [35,36]. Simpler life forms, such as viruses, bacteria or protozoa, could be generated according to safety and security regulations.

Difference between Artificial "Copies" and Artificial New Species

What makes an artificial multicellular animal-like organism different to a lab mouse born in order to be used for experimental reasons is that, although this specific mouse was created or born in order to be used in an experiment (and therefore is quasi-objectified), being part of an experiment is not an inherent characteristic of its nature. Mice are not naturally lab animals, designed for research purposes. It could very well be released without that making any difference to the aim of its existence: to survive and reproduce. The same goes for an artificial mouse. On the other hand, a new artificial entity will always be partially instrumental, created as a lab organism—an object for experimental use. Even if one believes that the ecosystem, or organisms in particular, have no specific "telos" and therefore a natural or artificial organism has no specific purpose, one should consider that in that case that artificial new life forms differ from the natural and their artificial copies in that they do have a purpose—they were created for a reason.

One can think that an artificial mouse generated to be part of an experiment and an artificial animal-entity generated for the same reason are similar, as they are both synthetic and both are used in a lab. In that case, what is the difference between a synthetic mouse which, as we argued, carries the same moral value as a natural one, and an artificial animal entity designed and created for experimental reasons? Is it mere appearance, an issue of DNA?

We already have legislation preventing harm to animals in research and regulating their use in experiments [37]. An artificial being may have moral significance based on the fact that it resembles a natural being. An entirely new life form on the other hand may draw its moral status from its complexity, its level of consciousness. A living being will always develop its own goals: to self-sustain and reproduce. Moreover, a complex multicellular organism capable to feel pain and agony and conscious of a part of its identity or at least able to create a primary concept of a "self" [38], will also develop further interests, such as avoiding circumstances which may cause pain. One needs to find a strong moral reason why it should be manipulated in a way which may be contrary to its will. Such a reason cannot be but experiments concerning subjects of higher moral value, such as the ones addressing health or environmental problems.

We believe that the use of (natural) animals for experimental reasons is morally problematic and should be avoided if possible. For the same reasons, the creation of beings complex enough to feel pain and agony in order to experiment with constitutes a moral step backwards. What we should aim to do is avoid causing pain and suffering to anything and not just change the object of our potentially painful operations.

A crucial issue which might emerge in the synthesis of a complex moral being is that its creators may argue that it might be used in order to save a human life, through organ transplantation for example. In that case, we believe that a generation of such an entity is also morally problematic: to generate life in order to use or even destroy it is by itself morally impermissible. It will be different than a case of xenotransplantation (which by itself is a controversial subject). We find that this use may lead to reductionism, reducing living beings into sums of biologically functional parts.

5. Conclusions

We have argued that synthetic biology is not a novel scientific discipline, it emerged from the development of biotechnological research under the influence of the systemic biology's approach and the scientific and engineering tools which were developed during the Human Genome Project research. In addition, amongst the various research strategies used in synthetic biology, only the bottom-up approach can be related with the construction of artificial synthetic life forms. Secondly, we presented an opinion in favor of the evolution of technologies permitting the creation of synthetic life forms and claimed that synthetic beings possess moral status. On the other hand, we disapproved the potential creation of multicellular complex and conscious beings for reasons other than scientific research concerning human health or environmental sustainability, as we support the idea that this type of organisms' status does not permit ignoring their interests and/or causing unnecessary pain. We believe that the objectives of synthetic biology in general, and life –synthesis in particular, must be the promotion of humanity's health and the protection of the environment, and hope for a just and sustainable distribution of scientific benefits. Although the science of biology has entered a new era, we must not abandon principles such as the respect of life and dignity, which lead us so far. Biologists need to remember that justice and virtue is what separates "science from roguery" [39].

Author Contributions: Conceptualization, N.K.; investigation, N.K. and F.K.; writing—original draft preparation—review and editing, N.K. and F.K. Both authors have read and agreed to the published version of the manuscript.

Funding: This work received no external funding.

Conflicts of Interest: The authors declare no conflict of interest.

References

1. Westerhoff, H.V.; Winder, C.; Messiha, H.; Simeonidis, V.; Adamczyk, M.; Verma, M.; Bruggeman, F.J.; Dunn, W. Systems Biology: The elements and principles of Life. *FEBS Lett.* **2009**, *583*, 3882–3890. [CrossRef]
2. Atlan, H. *Le Vivant Post-Genomic: Ou Qu'est-ce que l'Auto-Organisation?* Odile Jacob Sciences: Paris, France, 2011; pp. 39–60.
3. Kitano, H. Systems Biology: A Brief Overview. *Science* **2002**, *295*, 1662–1664. [CrossRef]
4. Kitano, H. Computational systems biology. *Nature* **2002**, *420*, 206–210. [CrossRef] [PubMed]
5. Marcus, W. *Covert, Fundamentals of Systems Biology: From Synthetic Circuits to Whole-Cell Models*; CRC Press: Boca Raton, FL, USA; Taylor & Francis Group: Abingdon, UK, 2015.
6. Baldwin, G.; Bayer, T.; Dickinson, R.; Ellis, T.; Freemont, P.S.; Kitney, R.I.; Polizzi, K.; Stan, G.-B. *Synthetic Biology: A Primer*; World Scientific Publishing: Singapore, 2016.
7. Royal Academy of Engineers. 2009. Available online: https://www.google.com/url?client=internal-element-cse&cx=005135733883558849575:cfmytgziwsk&q=https://www.raeng.org.uk/publications/reports/synthetic-biology-report&sa=U&ved=2ahUKEwiy_6eZhPDxAhXpgP0HHTIpCU8QFjAAegQICBAC&usg=AOvVaw1WuUJ9r5TWOBTR6sNsgIlF (accessed on 19 July 2021).
8. Report Tessy, 2008. Available online: http://www.tessy-europe.eu/public_docs/TESSY-Final-Report_D5-3.pdf (accessed on 16 December 2008).
9. Synthetic Biology and the Convention on Biological Diversity. In Proceedings of the Conference of the Parties to the Convention on Biological Diversity, Cancun, Mexico, 4–17 December 2016. Available online: https://www.iucn.org/theme/science-and-economics (accessed on 14 July 2021).
10. De Lorenzo, V.; Krasnogor, N.; Schmidt, M. For the sake of the Bioeconomy: Define what a Synthetic Biology Chassis is! *New Biotechnol.* **2021**, *60*, 44–51. [CrossRef] [PubMed]
11. Solé, R.V.; Munteanu, A.; Rodriguez-Caso, C.; Macía, J. Synthetic protocell biology: From reproduction to computation. *Philos. Trans. R. Soc. B Biol. Sci.* **2007**, *362*, 1727–1739. [CrossRef] [PubMed]
12. Cho, E.; Lu, Y. Compartmentalizing Cell-Free Systems: Toward Creating Life-Like Artificial Cells and Beyond. *ACS Synth. Biol.* **2020**, *9*, 2881–2901. [CrossRef] [PubMed]
13. Stuart, F.J. Craig Venter Institute Creates First Synthetic Life. *Christian Science Monitor*, 21 May 2010.
14. Pelletier, J.F.; Sun, L.; Wise, K.S.; Assad-Garcia, N.; Karas, B.J.; Deerinck, T.J.; Ellisman, M.H.; Mershin, A.; Gershenfeld, N.; Chuang, R.-Y.; et al. Genetic requirements for cell division in a genomically minimal cell. *Cell* **2021**, *184*, 2430–2440.e16. [CrossRef]
15. Coyne, L. The Ethics and Ontology of Synthetic Biology: A Neo-Aristotelian Perspective. *NanoEthics* **2020**, *14*, 43–55. [CrossRef]
16. Nurse, P. *What Is Life? Five Great Ideas in Biology, Kindle Edition*; W.W. Norton & Company: New York, NY, USA, 2021.
17. Taylor, P.W. *Respect for Nature a Theory of Environmental Ethics*; Princeton University Press: Princeton, NJ, USA, 1986.
18. Mill, J.S. Nature. In *Essential Works of John Stuart Mill*; Bantam Books: New York, NY, USA, 1961.
19. Soper, K. *What Is Nature? Culture, Politics and the Non-Human*; Blackwell: Oxford, UK, 1995.
20. Kaebnick, G.E. *Humans in Nature: The World as We Find It and the World as We Create It*; Oxford University Press: New York, NY, USA, 2013.
21. Deplazes-Zemp, A. The Moral Impact of Synthesising Living Organisms: Biocentric Views on Synthetic Biology. *Environ. Values* **2012**, *21*, 63–82. [CrossRef]
22. Boldt, J. Machine metaphors and ethics in synthetic biology. *LifeSci. Soc. Policy* **2018**, *14*, 12. [CrossRef]
23. Calvert, J. Synthetic Biology: Constructing Nature? *Sociol. Rev.* **2010**, *58*, 95–112. [CrossRef]
24. Kass, L. Ageless bodies, happy souls: Biotechnology and the pursuit of perfection. *New Atlantis* **2003**, *1*, 9–28.
25. Buchanan, A. *Beyond Humanity*; Oxford University Press: Oxford, UK, 2011.
26. Baertschi, B. The Moral Status of Artificial Life. *Environ. Values* **2012**, *21*, 5–18. [CrossRef]
27. Attfield, R.A. Biocentrism and Artificial Life. *Environ. Values* **2012**, *21*, 83–94. [CrossRef]

28. Douglas, T.; Savulescu, J. Synthetic biology and the ethics of knowledge. *J. Med. Ethics* **2010**, *36*, 687–693. [CrossRef] [PubMed]
29. Nicholson, D.J. Organisms ≠ Machines. *Stud. Hist. Philos. Sci. Part C Stud. Hist. Philos. Biol. Biomed. Sci.* **2013**, *44*, 669–678. [CrossRef] [PubMed]
30. Schark, M. Synthetic Biology and the Distinction between Organisms and Machines. *Environ. Values* **2012**, *21*, 19–41. [CrossRef]
31. Charles, T.W. The organism as ontological go-between: Hybridity, boundaries and degrees of reality in its conceptual history. *Stud. Hist. Philos. Sci. Part C Stud. Hist. Philos. Biol. Biomed. Sci.* **2014**, *48*, 151–161.
32. Cengiz, N.; Wareham, C.S. Ethical considerations in xenotransplantation. *Curr. Opin. Organ Transplant.* **2020**, *25*, 483–488. [CrossRef]
33. Koplin, J.J.; Savulescu, J. Time to rethink the law on part-human chimeras. *J. Law Biosci.* **2019**, *6*, 37–50. [CrossRef]
34. Keiper, F.; Atanassova, A. Regulation of Synthetic Biology: Developments under the Convention on Biological Diversity and Its Protocols. *Front. Bioeng. Biotechnol.* **2020**, *8*, 310. [CrossRef] [PubMed]
35. Braun, C.M.; Lovejoy, S. The biology of consciousness from the bottom up. *Adapt. Behav.* **2018**, *26*, 91–109. [CrossRef]
36. Leung, A.; Cohen, D.; van Swinderen, B.; Tsuchiya, N. Integrated information structure collapses with anesthetic loss of conscious arousal in Drosophila melanogaster. *PloS Comput. Biol.* **2021**, *17*, e1008722. [CrossRef]
37. Directive 2010/63/EU of the European Parliament and of the Council of 22 September 2010 on the protection of animals used for scientific purposes. *Off. J. Eur. Union* **2020**, *276*, 33–79. Available online: https://eur-lex.europa.eu/legal-content/EN/TXT/?uri=uriserv%3AOJ.L_.2010.276.01.0033.01.ENG&toc=OJ%3AL%3A2010%3A276%3ATOC (accessed on 15 July 2021).
38. Pettit, P. My Three Selves. *Philosophy* **2020**, *95*, 363–389. [CrossRef]
39. Plato. "Menexenus". In *Platonis Opera*; Burnet, J., Ed.; Oxford University Press: Oxford, UK, 1903; pp. 246e–247a.

BioTech

Article

Privacy Implications of Contacting the At-Risk Relatives of Patients with Medically Actionable Genetic Predisposition, with Patient Consent: A Hypothetical Australian Case Study

Jane Tiller [1,2,3,*], Kristen Nowak [4], Tiffany Boughtwood [1,2] and Margaret Otlowski [5]

1 Australian Genomics, Parkville, VIC 3052, Australia
2 Murdoch Children's Research Institute, Parkville, VIC 3052, Australia
3 School of Public Health and Preventive Medicine, Monash University, Melbourne, VIC 3004, Australia
4 Office of Population Health Genomics, Department of Health, Perth, WA 6004, Australia
5 Centre for Law and Genetics, University of Tasmania, Hobart, TAS 7000, Australia
* Correspondence: jane.tiller@mcri.edu.au

Abstract: Genetic risk information has relevance for patients' blood relatives. However, cascade testing uptake in at-risk families is <50%. International research supports direct notification of at-risk relatives by health professionals (HPs), with patient consent. However, HPs express concerns about the privacy implications of this practice. Our privacy analysis, grounded in a clinically relevant hypothetical scenario, considers the types of personal information involved in direct notification of at-risk relatives and the application of Australian privacy regulations. It finds that collecting relatives' contact details, and using those details (with patient consent) to notify relatives of possible genetic risk, does not breach Australian privacy law, providing that HPs adhere to regulatory requirements. It finds the purported "right to know" does not prevent disclosure of genetic information to at-risk relatives. Finally, the analysis confirms that the discretion available to HPs does not equate to a positive duty to warn at-risk relatives. Thus, direct notification of a patient's at-risk relatives regarding medically actionable genetic information, with patient consent, is not a breach of Australian privacy regulations, providing it is conducted in accordance with the applicable principles set out. Clinical services should consider offering this service to patients where appropriate. National guidelines would assist with the clarification of the discretion for HPs.

Keywords: privacy; genetics; ethics; genetic testing; cascade testing; medically actionable; risk notification; prevention

Key Contribution: Direct notification of patients' relatives about their possible genetic risk by health professionals can support family communication and increase the uptake of cascade genetic testing for medically actionable conditions. Health professionals have historically had concerns about the privacy implications of this practice. This legal analysis considers the Commonwealth and state/territory privacy regulations in Australia; and concludes that this practice can be conducted in accordance with regulations in all jurisdictions.

Citation: Tiller, J.; Nowak, K.; Boughtwood, T.; Otlowski, M. Privacy Implications of Contacting the At-Risk Relatives of Patients with Medically Actionable Genetic Predisposition, with Patient Consent: A Hypothetical Australian Case Study. *BioTech* **2023**, *12*, 45. https://doi.org/10.3390/biotech12020045

Academic Editors: Vasiliki Mollaki and Massimo Negrini

Received: 27 January 2023
Revised: 31 May 2023
Accepted: 1 June 2023
Published: 2 June 2023

1. Introduction

Genetic risk information has relevance for patients' blood relatives, especially for medically actionable conditions. Health professionals (HPs) discuss the importance of risk notification with patients and commonly provide "family letters" for distribution to at-risk relatives. However, the uptake of cascade testing in at-risk families is <50% [1]. A recent Australian study [2] found relatives had not been notified of genetic risk in >50% of families. The burden of contacting relatives was identified as a significant barrier to notification, especially for affected patients, indicating a need for supported communication. One mechanism to assist with increased cascade testing uptake is direct notification of at-risk relatives by HPs, ***with patients' consent***. We note that disclosure of genetic results without patient consent is an important but separate topic, about which we have separately published [3].

The international literature supports the effectiveness of this practice, including strong public and patient support in multiple countries [1,4–11], with many studies recommending the consideration of direct contact of at-risk relatives by HPs. A 2022 systematic review and meta-analysis of 87 international studies found that direct contact increased the uptake of cascade genetic testing from 40% to 62% [12]. A 2016 Belgian study of *BRCA1/2* families found that direct notification almost doubled the cascade testing rate [4]. Australian studies about familial hypercholesterolaemia (FH) (genetic high cholesterol), show strong support from the public [13] and patients [14] for direct notification. A 2006 South Australian study also demonstrated a significant increase in cascade testing uptake for cancer variants after direct notification by HPs, and received no complaints about breach of privacy from individuals who were contacted directly [15]. A recently published study by authors of this manuscript also demonstrated strong support for direct notification amongst >1000 members of the Australian public, including very few privacy concerns [16].

Despite strong international evidence for the effectiveness and acceptability of this practice, Australian HPs anecdotally express concerns about its privacy implications. There are no published legal analyses of this practice from an Australian privacy perspective, or published national guidelines, to guide and inform HPs regarding their discretion and obligations in this area.

2. Materials and Methods

Hypothetical case study

The following hypothetical case study (Figure 1) is used as the basis for this privacy analysis.

- A patient, **Simon**, has had clinical genetic testing and has a *BRCA1* pathogenic variant.
- **Simon's** sister, **Darcy,** has a 50% chance of having inherited the same variant.
- The genetic health service who conducted **Simon's** testing advised him that he should notify certain relatives, including **Darcy**, that they are also at-risk of having inherited this variant.
- **Simon** is not in regular contact with **Darcy** and prefers not to speak with her; however, he has her current contact details and feels she should be aware of her genetic risk, and asks the genetics service to write to her on his behalf.
- **Simon** provides the service with **Darcy's** name and address details, and consents to the health service writing to Darcy to share risk information, including naming the genetic variant found in him. The health service writes to **Darcy** as set out in letters S1 (*scenario 1*) or S2 (*scenario 2*).
- *Letters S1 and S2* (see Supplementary Files S1 and S2) have been adapted from real letters sent by Australian health professionals:
  - *Letter S1 (Scenario 1)* does not name the genetic variant found in **Simon**
  - *Letter S2 (scenario 2)* names the genetic variant (*BRCA1*) found in **Simon**

Figure 1. Case study (hypothetical).

Legal analysis

This analysis will answer the following questions:

1. What are the relevant Australian Commonwealth and state/territory privacy regulations?
2. Are the types of information collected and used in ***Letters S1/S2*** protected under privacy regulations?
3. Has the genetics service breached its privacy obligations by notifying **Darcy** directly in the hypothetical case study provided (Figure 1)?

This analysis is restricted to considering privacy implications of the collection, use and disclosure of personal information by HPs. It does not consider the impact of other regulations, such as restrictions on advertising or solicitation of business, that may apply to private HPs operating in a commercial setting.

3. Results

3.1. What Are the Relevant Australian Commonwealth and State/Territory Privacy Regulations?

The *Privacy Act 1988* (Cth) (PA) is the key privacy legislation applicable to HPs working in the private sector in Australia, and includes 13 Australian Privacy Principles (APPs). Relevant regulations also exist in all Australian states and territories (some of which have specific privacy regimes) and apply to HPs working in the public (and, sometimes, private) sector.

Table 1 sets out the various pieces of legislation and regulations that apply across various states and territories in Australia.

Table 1. Commonwealth, State and Territory regulations relevant to collection, use and disclosure of personal information (applied in Table 2).

Jurisdiction	Act	Privacy Principles
Commonwealth (CTH)	*Privacy Act 1988* (Cth)	Schedule 1—Australian Privacy Principles (APP)
Australian Capital Territory (ACT)	*Information Privacy Act 2014* (ACT)	Schedule 1—Territory Privacy Principles (TPP)
	Health Records (Privacy and Access) Act 1997 (ACT)	Schedule 1—Privacy Principles (PP)
New South Wales (NSW)	*Privacy and Personal Information Protection Act 1998* (NSW) (**PRIPA**)	N/A—applicable sections listed
	Health Records and Information Privacy Act 2002 (NSW)	Schedule 1—Health Privacy Principles (HPP)
Northern Territory (NT)	*Information Act 2002* (NT)	Schedule 2—Information Privacy Principles (IPP)
Queensland (QLD)	*Information Privacy Act* 2009 (QLD)	Schedule 3—Information Privacy Principles (IPP) and
		Schedule 4—National Privacy Principles (IPP)
South Australia (SA)	Premier and Cabinet Circular PC 012—Information Privacy Principles (IPPs) Instruction (2020)	Part II—Information Privacy Principles (IPP)
Tasmania (TAS)	*Personal Information Protection Act 2004* (TAS)	Schedule 1—Personal Information Protection Principles (PIPP)
Victoria (VIC)	*Health Records Act 2001* (VIC)	Schedule 1—Health Privacy Principles (HPP)
	Privacy and Data Collection Act 2014 (VIC)	Schedule 1—Information Privacy Principles (IPP)
Western Australia (WA)	*Health Services Act 2016* (WA)	N/A—applicable sections listed
	Health Services (Information) Regulations 2017 (WA)	N/A—applicable sections listed

It is clear that where patients freely consent to use or disclosure of their own personal information, there is no breach of their privacy. This assumes that consent to the disclosure has been properly obtained. In Supplementary Files S1 and S2, **Simon** has consented to the disclosure of his information and it is reasonable to assume that consent was properly obtained. Accordingly, this analysis will focus on **Darcy's** privacy.

Table 2. Application of privacy regulations to collection, use or disclosure of contact information and health information (see Table 1 for relevant regulations).

CTH Privacy Act	Clause	Application to Contact of At-Risk Relatives with Patient Consent	Principles in State/Territory Regulations Applicable to Collection, Use or Disclosure of Contact Information	Additional State/Territory Principles Applicable to Collection, Use or Disclosure of Health Information	Notes
APP 3: Collection of solicited personal information	3.2: Entity must not collect personal information (other than sensitive information) unless the information is reasonably necessary for one or more of the entity's functions or activities.	Facilitating risk notification and cascade testing of relatives is one of the core functions of a clinical genetics service	ACT: TPP 3.1 NSW: PRIPA s8 NT: IPP 1.1 QLD: IPP1; NPP 1 VIC: IPP1.1 SA: IPP 4(1) TAS: PIPP 1		
	3.3: Entity must not collect sensitive information about an individual unless the individual consents to the collection of the information and the information is reasonably necessary for one or more of the entity's functions or activities.	Personal contact details are not sensitive information, thus it is not necessary that relatives' consent be obtained before the information is collected		VIC: IPP 10 ACT: TPP 3.3; PP 1 NSW: HPP 1 NT: IPP 10 TAS: PIPP 10	
	3.5: An APP entity must collect personal information only by lawful and fair means.	Collecting contact details of relatives directly from patients, with their consent, for the purpose of providing them with information about their genetic risk, is lawful and fair	VIC: IPP1.2 ACT: TPP 3.5 NSW: PRIPA s8 NT: IPP 1.2 QLD: IPP1 and NPP 1 SA: IPP 4(1) TAS: PIPP 1	VIC: HPP 1.2 NSW: HPP 1	

Table 2. *Cont.*

CTH Privacy Act	Clause	Application to Contact of At-Risk Relatives with Patient Consent	Principles in State/Territory Regulations Applicable to Collection, Use or Disclosure of Contact Information	Additional State/Territory Principles Applicable to Collection, Use or Disclosure of Health Information	Notes
APP 3: Collection of solicited personal information	3.6: An APP entity must collect personal information about an individual only from the individual unless it is unreasonable or impracticable to do so.	Given the purpose is to facilitate risk notification of relatives with whom the service has no contact, it is impracticable to collect contact details directly from those relatives	VIC: IPP 1.4 ACT: TPP 3.6 NSW: PRIPA s9 (and s26) NT: IPP 1.4 QLD: NPP 1 TAS: PIPP 1	VIC: HPP 1.2 NSW: HPP 1	NSW: PRIP s9 does not allow for exception to the requirement that personal information must be collected from the individual unless unreasonable or impracticable. However, s26(1) allows for an exemption where compliance would prejudice the interests of the individual to whom the information relates. Clearly, at-risk relatives' interests will be prejudiced if they cannot be notified of their medically actionable genomic risk. WA: Collection, use or disclosure of personal information is authorised if done with the consent of the person to whom it relates (HSA s220(1)(a)). However, under HSIR s5(1)(a), collection, use or disclosure is authorised if reasonably necessary to lessen or prevent a serious risk to the life, health or safety of an individual.

Table 2. *Cont.*

CTH Privacy Act	Clause	Application to Contact of At-Risk Relatives with Patient Consent	Principles in State/Territory Regulations Applicable to Collection, Use or Disclosure of Contact Information	Additional State/Territory Principles Applicable to Collection, Use or Disclosure of Health Information	Notes
APP 5: Notification of the collection of personal information	5.1 and 5.2: As soon as practicable after collecting personal information about an individual, the entity must take reasonable steps to notify the individual of the circumstances of the collection, the entity's identity and contact details, the purpose of the collection and any consequences of not collecting the information, details of the entity's privacy policy, mechanisms to correct information and avenues for complaints about breach of privacy, and any other bodies to which the information may be disclosed	These considerations should inform the content of the letter (or other form of communication) sent to relatives, but do not prevent the collection and use of the contact details for this purpose	VIC: IPP 1.3 and 1.5 ACT: TPP 5 NSW: PRIPA s10 NT: IPP 1.3 and 1.5 QLD: NPP 1 SA: IPP 4(2) TAS: PIPP 1	ACT: PP 2 VIC: HPP 1.4 and 1.5 NSW: HPP 4	VIC: HPP 1.7 requires that reasonable steps are taken to ensure that health information remains confidential where it is received from a recipient who is not the individual that the health information is about (for general obligations to take reasonable steps to protect personal information, see APP 11.1, VIC IPP 4.1/HPP 4.1; ACT TPP 11/PP 4.1; NSW HPP 5/PRIPA s12; NT IPP 4.1; QLD IPP 4/NPP 4; SA IPP 4(4); TAS PIPP 4).
APP 6: Use or disclosure of personal information	6.1: Personal information about an individual collected for a particular purpose (the *primary purpose*), must not be used or disclosed for another purpose (the *secondary purpose*) unless the individual consents or an exception applies	Contact details can only be used to contact relatives to notify them of their possible genetic risk and options for testing, not for any other purpose (without their subsequent consent)	VIC: IPP 2 ACT: TPP 6 NSW: PRIPA s17 NT: IPP 2.1 VIC: IPP10 QLD: NPP 2 SA: IPP 4(8) and IPP 4(10) TAS: PIPP 2	VIC: HPP 2 ACT: PP 9 and PP 10 NSW: HPP 1	VIC: IPP 1 applies to the use or disclosure of contact information (personal information that is not health information) VIC: IPP2 and HPP 2 applies to the use or disclosure of the health information. TAS: PIPP 9 has special provisions regarding the disclosure of personal information about an individual to an entity outside of Tasmania.

3.2. Are the Types of Information Collected and Used in Letters S1/S2 Protected under Privacy Regulations?

All "personal information" is protected under the PA. "Sensitive information" is a subset of personal information, and greater protection exists for information that is considered to be sensitive information (Figure 2). The State/Territory definitions are very similar.

Section 6(1) of the *Privacy Act 1988* (Cth) defines "personal information", "sensitive information" and "health information" as:

Personal information:

"Information or an opinion about an identified individual, or an individual who is reasonably identifiable:

a) whether the information or opinion is true or not; and

b) whether the information or opinion is recorded in a material form or not." (s6(1)).

Sensitive information:

"(a) information or an opinion about an individual's racial or ethnic origin; political opinions; membership of a political association; religious beliefs or affiliations; philosophical beliefs; membership of a professional or trade association; membership of a trade union; sexual orientation or practices; criminal record; that is also personal information; or

(b) health information about an individual; or

(c) genetic information about an individual that is not otherwise health information; or

(d) biometric information that is to be used for the purpose of automated biometric verification or biometric identification; or

(e) biometric templates."

Health information:

a) information or an opinion about:

(i) the health or a disability (at any time) of an individual; or

(ii) an individual's expressed wishes about the future provision of health services to him or her; or

(iii) a health service provided, or to be provided, to an individual; that is also personal information; or

(b) other personal information collected to provide, or in providing, a health service; or

(c) other personal information about an individual collected in connection with the donation, or intended donation, by the individual of his or her body parts, organs or body substances; or

(d) genetic information about an individual in a form that is, or could be, predictive of the health of the individual or a genetic relative of the individual.

Figure 2. Definitions of personal information, sensitive information, and health information.

There are two types of information that are being collected, used, and/or disclosed in this case study. The first type of information is **Darcy's** contact details, and the second is the genetic information being included in the letter. This genetic information is both about **Simon's** genetic status, and about **Darcy's** possible genetic risk. In the discussion section we consider how the privacy regulations protect and regulate the use of this information.

The relevant Commonwealth APPs which apply to the collection, use, and/or disclosure of personal information in this context are **APP 3** (Collection of solicited personal information), **APP 5** (Notification of the collection of personal information) and **APP 6** (Use or disclosure of personal information). Table 2 summarizes these APPs and their application to this question, as well as listing the applicable state/territory principles. Although the language in the state/territory regulations is not identical, their effect is the same with a few notable exceptions. Those exceptions are noted in Table 2 and described, where applicable, below.

4. Discussion

Has the genetics service breached its statutory privacy obligations by notifying Darcy directly in the hypothetical case study provided* (Figure 1)*?

4.1. *How Is the Use of Each Type of Information Identified in the Case Study Regulated by the Relevant Regulations?*

4.1.1. **Darcy's** Contact Details

Individuals' contact details, such as addresses and telephone numbers, are generally accepted to be personal information [17] (but not sensitive information), so their collection and/or use must comply with the requirements applicable to personal information.

4.1.2. The Genetic Information

Simon has consented to the disclosure of his genetic information in both scenarios, so the question to be addressed is whether the genetic information in the letters (that **Darcy** is *at risk* of inheriting a familial variant) is (a) sensitive information and (b) genetic information *belonging to* **Darcy**. Given the definition of personal information (see Figure 2) includes information or an opinion about an identified individual, whether it is true or not, information that identifies an individual's risk of developing disease appears to be personal information. The definition of "sensitive information" clearly includes genetic information (whether it is health information or not), so any genetic information about **Darcy** will also be sensitive information.

Health information is defined to include, "*genetic information about an individual in a form that is, or could be, predictive of the health of the individual or a genetic relative of the individual*". ***Letter S2*** includes specific information about the familial genetic condition, that seems to fall within this definition as it is in a form that could be predictive of the health of **Darcy** or her genetic relative (**Simon**). However, ***Letter S1***, which only refers generally to a relative having "a DNA change that increases the risk of developing an inherited medical condition", is less obvious. Arguably, the fact that **Darcy** is at risk of inheriting an unnamed DNA variant is not specific enough to be health information about **Darcy** as it is not in a form that could be predictive of her health or her genetic relative's health.

The question, then, is whether **Darcy's** risk of inheriting an unnamed DNA variant from an unnamed relative is genetic information (that is not health information) about her. The PA and explanatory material do not consider what constitutes genetic information that is not health information [18], and there is no judicial interpretation to assist. However, the 2006 amendment of the PA to insert genetic information that is not health information into the definition of sensitive information arose from the recommendations of the Australian Law Reform Commission and Australian Health Ethics report *Essentially Yours* (ALRC 96) [19]. These recommendations were intended to cover, for example, "genetic information derived from parentage or other identification testing that is not predictive of health".

The recent recommendations arising from the Australian Attorney General's review of the PA, which recommend adding "genomic information" to the definition of sensitive information, do not further clarify this question [20]. This means that the information in ***Letter S2*** is likely to be personal and sensitive information about **Darcy**, whereas the information in ***Letter S1*** is likely to be personal information (as it is information about her), but it is unclear whether it is sensitive information. For this reason, it should be treated as sensitive information in this context to be prudent. Next, we will consider how the requirement that information must be about an "identified or reasonably identifiable" individual affects this categorization.

The definition of personal information (see Figure 2) applies to "Information or an opinion about an identified individual, or an individual who is reasonably identifiable". Since (i) **Darcy** is identified and named and (ii) the familial genetic information is linked to her and used to inform the assessment of **Darcy's** risk, the argument that the information contained in ***Letter S2*** is **Darcy's** personal (and sensitive) information is further supported. However, the information about **Simon** would not be **Darcy's** personal information without this additional link to her risk, as a reasonably identifiable individual she needs to be "a subject matter of the information or opinion" [21]. If information about **Simon's** genetic variant on its own became **Darcy's** personal information through the sharing of the information in either letter, this would raise the question of whether **Darcy** could control **Simon's** sharing of his own genetic information without her consent.

It is clear that the parliamentary intention does not support an interpretation that **Darcy** could interfere with **Simon's** sharing of his *own* genetic information. Although statutory interpretation must prioritize the word of the text, parliamentary materials may be used to provide context [22]. The Explanatory Memorandum for the *Privacy Legislation Amendment Bill 2006* (Cth) indicates that expressly including genetic information in the definitions (Figure 2) was intended to allow HPs' discretion to advise relatives of genetic risk, even without patient consent [23]. However, this does not support an interpretation that Parliament intended to restrict individuals' own autonomy with respect to their individual information. **Darcy** has no right to control the sharing of **Simon's** personal information with others—that is **Simon's** decision.

In summary:

- **Darcy's** contact details <u>are</u> *personal information* and must be collected and used in accordance with the regulations applicable to personal information.
- The information contained in ***Letters S1 and S2*** <u>is</u> **Darcy's** *personal information.*
- The genetic information contained in ***Letter S2*** (which names the specific gene) <u>is likely to also be</u> **Darcy's** *sensitive information,* and must be used and/or disclosed in accordance with the regulations applicable to sensitive information.
- It is unclear whether the information contained in ***Letter S1*** (which does not name the specific gene and provides general information only) is *sensitive information,* but to be prudent it should be used and/or disclosed in accordance with the regulations applicable to sensitive information.
- **Simon's** genetic information alone is <u>not</u> **Darcy's** *personal information.*

Next, we consider whether the collection, use and/or disclosure of the personal information was a breach of privacy, or conducted in accordance with the relevant regulations (Table 2).

4.2. Are the Proposed Uses a Breach of Privacy?

We have concluded that **Darcy's** contact details and the information in ***Letters S1*** and ***S2*** are *personal information,* and the genetic information in ***Letter S2*** (and potentially the information in ***Letter S1***) is *sensitive information* belonging to **Darcy**. The purpose of the collection and use of the contact details, and the use and disclosure of the genetic information in the letter, was to notify **Darcy** about her potential genetic risk. Facilitating the use of personal information to advise genetic relatives of their potential genetic risk was the primary reason behind the amendments which were made to the PA in 2006 to include genetic information in the PA framework [23].

4.2.1. APP 3: Collection of Solicited Personal Information

APP 3 prohibits the collection of personal information unless reasonably necessary for the entity's functions. Facilitation of cascade testing of at-risk relatives is a core function of genetics services [12,24–32], and communication of risk information to relatives by patients directly is frequently inadequate [2,29]. Accordingly, collecting **Darcy's** personal information for this purpose sits squarely within its core functions. For sensitive information, APP 3 also requires the individual's consent to collection. As contact details are not sensitive information, this aspect of APP 3 does not require **Darcy's** consent for the collection of her contact information (although APP 5 requires her to be notified of certain things, as discussed below). This is consistent across all state/territory regulations other than in Western Australia (considered further below).

APP 3 also requires personal information be collected from individuals directly, unless unreasonable or impracticable to do so. The genetics service has no pre-existing relationship with **Darcy**, so collecting her contact details directly is clearly impracticable. Most states/territory regimes have similar effect, although Table 2 notes some differences in New South Wales and Western Australia. In New South Wales, s9 of the *Privacy and Personal Information Protection Act 1998* (NSW) (**PRIPA**) does not include the "unless unreasonable or impracticable' exemption. However, s26(1) allows for an exemption where compliance would prejudice the interests of the individual to whom the information relates. Clearly, at-risk relatives' interests will be prejudiced if they cannot be notified of their medically actionable genomic risk [12,24,25,32,33].

In Western Australia, which does not have a privacy regime, the collection, use, and disclosure of personal information are regulated under the *Health Services Act 2016* (WA), and is authorized if done with the consent of the person to whom it relates (s220(1)(a)). However, they can also be authorized under s220(1)(i) if any circumstances prescribed in the *Health Services (Information) Regulations 2017* (WA) apply. Under s5(1)(a) of those regulations, collection, use, or disclosure is authorized if reasonably necessary to lessen or prevent a serious risk to the life, health, or safety of an individual. Although genetic information is not explicitly mentioned in the WA Regulations, these are almost the exact words that were inserted into the PA to allow the disclosure of information to a genetic relative regarding their genetic risk [23]. This supports the conclusion that the WA regulations allow the collection of **Darcy's** contact information from **Simon** without her consent, for the purpose of lessening or preventing a serious risk to her health, due to genetic risk.

Accordingly, in all jurisdictions, there is support for the argument that the collection of contact details without **Darcy's** consent for the purposes of notification to her about her potential genetic risk is allowed.

4.2.2. APP 5: Notification of Individuals

APP 5 requires entities who have collected personal information to take reasonable steps to notify individuals of matters including the entity's contact details, the purpose of the collection (and any consequences flowing from not collecting the information), and mechanisms to complain about breach of privacy. These matters do not prevent the collection/use of contact details for risk notification, but must inform the content of any communication by HPs. ***Letters S1*** and ***S2*** have incorporated these requirements.

In addition to these Commonwealth PA obligations, which are largely mirrored by the various state/territory regulations, the Victorian Health Privacy Principles (HPP 1.7), require that reasonable steps are taken to ensure health information remains confidential when received from a recipient who is not the individual the health information is about. Some further general obligations to take reasonable steps to protect personal information are also found in the Commonwealth Australian Privacy Principles (APP 11.1); as well as those in Victoria (IPP 4.1/HPP 4.1); Australian Capital Territory (TPP 11/PP 4.1); New South Wales (HPP 5/PRIPA s12); Northern Territory (IPP 4.1); Queensland (IPP 4/NPP 4); South Australia (IPP 4(4)); and Tasmania (PIPP 4).

4.2.3. APP 6: Use or Disclosure of Personal Information

APP 6 (and similar state/territory principles) limits use of **Darcy's** personal information once collected. Personal information collected for one purpose (the primary purpose) cannot be used for another purpose (a *secondary purpose*) without consent, unless an exception applies.

Adding **Darcy's** contact details (without consent) to a mailing list, for example, would not be related to the primary purpose and would be a privacy breach. Contacting her as a follow-up to the letter that was sent would be related to the primary purpose, and would not be a breach of privacy unless she had expressly requested not to be contacted further.

The use of the genetic information about **Darcy** (her genetic risk) is also governed by APP 6. However, there is no breach of privacy in disclosing **Darcy's** *own* personal information (her potential genetic risk) to her. The "right not to know" might be raised here to argue that it is a breach of **Darcy's** rights to directly contact her with this information, without her consent. However, this purported "right" is not an element of statutory privacy obligations, or a right recognized under Australian privacy regimes. Rather, it is an ethical element (linked to autonomy) to be balanced against other elements (including the ethical imperative to provide access to medically actionable risk information) [34,35]. Because of the significant preventive potential of medically actionable risk information, the "right not to know" is significantly outweighed by the ethical imperative to offer this information to at-risk individuals [10].

Further, s16B(4) of the PA further supports disclosing to **Darcy** her potential genetic risk. Even *without* **Simon's** consent, disclosure to **Darcy** is permitted if "necessary to lessen or prevent a serious threat to [her] life, health or safety". A genetic predisposition to cancer has been specifically recognized as a serious threat to life, health, or safety, "*even where such a threat is not imminent*" [23]. Thus, the purported "right not to know" does not prevent the disclosure of this information directly to **Darcy**, especially with **Simon's** consent. However, informing other entities or individuals of **Darcy's** risk, without her consent, would be a privacy breach (unless another statutory exception applies). Furthermore, if **Darcy** asked not to be contacted further after the initial contact was made the HP should respect her wishes.

An important final point is that the discretion to contact at-risk relatives directly with patient consent, as discussed throughout this analysis, does <u>not</u> equate to a positive duty on HPs to contact relatives directly and notify them of their risk. No such obligation has been created in Australia, either through legislative instruments or Australian judicial findings. Rather, this analysis has confirmed that the discretion to do so (with the patient's consent) exists, and is supported by the regulations governing HPs' collection, use, and disclosure of personal information in all jurisdictions in Australia.

In summary:

- This analysis supports a conclusion that collection of **Darcy's** contact details without her consent is allowed under all Australian privacy regulations, for the purpose of notifying her of her possible genetic risk.
- Reasonable steps should be taken to protect **Darcy's** personal information once collected.
- **Darcy** should be notified as soon as possible after her contact details are collected, about the purpose of the collection and avenues to complain about breach of privacy.
- **Darcy's** personal information (her contact details) can only be used for the primary purpose for which it was collected (to notify her about her possible genetic risk), not for any other purpose (without her consent).
- Disclosure of **Simon's** genetic information to **Darcy** is permitted with his consent.
- Disclosure of **Darcy's** *own* genetic information to her is permitted, and the purported "right not to know" does not prevent the disclosure of this information to **Darcy**, though her autonomy should be respected if she chooses not to pursue this further once notified.
- There is no positive duty on HPs to contact relatives directly to notify them of their risk—the discretion available to HPs to notify patients' at-risk relatives directly is not an obligation.

5. Conclusions

Direct notification of patients' at-risk relatives regarding medically actionable genetic information, with patient consent, is not a breach of Australian privacy law, providing it is conducted in accordance with the applicable regulatory principles as discussed throughout this analysis. Australian clinical services should consider offering direct notification of at-risk relatives to assist patients with family communication. This analysis provides an important resource for clinical services and HPs considering their obligations and discretion in this area; however, harmonized national guidelines would assist with the clarification of the discretion for HPs.

Supplementary Materials: The following supporting information can be downloaded at: https://www.mdpi.com/article/10.3390/biotech12020045/s1, Supplementary file S1: Scenario 1 Letter; Supplementary file S2: Scenario 2 Letter.

Author Contributions: Conceptualization: J.T.; Methodology: J.T. and M.O.; formal analysis: J.T.; writing—original draft preparation: J.T.; writing—review and editing: K.N., T.B., and M.O.; supervision: M.O. All authors have read and agreed to the published version of the manuscript.

Funding: Australian Genomics receives funding from the National Health and Medical Research Council (Grants GNT1113531 and GNT2000001) and the Australian Government's Medical Research Future Fund (MRFF).

Institutional Review Board Statement: Not applicable.

Informed Consent Statement: Not applicable.

Data Availability Statement: There is no associated data.

Conflicts of Interest: The authors declare no conflict of interest.

References

1. Marleen van den Heuvel, L.; Stemkens, D.; van Zelst-Stams, W.A.G.; Willeboordse, F.; Christiaans, I. How to inform at-risk relatives? Attitudes of 1379 Dutch patients, relatives, and members of the general population. *J. Genet. Couns.* **2020**, *29*, 786–799. [CrossRef] [PubMed]
2. Healey, E.; Taylor, N.; Greening, S.; Wakefield, C.E.; Warwick, L.; Williams, R.; Tucker, K. Quantifying family dissemination and identifying barriers to communication of risk information in Australian BRCA families. *Genet. Med.* **2017**, *19*, 1323–1331. [CrossRef]
3. Tiller, J.; Bilkey, G.; Macintosh, R.; O'Sullivan, S.; Groube, S.; Palover, M.; Pachter, N.; Rothstein, M.; Lacaze, P.; Otlowski, M. Disclosing genetic information to family members without consent: Five Australian case studies. *Eur. J. Med. Genet.* **2020**, *63*, 104035. [CrossRef] [PubMed]
4. Sermijn, E.; Delesie, L.; Deschepper, E.; Pauwels, I.; Bonduelle, M.; Teugels, E.; De Greve, J. The impact of an interventional counselling procedure in families with a BRCA1/2 gene mutation: Efficacy and safety. *Fam. Cancer* **2016**, *15*, 155–162. [CrossRef] [PubMed]
5. Roberts, M.C.; Dotson, W.D.; DeVore, C.S.; Bednar, E.M.; Bowen, D.J.; Ganiats, T.G.; Green, R.F.; Hurst, G.M.; Philp, A.R.; Ricker, C.N.; et al. Delivery of Cascade Screening for Hereditary Conditions: A Scoping Review of the Literature. *Health Affairs* **2018**, *37*, 801–808. [CrossRef]
6. Henrikson, N.B.; Blasi, P.; Figueroa Gray, M.; Tiffany, B.T.; Scrol, A.; Ralston, J.D.; Fullerton, S.M.; Lim, C.Y.; Ewing, J.; Leppig, K.A. Patient and Family Preferences on Health System-Led Direct Contact for Cascade Screening. *J. Pers. Med.* **2021**, *11*, 538. [CrossRef]
7. Dheensa, S.; Lucassen, A.; Fenwick, A. Limitations and Pitfalls of Using Family Letters to Communicate Genetic Risk: A Qualitative Study with Patients and Healthcare Professionals. *J. Genet. Couns.* **2018**, *27*, 689–701. [CrossRef]
8. Aktan-Collan, K.; Haukkala, A.; Pylvänäinen, K.; Järvinen, H.J.; Aaltonen, L.A.; Peltomäki, P.; Rantanen, E.; Kääriäinen, H.; Mecklin, J.P. Direct contact in inviting high-risk members of hereditary colon cancer families to genetic counselling and DNA testing. *J. Med. Genet.* **2007**, *44*, 732–738. [CrossRef]
9. Van den Heuvel, L.M.; Hoedemaekers, Y.M.; Baas, A.F.; Baars, M.J.; van Tintelen, J.P.; Smets, E.M.; Christiaans, I. A tailored approach to informing relatives at risk of inherited cardiac conditions: Results of a randomised controlled trial. *Eur. J. Hum. Genet.* **2022**, *30*, 203–210. [CrossRef]
10. Newson, A.J. Why Genetics Services Should Contact At-Risk Relatives Directly. 2006. Available online: http://hdl.handle.net/2123/12242 (accessed on 1 November 2022).
11. Marks, D.; Thorogood, M.; Neil, S.M. Cascade screening for familial hypercholesterolaemia: Implications of a pilot study for national screening programmes. *J. Med. Screen.* **2006**, *13*, 156–159. [CrossRef]
12. Frey, M.K.; Ahsan, M.D.; Bergeron, H.; Lin, J.; Li, X.; Fowlkes, R.K.; Narayan, P.; Nitecki, R.; Rauh-Hain, J.A.; Moss, H.A.; et al. Cascade Testing for Hereditary Cancer Syndromes: Should We Move Toward Direct Relative Contact? A Systematic Review and Meta-Analysis. *J. Clin. Oncol.* **2022**, *40*, 4129–4143. [CrossRef] [PubMed]
13. Maxwell, S.; Molster, C.; Poke, S.; O'leary, P. Communicating Familial Hypercholesterolemia Genetic Information within Families. *Genet. Test. Mol. Biomark.* **2009**, *13*, 301–306. [CrossRef]

14. Hardcastle, S.J.; Legge, E.; Laundy, C.S.; Egan, S.J.; French, R.; Watts, G.F.; Hagger, M.S. Patients' Perceptions and Experiences of Familial Hypercholesterolemia, Cascade Genetic Screening and Treatment. *Int. J. Behav. Med.* **2015**, *22*, 92–100. [CrossRef]
15. Suthers, G.K.; Armstrong, J.; McCormack, J.; Trott, D. Letting the family know: Balancing ethics and effectiveness when notifying relatives about genetic testing for a familial disorder. *J. Med. Genet.* **2006**, *43*, 665–670. [CrossRef]
16. Tiller, J.; Stott, A.; Finlay, K.; Boughtwood, T.; Madelli, E.; Horton, A.; Winship, I.; Nowak, K.; Otlowski, M. Direct notification by health professionals of relatives at-risk of genetic conditions (with patient consent): Views of the Australian public. *Eur. J. Hum. Genet*, 2023; *accepted*.
17. Australian Government Office of the Australian Information Commissioner. *What Is Personal Information?* Australian Government Office of the Australian Information Commissioner: Canberra, Australia, 2017.
18. Paltiel, M.; Taylor, M.; Newson, A. Protection of genomic data and the Australian Privacy Act: When are genomic data 'personal information'? *Int. Data Priv. Law.* **2023**, *13*, 47–62. [CrossRef]
19. Australian Law Reform Commission. *Essentially Yours: The Protection of Human. Genetic Information in Australia*; Australian Law Reform Commission: Sydney, Australia, 2003. Available online: http://www.alrc.gov.au/publications/report-96 (accessed on 1 November 2022).
20. Australian Government Attorney General's Department. Privacy Act Review Report; Australian Government Attorney General's Department. 2022. Available online: https://www.ag.gov.au/rights-and-protections/publications/privacy-act-review-report (accessed on 1 May 2023).
21. Privacy Commissioner v Telstra Corp Ltd. FCAFC 4. 2017. Available online: https://www.ags.gov.au/sites/default/files/el253.pdf (accessed on 1 November 2022).
22. Dharmananda, J. Using parliamentary materials in interpretation: Insights from parliamentary process. *Univ. N. S. W. Law J.* **2018**, *41*, 4–39. [CrossRef]
23. Parliament of Australia. Bills Digest No. 9 2006–2007: Privacy Legislation Amendment Bill 2006. 2006. Available online: https://www.aph.gov.au/Parliamentary_Business/Bills_Legislation/bd/bd0607/07bd009 (accessed on 1 November 2022).
24. Ademi, Z.; Watts, G.F.; Pang, J.; Sijbrands, E.J.; van Bockxmeer, F.M.; O'Leary, P.; Geelhoed, E.; Liew, D. Cascade screening based on genetic testing is cost-effective: Evidence for the implementation of models of care for familial hypercholesterolemia. *J. Clin. Lipidol.* **2014**, *8*, 390–400. [CrossRef]
25. Bell, D.A.; Pang, J.; Burrows, S.; Bates, T.R.; van Bockxmeer, F.M.; Hooper, A.J.; O'Leary, P.; Burnett, J.R.; Watts, G.F. Effectiveness of genetic cascade screening for familial hypercholesterolaemia using a centrally co-ordinated clinical service: An Australian experience. *Atherosclerosis* **2015**, *239*, 93–100. [CrossRef]
26. Courtney, E.; Chok, A.K.L.; Ting Ang, Z.L.; Shaw, T.; Li, S.T.; Yuen, J.; Ngeow, J. Impact of free cancer predisposition cascade genetic testing on uptake in Singapore. *NPJ Genom. Med.* **2019**, *4*, 22. [CrossRef]
27. Frey, M.K.; Kahn, R.M.; Chapman-Davis, E.; Tubito, F.; Pires, M.; Christos, P.; Anderson, S.; Mukherjee, S.; Jordan, B.; Blank, S.V.; et al. Prospective Feasibility Trial of a Novel Strategy of Facilitated Cascade Genetic Testing Using Telephone Counseling. *J. Clin. Oncol.* **2020**, *38*, 1389–1397. [CrossRef] [PubMed]
28. Ho, A.; Leach, E.; Virani, A.; Arbour, L.; Bartels, K.; Wong, E.K. Cascade testing for inherited arrhythmia conditions: Experiences and attitudes of family communication approaches for a Canadian cohort. *J. Genet. Counsel.* **2022**, *31*, 815–828. [CrossRef] [PubMed]
29. Srinivasan, S.; Won, N.Y.; Dotson, W.D.; Wright, S.T.; Roberts, M.C. Barriers and facilitators for cascade testing in genetic conditions: A systematic review. *Eur. J. Hum. Genet.* **2020**, *28*, 1631–1644. [CrossRef]
30. Tuffaha, H.W.; Mitchell, A.; Ward, R.L.; Connelly, L.; Butler, J.R.; Norris, S.; Scuffham, P.A. Cost-effectiveness analysis of germ-line BRCA testing in women with breast cancer and cascade testing in family members of mutation carriers. *Genet. Med.* **2018**, *20*, 985–994. [CrossRef]
31. Human Genetics Society of Australasia. Submission to the Commonwealth Department of Health MBS Review Advisory Committee: Provision of Services by FHGSA Registered Clinical Genetic Counsellors. 2021. Available online: https://consultations.health.gov.au/medicare-reviews-unit/medicare-benefits-schedule-mbs-review-advisory-com/supporting_documents/HGSA%20Submission%20for%20MRAC%20Review.pdf (accessed on 1 January 2023).
32. Forrest, L.E.; Delatycki, M.B.; Curnow, L.; Skene, L.; Aitken, M. Genetic health professionals and the communication of genetic information in families: Practice during and after a genetic consultation. *Am. J. Med. Genet. Part A* **2010**, *152A*, 1458–1466. [CrossRef] [PubMed]
33. George, R.; Kovak, K.; Cox, S.L. Aligning policy to promote cascade genetic screening for prevention and early diagnosis of heritable diseases. *J. Genet. Counsel.* **2015**, *24*, 388–399. [CrossRef]
34. Tiller, J.; Trainer, A.H.; Campbell, I.; Lacaze, P.A. Ethical and practical implications of returning genetic research results: Two Australian case studies. *Med. J. Aust.* **2021**, *214*, 259–262.e1. [CrossRef]
35. Newson, A.J.; Humphries, S.E. Cascade testing in familial hypercholesterolaemia: How should family members be contacted? *Eur. J. Hum. Genet.* **2005**, *13*, 401–408. [CrossRef]

BioTech MDPI

Review

Gene Therapy for Genetic Syndromes: Understanding the Current State to Guide Future Care

Marian L. Henderson [1,2], Jacob K. Zieba [2], Xiaopeng Li [2], Daniel B. Campbell [2], Michael R. Williams [2], Daniel L. Vogt [2], Caleb P. Bupp [2,3], Yvonne M. Edgerly [4], Surender Rajasekaran [2,4,5], Nicholas L. Hartog [2,6], Jeremy W. Prokop [2,4,*] and Jena M. Krueger [2,7,*]

1 The Department of Biology, Calvin University, Grand Rapids, MI 49546, USA; hendemar2000@outlook.com
2 Department of Pediatrics and Human Development, College of Human Medicine, Michigan State University, Grand Rapids, MI 48824, USA; ziebajac@msu.edu (J.K.Z.); lixiao@msu.edu (X.L.); campb971@msu.edu (D.B.C.); will3434@msu.edu (M.R.W.); vogtdan2@msu.edu (D.L.V.); caleb.bupp@corewellhealth.org (C.P.B.); surender.rajasekaran@corewellhealth.org (S.R.); nicholas.hartog@corewellhealth.org (N.L.H.)
3 Medical Genetics, Corewell Health, Grand Rapids, MI 49503, USA
4 Office of Research, Corewell Health, Grand Rapids, MI 49503, USA; yvonne.edgerly@corewellhealth.org
5 Pediatric Intensive Care Unit, Helen DeVos Children's Hospital, Corewell Health, Grand Rapids, MI 49503, USA
6 Allergy & Immunology, Corewell Health, Grand Rapids, MI 49503, USA
7 Department of Neurology, Helen DeVos Children's Hospital, Corewell Health, Grand Rapids, MI 49503, USA
* Correspondence: jprokop54@gmail.com (J.W.P.); jena.krueger@helendevoschildrens.org (J.M.K.)

Abstract: Gene therapy holds promise as a life-changing option for individuals with genetic variants that give rise to disease. FDA-approved gene therapies for Spinal Muscular Atrophy (SMA), cerebral adrenoleukodystrophy, β-Thalassemia, hemophilia A/B, retinal dystrophy, and Duchenne Muscular Dystrophy have generated buzz around the ability to change the course of genetic syndromes. However, this excitement risks over-expansion into areas of genetic disease that may not fit the current state of gene therapy. While in situ (targeted to an area) and ex vivo (removal of cells, delivery, and administration of cells) approaches show promise, they have a limited target ability. Broader in vivo gene therapy trials have shown various continued challenges, including immune response, use of immune suppressants correlating to secondary infections, unknown outcomes of overexpression, and challenges in driving tissue-specific corrections. Viral delivery systems can be associated with adverse outcomes such as hepatotoxicity and lethality if uncontrolled. In some cases, these risks are far outweighed by the potentially lethal syndromes for which these systems are being developed. Therefore, it is critical to evaluate the field of genetic diseases to perform cost–benefit analyses for gene therapy. In this work, we present the current state while setting forth tools and resources to guide informed directions to avoid foreseeable issues in gene therapy that could prevent the field from continued success.

Keywords: gene therapy; genetic syndromes; clinical trials

Key Contribution: The promise of gene therapy is reflected through the FDA approvals for multiple genomic syndromes. This work reflects on the field's current state while providing topics that must be considered as the field progresses with more clinical usages.

Citation: Henderson, M.L.; Zieba, J.K.; Li, X.; Campbell, D.B.; Williams, M.R.; Vogt, D.L.; Bupp, C.P.; Edgerly, Y.M.; Rajasekaran, S.; Hartog, N.L.; et al. Gene Therapy for Genetic Syndromes: Understanding the Current State to Guide Future Care. *BioTech* **2024**, *13*, 1. https://doi.org/10.3390/biotech13010001

Academic Editor: Vasiliki Mollaki

Received: 24 August 2023
Revised: 8 December 2023
Accepted: 21 December 2023
Published: 3 January 2024

1. Introduction

With the discoveries that DNA codes for genes and that a DNA sequence can have variants that increase disease susceptibility, a future was envisioned in which modifying genetic material to reduce disease risk/progression is achievable. Multiple possibilities arose to modify genetic material (Figure 1) [1,2], including taking cells out of the body to correct genetics followed by delivery back to the individual (ex vivo gene therapy), packaging material to make the changes systemically (in vivo gene therapy), or targeting a tissue or cell to be edited (in situ gene therapy). Gene therapy consists of packaging nucleic acids (plasmid, DNA, RNA, antisense oligonucleotides) or gene editing machinery such as clustered regularly interspaced short palindromic repeats—CRISPR- and CRISPR-associated protein 9 (Cas9)—with guide RNA within a particle, often formed by an attenuated virus or nanoparticle, and delivering it to a cell or tissue to modulate a desired gene [3–7]. While animal models showed incredible promise for gene therapy in the 1970s and 1980s, there were early signs of safety risks posed by delivering biomaterials to humans [8].

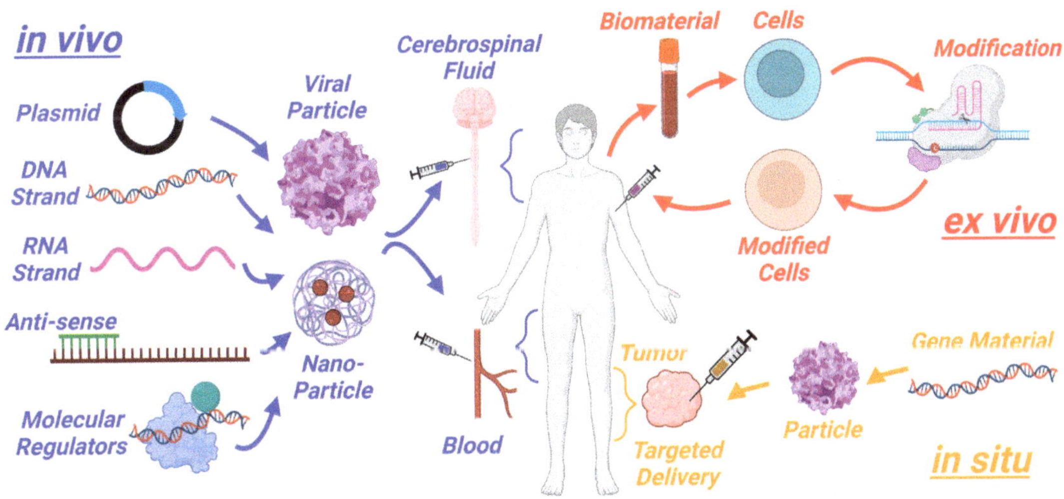

Figure 1. Schematic of three gene therapy approaches: in vivo, ex vivo, and in situ. Generated with BioRender (www.biorender.com/).

One of the first human gene therapy clinical trials, completed in 1990 by Rosenberg et al., involved the transfer of tumor-infiltrating lymphocytes modified with a neomycin resistance gene via a retroviral vector to patients with advanced melanoma [9]. The success of this trial provided proof of concept for the clinical application of gene therapy. With that promise of gene therapy, it is rather surprising to follow the complex multiple-decade history of gene therapy setbacks and complications [1]. However, the excitement associated with gene therapy has finally translated into clinical utility within the past few years, with the FDA and other world regulators approving their use, opening the door for correcting or replacing broader disease genetics [2].

Within rare diseases, genomic sequencing has increased to identify pathogenic variants [5,6], which yields an increasing hope of gene therapy to correct the variants. Rare diseases account for USD 997 billion in healthcare costs annually, impacting 15.5 million people within the U.S. [10]. Internationally, the frequency of rare diseases is uncertain due to limitations in diagnosis, but estimates are greater than 100 million individuals. While each rare disease occurs in less than 200,000 individuals (United States) and in 1/2000 births (European Union) [11], more than 5000 unique, rare diseases add up to a considerable fraction of healthcare costs internationally [12]. As international sequencing initiatives have expanded, so has the number of diagnosed individuals for each rare disease, largely contributed to the sharing of flagged genomic variants across borders [13–15]. The International Rare Diseases Research Consortium (IRDiRC), founded in 2011, has set forth a critical mission of expanding therapeutics for international usage through integrating international efforts into funding within each country or foundation [16,17]. This international partnership highlights the growing efforts to expand access across borders, which is critical to growing the number of patients with each rare disease to grow the demand and offset drug development costs [18]. The international efforts must continue to translate the United States and European union clinical trials into cross-border initiatives to increase clinical trial implementation for rare diseases [19].

As diagnoses of rare diseases have improved with the implementation of genome sequencing [20–22], the knowledge of the exact variant for each individual yields details of how to best treat each case [23–25]. If a variant results in loss of function of a protein, it is possible to replace that protein with a functional gene (gene delivery) or remove the cell, followed by CRISPR editing. If a variant causes a gain of function, one can reduce the function using antisense oligonucleotides. Thus, rare diseases are one of the areas where gene therapy holds incredible promise. However, a balance must be maintained between evaluating gene therapy benefits and safety risks to have a sustainable gene therapy ecosystem moving forward. Within this review article, we address the field's current state in rare diseases and provide insights and guidance to advance the clinical use of gene therapy sustainably and safely. The article consists of an analysis of gene therapy based on publications, funding, status of clinical trials, and approved clinical usages while expanding considerations for additional rare disease genes, immune modulation, cost of therapy, and the need for increased transparency. At the end, the work is concluded through a discussion of the current and future ethical considerations for gene therapy advancement.

2. Past and Current Work in Gene Therapy

2.1. Publications

The advancements and applications of gene therapy can be reflected in yearly publications (Figure 2). Publications mentioning "gene therapy" date back to the 1970s (1922 total papers) but expanded rapidly in the 1990s (76,314 papers) to the 2000s (317,383 papers) and 2010s (637,126 papers). The number of papers per year seems to have stabilized at the beginning of the 2020s, with 2020 having 88,853 papers, 2021 having 98,207 papers, and 2022 having 99,992 papers. In 2022, the gene therapy papers reflected diverse topics based on a Web of Science analysis. These include general fields like genetic heredity, biochemistry, and pharmacology. More specialized fields such as oncology, immunology, and neurosciences rank the highest in 2022 publications (Figure 2). There are a total of 802,029 papers for "gene therapy" and "Genetic Heredity" over all years, with 25,280 of those articles also containing "Rare Disease." A similar search within PubMed for "gene therapy" and "rare disease" returns 16,032 papers.

Literature analysis provides valuable insights, especially those of nucleotide delivery systems for studying animal modeling of rare diseases. In the 2000s, a strategy known as morpholino oligonucleotides was widely used in research to knockdown genes in animal models [26]. Building on the toxic nature of oligonucleotides in developmental studies [27], morpholinos were developed to inhibit gene translation using chemical alterations of the oligonucleotide that allow for complementation with the transcript to prevent ribosome engagement [28]. In 2000, these morpholinos were shown to be functional in the knockdown of zebrafish genes during development, mimicking rare disease phenotypes [29]. This novel animal modeling tool progressed with hundreds of papers defining knockdown to phenotype correlations for rare genetic disorders [30]. However, in 2007, the same group that had presented the promise of zebrafish morpholinos showed that the system also regulated the tumor protein p53 (TP53, coded by the *p53* gene) cascade and induced phenotypes independent of the targeted morpholino [31], a finding also shown through small interfering RNA (siRNA) [32] and phosphorothioate-linked DNA [33]. While there are off-target oligonucleotide functions in gene regulation, the tools continue to be used through understanding mechanisms and the growth of control datasets [34,35]. For example, our group has shown morpholino use in zebrafish followed by human mRNA recovery allows for definitive outcomes of human genotype-to-phenotype insights and gene therapy modeling for kidney disease [36]. While these techniques are being phased out with newer

CRISPR-based animal modeling [37], they still provide a valuable lesson in considering off-target impacts for delivering nucleic acids. These findings highlight the persistent need for refined knowledge of how foreign nucleotides can impact cellular processes to better predict unexpected, off-target outcomes.

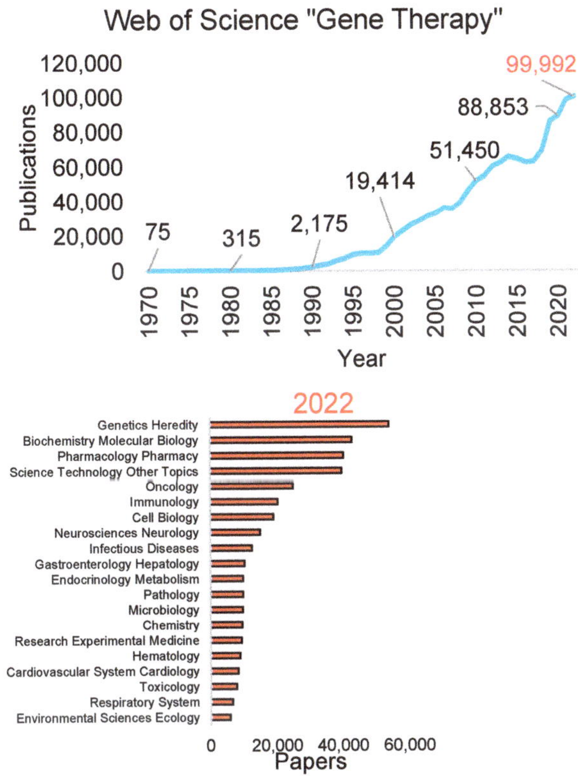

Figure 2. Publications on "gene therapy." The first panel shows the number of publications found on Web of Science per year for the search "gene therapy," with every five years labeled in black. The number of publications in 2022 is in red. The second panel shows the breakdown of the top 20 research areas of the 2022 papers. The analysis was performed on 18 April 2023.

2.2. Funding

Similar to publications, funding can establish the trajectory of the gene therapy field. The top funder of worldwide science, the National Institutes of Health (NIH), is experiencing rapid funding growth in "gene therapy," based on an analysis of NIH reporter. Beginning in 2016, funding mentioning "gene therapy" could be found in the project terms of NIH grants (Figure 3). In 2018, the term could be found in project abstracts, and in 2019 within project titles, with a fast elevation to the USD 8.279 billion in total funding for 2022. The 2022 levels of NIH funding broken down by institutes show the top to be the National Cancer Institute (NCI, USD 1.8 billion), followed by the National Institute of Allergy and Infectious Diseases (NIAID, USD 1.5 billion), National Heart Lung and Blood Institute (NHLBI, USD 885 million), and the National Institute of Aging (NIA, USD 669 million).

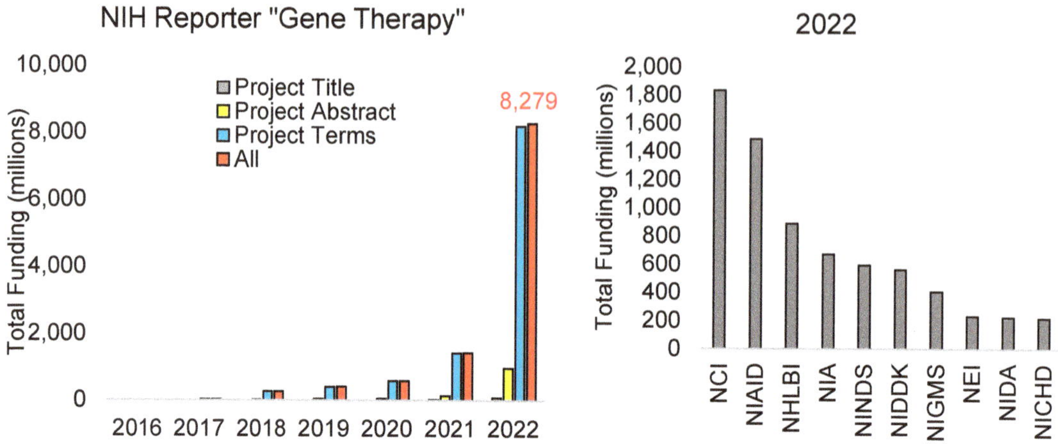

Figure 3. NIH funding mentioning "Gene Therapy." The first panel shows the funding (in millions of USD) per year by the National Institutes of Health (NIH) mentioning the term "gene therapy" in various annotation bins (mentioned in project: gray—title, yellow—abstract, cyan—terms, red—any of the three). The total annotated funding in 2022 is in red text. The second panel shows the breakdown of the top NIH institutes of the 2022 NIH funding for "Gene Therapy." Abbreviations: NCI—National Cancer Institute, NIAID—National Institute of Allergy and Infectious Diseases, NHLBI—National Heart, Lung, and Blood Institute, NIA—National Institute on Aging, NINDS—National Institute of Neurological Disorders and Stroke, NIDDK—National Institute of Diabetes and Digestive and Kidney Diseases, NIGMS—National Institute of General Medical Sciences, NEI—National Eye Institute, NIDA—National Institute on Drug Abuse, NICHD—Eunice Kennedy Shriver National Institute of Child Health and Human Development. The analysis was performed on 1 May 2023 using NIH reporter.

The top ten highest funded awards from NIH represent a diversity of institutes and initiatives (Table 1). Many of these awards were for mRNA vaccine programs and testing sites (1ZIATR000437, 1U19AI171421, 1U19AI171443, 1U19AI171110, 1U19AI171954, 1U19AI171292, 1U19AI171403), which primarily reflects the SARS-CoV-2 pandemic response. This mRNA vaccine expansion is likely the most significant factor in the rapid funding investments for gene therapy in 2022. A few of these large projects also reflect the growth of gene therapy within oncology (75N91019D00024-0-759102200019-1, 1U24CA224319) and neurodegeneration (5U01AG059798, 1UF1NS131791, 5R01AG068319, 5U19NS120384).

Further refining NIH investments using a co-search with "rare disease" identified 787 funded awards (Figure 4) with 728 unique project numbers totaling USD 526,396,101. Of these awards, 276 are traditional R01 NIH research awards, summing USD 155,491,503 in research. Additional funding for gene therapy comes from intramural awards (ZIA, 76 awards, USD 109,812,041), contract awards (U54, 63 awards, USD 36,059,350; U01, 47 awards, USD 48,207,117), and small research pilot grants (R21, 57 awards, USD 13,314,891). There is a surprisingly low number amongst these awards of trainee funding, such as K08 clinician scientist awards (24 awards for USD 3,829,993), K23 patient-oriented training (12 awards, USD 2,235,855), F30/F31 predoctoral awards (18 awards, USD 755,681), and F32 postdoctoral awards (3 awards, USD 235,260). As gene therapy is one of the most promising clinical tools, there seems to be a need for elevating targeted training awards.

Table 1. Top ten highest NIH-funded projects mentioning "gene therapy". The analysis was performed on 1 May 2023 using NIH reporter.

Application ID	Project Number	Total Cost I.C.	Administering I.C.	Organization Name	Project Title
10695742	1ZIATR000437-01	USD 77,500,000	NCATS	National Center for Advancing Translational Sciences	Antiviral Program for Pandemics (App) and Ncats: Accelerating Antiviral Development
10514264	1U19AI171421-01	USD 69,058,677	NIAID	Stanford University	Development of Outpatient Antiviral Cocktails Against SARS-CoV-2 and Other Potential Pandemic Rna Viruses.
10514317	1U19AI171443-01	USD 67,624,156	NIAID	Scripps Research Institute, The	Center For Antiviral Medicines and Pandemic Preparedness (Campp)
10512617	1U19AI171110-01	USD 67,452,049	NIAID	University of California, San Francisco	Qcrg Pandemic Response Program
10522804	1U19AI171954-01	USD 66,431,207	NIAID	University of Minnesota	Midwest Avidd Center
10513679	1U19AI171292-01	USD 65,483,194	NIAID	Univ of North Carolina Chapel Hill	Rapidly Emerging Antiviral Drug Development Initiative—Avidd Center (Readdi-Ac)
10513935	1U19AI171403-01	USD 51,914,880	NIAID	Emory University	Antiviral Countermeasures Development Center (Ac/Dc)
10716676	75N91019D00024-0-759102200019-1	USD 22,364,766	NCI	Leidos Biomedical Research, Inc.	Discovery and Development of Cancer Therapeutics for Next Program
10446989	5U01AG059798-03	USD 20,263,304	NIA	Washington University	Dian-Tu Primary Prevention Trial
10649756	1UF1NS131791-01	USD 18,136,504	NINDS	Massachusetts General Hospital	An Expanded Access Protocol of Intravenous Trehalose Injection 90 mg/mL Treatment of Patients with Amyotrophic Lateral Sclerosis
10693707	1ZIAHD002400-31	USD 17,942,380	NICHD	Eunice Kennedy Shriver National Institute of Child Health and Human Development	The Role of Subclinical Infection and Cytokines in Preterm Parturition
10452692	5R01AG068319-03	USD 16,720,909	NIA	Washington University	Dian-Tu: Tau Next Generation Prevention Trial
9457012	1U24CA224319-01	USD 13,559,983	NCI	Icahn School of Medicine at Mount Sinai	High-Dimensional Immune Monitoring of Nci-Supported Immunotherapy Trials
10266149	5U19NS120384-02	USD 13,212,214	NINDS	University Of California at Davis	The Clinical Significance of Incidental White Matter Lesions on Mri Amongst a Diverse Population with Cognitive Complaints (Indeed)

Based on the titles and the public health relevance statements of "gene therapy" and "rare disease" funded grants, there is a diverse clinical perspective (Figure 4). The mention of genes within the abstracts of the projects also reflects this diverse perspective. From the list of genes, funding is in the areas of neuroscience (*TSC, MTOR, CLN1, CMT1A, NF1*), neurodegeneration (*APOE, TAU, TREM2*), cancer (*RUNX1, P53, MDM2, KRAS*), and cystic fibrosis (*CFTR*). As rare diseases are dispersed between the NIH units, with no primary home that focuses on all rare diseases as a single pathology, it is unsurprising that the funding is spread across different institutes. As gene therapy grows in development, it is critical to consider new cross-NIH initiatives focusing on funding gene therapy advancements, especially those outside of oncology or vaccine designs. As the new ARPA-H (Advanced Research Projects Agency for Health) is established in the United States, gene therapy will likely be a significant component of agency design.

Figure 4. Word usage for "gene therapy" and "rare disease" within all NIH-funded projects. The analysis was performed using WordClouds.com. The first panel shows words enriched within the 787 funded project titles. The second panel shows words enriched from their public health relevance statements. The analysis was performed on 1 May 2023 using NIH reporter.

2.3. Clinical Trials

The translational advancement of gene therapy is reflected through clinical trials and approved therapies. Since 1990, the field has proliferated, with over 2000 completed clinical trials registered on ClinicalTrials.gov (Figure 5, as of 18 April 2023). The first registered trial returned for "gene therapy" (ClinicalTrials.gov Identifier: NCT00001166) was initiated in 1978, an observational trial of "Gyrate Atrophy of the Choroid and Retina" that focused on genetic determination of disease. In the 1990s, trials began expanding, with fast growth in the 2010s to the 2022 level of 397 trials initiated (Figure 5A). Of the studies, 37% of the total results have been marked as completed, 21% are recruiting, 9% are active but not recruiting, 9% have been terminated, and 5% are not yet recruiting (Figure 5B).

Among the completed studies, cancer was the primary target of most trials, as determined by an analysis of the disease categories provided by ClinicalTrials.gov. Monogenic disorders follow. The FDA breaks human clinical trials into four phases [38]. Phase I trials aim to answer whether a treatment may be given safely, assessing for toxicity in a small population. Phase II trials determine if the treatment is effective at different dosages, such as if adequate protein expression is obtained following gene therapy. Phase III trials compare the new treatment to those already utilized or a placebo, often in a larger population, where it is determined if it will be sent for federal approval as a new therapy. Once approved, interventions are continually monitored for adverse events in phase IV. Rare disease trials, particularly those utilizing gene therapy, often combine phases I and II and utilize a stepwise approach.

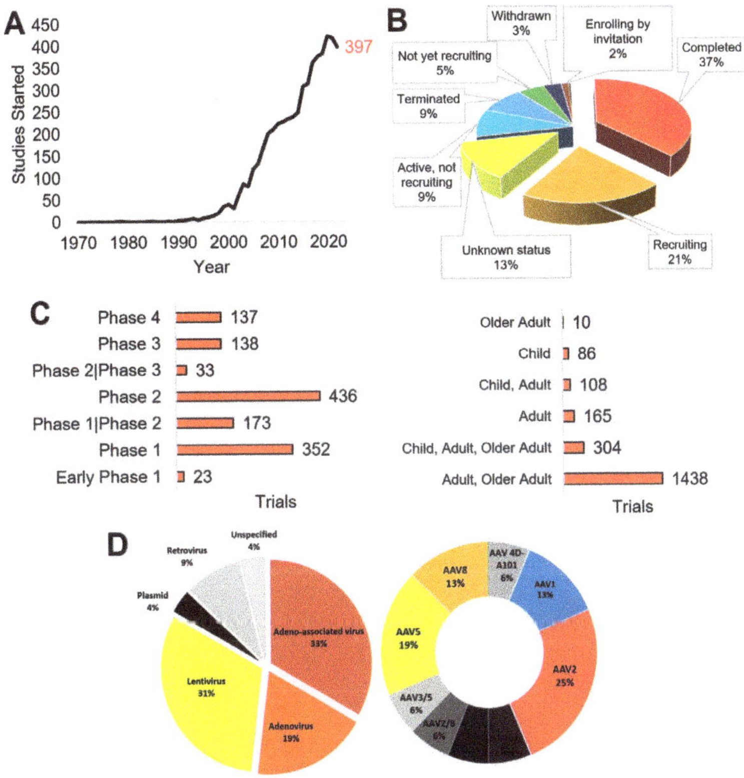

Figure 5. Analysis of ClinicalTrials.gov for "gene therapy." All analyses were performed on 18 April 2023 using the ClinicalTrial.gov site. (**A**) Number of trials started each year, with the 2022 number in red. (**B**) Breakdown of trial status. Groups below 2% are not shown. (**C**) Breakdown of completed trials for FDA phase and age group inclusion. (**D**) Breakdown of the delivery system used, with a call out of adeno-associated virus subtypes shown to the right.

Among the clinical trials returned when searching for "gene therapy" and marked as complete, most fall under phase I or II trials (Figure 5C). In addition, most of these were only tested in adults (18 years and older). Viral vectors are the most utilized delivery system in gene therapy clinical trials, the most common being adenoviruses, retroviruses, lentiviruses, and adeno-associated viruses (Figure 5D). Of the adeno-associated viruses, AAV2 and AAV5 were the most selected for use. Plasmid DNA delivery, lipofection, and RNA transfer are the most utilized among nonviral vectors.

As "gene therapy" returns trial data irrelevant to interventions, we further filtered genetic diseases with intervention therapies (Table 2). Multiple disorders have completed phase III trials, including cystic fibrosis, hemophilia B, retinal dystrophy, cerebral adrenoleukodystrophy, Spinal Muscular Atrophy (SMA), and β-Thalassemia. It should be noted that enrollment numbers are minimal for many rare diseases due to the low frequency of disorders within the population. This makes it challenging to build placebo control systems and generate sufficient data for FDA approval processes. These issues suggest the need for thoughtful reconsiderations in gene therapy authorization processes in the future [39] in addition to international cooperation efforts.

Table 2. Top genetic diseases with interventional "gene therapy" clinical trials. A "-" is used in the FDA-authorized treatment column when no treatments are authorized. The "*" indicates drugs that are not gene therapy.

Disorder	Trials	Total Enroll-ment	Trials with under 18	Phase I	Phase I I Phase II	Phase II	Phase II I Phase III	Phase III	FDA-Authorized Treatment
Cystic Fibrosis	43	4080	27	7	3	15	2	10	Elexacaftor–Tezacaftor–Ivacaftor *
Hemophilia B	26	666	2	5	11	4	0	3	Hemgenix
Retinal Dystrophy	2	35	2	0	0	0	0	2	Luxturna
Cerebral Adrenoleukodystrophy	2	67	2	0	0	0	1	1	Skysona
Spinal Muscular Atrophy	14	713	13	2	1	0	0	8	Zolgensma
β-Thalassemia	25	604	17	2	7	3	1	2	Zynteglo
Muscular Dystrophy	42	1837	37	9	12	12	0	7	Elevidys
Hemophilia A	22	678	1	5	7	2	0	5	Roctavian
Epidermolysis Bullosa	18	228	15	0	12	2	0	2	Vyjuvek
Fabry Disease	12	377	5	1	7	1	0	1	-
Sickle Cell Anemia	5	245	2	0	0	2	0	1	-
Mucopolysaccharidosis	17	186	17	1	13	0	2	0	-
Gaucher Disease	13	366	8	0	6	0	2	5	-
Retinitis Pigmentosa	27	1713	13	1	14	3	3	3	-
Leber Congenital Amaurosis	11	178	11	2	6	0	2	1	-
Amyotrophic Lateral Sclerosis	5	308	0	0	1	2	0	1	-
Severe Combined Immunodeficiency	19	181	19	3	11	1	1	0	-
Fanconi Anemia	14	82	14	6	4	3	0	0	-
Alzheimer's Disease	4	43	0	3	1	0	0	0	-

Table 3 shows a curated list of phase III trials with gene therapy for rare diseases. Among these nine completed studies, four were for SMA using Onasemnogene Abeparvovec (also known as Zolgensma) for different inclusion criteria (NCT03306277, NCT03461289, NCT03505099, NCT03837184). SMA is characterized by an autosomal recessive dysfunction to exons 7 and 8 of the *SMN1* gene, resulting in progressive spinal cord motor neuron degeneration and muscle atrophy [40]. Type 1 SMA decreases muscle tone so severely that children are never able to sit independently. Without intervention, type 1 SMA patients die of respiratory failure prior to their second birthday. The known genetic mechanisms and the progressive debilitating phenotype have resulted in SMA inclusion in many newborn screenings for early detection before the phenotype manifests [41], making it a compelling target for gene therapy intervention. NCT03306277, known as STR1VE, was the first completed gene therapy phase III study, showing in 22 participants that a single AAV9 cDNA intravenous delivery of the *SMN1* gene (Zolgensma) could prevent the phenotype of SMA type 1 [42]. Of the 22 participants, 3 were withdrawn, with 1 due to an unrelated death and 1 due to an adverse event. Of the patients enrolled, they had an average age of 3.7 months at gene delivery, with half identifying as white and 12 as female. All patients with therapy showed marked clinical improvement and achieved independent sitting at 18 months. Of the 22 individuals, 4 showed signs of respiratory distress, 1 with signs of secondary sepsis, and 2 with hepatic elevated enzymes. Presymptomatic genetically screened *SMN1* variant-positive individuals were assessed for earlier delivery of this therapy (NCT03505099), where all 14 patients had marked clinical improvements [43].

Table 3. Curated phase III intervention studies for genetic syndromes.

Trial	Status	Phases	Start Date	Completion Date	Age	Enrollment #	Conditions	Interventions
NCT02292537	Completed	Phase III	24 November 2014	20 February 2017	2–12 years	126	Spinal Muscular Atrophy	Nusinersen (Spinraza)
NCT03306277	Completed	Phase III	24 October 2017	12 November 2019	up to 180 Days	22	Spinal Muscular Atrophy	Biological: Onasemnogene Abeparvovec
NCT03461289	Completed	Phase III	16 August 2018	11 September 2020	up to 6 Months	33	Spinal Muscular Atrophy	Biological: Onasemnogene Abeparvovec
NCT03496012	Completed	Phase III	11 December 2017	1 December 2020	18 Years and older	170	Choroideremia	Genetic: BIIB111
NCT01896102	Completed	Phase III Phase III	21 August 2013	26 March 2021	up to 17 Years	32	Cerebral Adrenoleukodys-trophy (CALD)	Genetic: Lenti-D Drug Product
NCT03505099	Completed	Phase III	2 April 2018	15 June 2021	up to 42 Days	30	Spinal Muscular Atrophy	Biological: Onasemnogene Abeparvovec
NCT03837184	Completed	Phase III	31 May 2019	29 June 2021	0 Days to 6 Months	2	Spinal Muscular Atrophy	Biological: Onasemnogene Abeparvovec
NCT02906202	Completed	Phase III	1 July 2016	31 March 2022	0 Years to 50 Years	23	β-Thalassemia	Genetic: LentiGlobin BB305
NCT03406104	Completed	Phase III	9 January 2018	4 July 2022	15 Years and older	61	Leber Hereditary Optic Neuropathy	Genetic: GS010
NCT03207009	Completed	Phase III	8 June 2017	15 November 2022	0 Years to 50 Years	18	β-Thalassemia	Genetic: LentiGlobin BB305
NCT00999609	Active, not recruiting	Phase III	1 October 12	-	3 Years and older	31	Inherited Retinal Dystrophy	Biological: AAV2-hRPE65v2
NCT03370913	Active, not recruiting	Phase III	19 December 2017	-	18 Years and older	134	Hemophilia A	Biological: valoctocogene roxaparvovec
NCT03293524	Active, not recruiting	Phase III	12 March 2018	-	15 Years and older	90	Leber Hereditary Optic Neuropathy	Genetic: GS010
NCT03392974	Active, not recruiting	Phase III	14 March 2018	-	18 Years and older	1	Hemophilia A	Biological: Valoctocogene Roxaparvovec
NCT03569891	Active, not recruiting	Phase III	27 June 2018	-	18 Years and older	67	Hemophilia B	Genetic: AAV5-hFIXco-Padua (Hemgenix)

Table 3. *Cont.*

Trial	Status	Phases	Start Date	Completion Date	Age	Enrollment #	Conditions	Interventions
NCT03837483	Active, not recruiting	Phase III	21 January 2019	-	up to 65 Years	10	Wiskott–Aldrich Syndrome	Genetic: OTL-103
NCT03852498	Active, not recruiting	Phase III	24 January 2019	-	up to 17 Years	35	Cerebral Adrenoleukodystrophy (CALD)	Genetic: Lenti-D
NCT04042025	Active, not recruiting	Phase III	10 February 2020	-	Child, Adult, Older Adult	85	Spinal Muscular Atrophy	Biological: Onasemnogene Abeparvovec
NCT04323098	Active, not recruiting	Phase III	10 November 2020	-	18 Years and older	22	Hemophilia A	Biological: valoctocogene roxaparvovec
NCT04516369	Active, not recruiting	Phase III	24 November 2020	-	4 Years and older	4	Retinal Dystrophy	Genetic: voretigene neparvovec (LUXTURNA)
NCT04851873	Active, not recruiting	Phase III	8 September 2021	-	up to 17 Years	24	Spinal Muscular Atrophy	Genetic: OAV101
NCT05096221	Active, not recruiting	Phase III	27 October 2021	-	4 Years to 7 Years	126	Duchenne Muscular Dystrophy	Genetic: SRP-9001
NCT05139316	Active, not recruiting	Phase III	8 November 2021	-	8 Years and older	50	Glycogen Storage Disease Type IA	Genetic: DTX401
NCT03566043	Recruiting	Phase II | Phase III	27 September 2018	-	4 Months to 5 Years	48	Mucopolysaccharidosis Type II (MPS II)	Genetic: RGX-121
NCT03861273	Recruiting	Phase III	29 July 2019	-	18 Years to 65 Years	55	Hemophilia B	Biological: fidanacogene elaparvovec
NCT04293185	Recruiting	Phase III	14 February 2020	-	2 Years to 50 Years	35	Sickle Cell Disease	Genetic: bb1111
NCT04370054	Recruiting	Phase III	18 August 2020	-	18 Years to 64 Years	63	Hemophilia A	Biological: PF-07055480
NCT04281485	Recruiting	Phase III	5 November 2020	-	4 Years to 7 Years	99	Duchenne Muscular Dystrophy	Genetic: PF-06939926
NCT04704921	Recruiting	Phase II | Phase III	29 December 2020	-	50 Years to 89 Years	300	Age-related Macular Degeneration	Genetic: RGX-314
NCT04671433	Recruiting	Phase III	16 March 2021	-	3 Years and older	96	X-Linked Retinitis Pigmentosa	Genetic: AAV5-RPGR
NCT04794101	Recruiting	Phase III	16 March 2021	-	3 Years and older	96	X-Linked Retinitis Pigmentosa	Genetic: AAV5-RPGR
NCT05407636	Recruiting	Phase III	28 December 2021	-	50 Years to 89 Years	465	Age-related Macular Degeneration	Genetic: RGX-314
NCT05089656	Recruiting	Phase III	12 January 2022	-	2 Years to 17 Years	125	Spinal Muscular Atrophy	Genetic: OAV101
NCT04283227	Recruiting	Phase III	17 January 2022	-	Child, Adult, Older Adult	6	Lysosomal Storage Diseases	Genetic: OTL-200

Table 3. *Cont.*

Trial	Status	Phases	Start Date	Completion Date	Age	Enrollment #	Conditions	Interventions
NCT05345171	Recruiting	Phase III	18 October 2022	-	12 Years and older	50	OTC Deficiency	Genetic: DTX301
NCT05335876	Recruiting	Phase III	19 December 2022	-	Child, Adult, Older Adult	260	Spinal Muscular Atrophy	Biological: onasemnogene abeparvovec
NCT05386680	Recruiting	Phase III	12 January 2023	-	2 Years to 12 Years	28	Spinal Muscular Atrophy	Genetic: OAV101
NCT05689164	Not yet recruiting	Phase III	14 April 2023	-	0 Years and older	250	Duchenne Muscular Dystrophy	Biological: fordadistrogene movaparvovec
NCT05815004	Not yet recruiting	Phase II	Phase III	1 October 2023	-	2 Years to 25 Years	40	Gaucher Disease, Type 3	Drug: Gene therapy
NCT00073463	Terminated	Phase II	Phase III	1 June 2003	-	12 Years and older	100	Cystic Fibrosis	Genetic: tgAAVCF

Additional phase III trials have been completed for Choroideremia, cerebral adrenoleukodystrophy, β-Thalassemia, and Leber Hereditary Optic Neuropathy. NCT03496012 showed that a single-dose delivery of an AAV2-encoded *REP1* gene targeted to the eye (in situ) with local injections was able to prevent monogenic inherited retinal dystrophies [44]. NCT01896102 showed the ex vivo delivery of CD34+ stem cells treated with lentiviral encoded *ABCD1* to treat males with cerebral adrenoleukodystrophy [45]. Within that study, there was one reported death, 47% of individuals identified as white, all patients were males, and there were eight events of febrile neutropenia, six with a severe fever, and an extensive list of nonserious adverse events. NCT02906202 and NCT03207009 showed the ex vivo delivery of CD34+ stem cells treated with lentiviral encoded βA-T87Q-Globin gene for β-Thalassemia, with a 91% success rate of individuals showing transfusion independence [46]. Four individuals had adverse events, including one case of thrombocytopenia. NCT03406104 showed the intravitreal delivery (in situ) of the AAV2-encoded *ND4* gene to improve vision in individuals with Leber Hereditary Optic Neuropathy [47]. In summary, it should be noted that SMA therapy is the only completed phase III trial with in vivo intravenous gene therapy results.

NCT00073463 started in 2003, aiming to test 100 participants age 12 or older for aerosolized AAV-encoded *CFTR* for the treatment of cystic fibrosis. While the phase I and II studies for this aerosolized therapy showed safety [48,49], the phase III trial showed no improvement in lung function [50]. The trial was terminated with the last enrolled participant in October 2005.

Below is a description of active trials with posted or published results, focusing on serious adverse responses reported. NCT00999609 used subretinal-injected AAV2-encoded *RPE65* to treat retinal dystrophy in 21 patients, where two of the cases showed adverse drug reactions, and one individual showed convulsions [51]. NCT03370913, NCT03392974, and NCT04323098 showed the use of AAV5-encoded Coagulation Factor VIII infusion in 134 males with hemophilia A, where 22 serious adverse events were reported [52]. NCT03569891 used AAV5-encoded Human Factor IX infusion (Hemgenix, etranacogene dezaparvovec) to treat 67 males with hemophilia B, with five severe events, including acute myocardial infarction, gastrointestinal hemorrhage, pseudarthrosis, and acute kidney injury. In nearly all of the recruiting studies, there is a lack of posted results, meaning until completed, most gene therapy clinical trials lack reported data on adverse events. A commonality of gene therapy studies is the prescreening of antibodies towards the AAV system with no reported issues with immunosuppressive agents.

2.4. Approved Therapies

The FDA classifies gene therapy products in combination with cellular therapies within the Office of Tissues and Advanced Therapies, where there are 32 approved licensed products (as of 2 August 2023), 8 of which are gene therapies.

Two therapies have been authorized for SMA treatment: Spinraza and Zolgensma. Spinraza (Nusinersen, Biogen) is an antisense oligonucleotide that targets the *SMN2* gene to alter splicing to recover SMN protein function [53]. The phase III trial (NCT02292537) for Spinraza showed success in preventing SMA in 84 patients, with severe adverse events similar to sham control [54]. It should be noted that Spinraza is delivered intrathecally to the cerebral spinal fluid, and one case of post-lumbar puncture syndrome was noted in the clinical trial. Spinraza requires repeat dosing every four months indefinitely to maintain clinical benefits. Spinraza therapy was submitted to the FDA and approved on 23 December 2016 under a fast-track and orphan drug designation. Zolgensma (Onasemnogene Abeparvovec, Novartis Gene Therapies Inc.) was submitted to the FDA on 1 October 2018 and approved on 24 May 2019, creating an intravenous gene therapy for SMA. Zolgensma is a functioning copy of the full human *SMN1* gene, which codes for the SMN protein that is lacking in SMA patients. Zolgensma currently requires only one dose.

Elevidys (delandistrogene moxeparvovec-rokl, Sarepta Theraputics, Inc.) was submitted to the FDA on 28 September 2022 and approved on 22 June 2023 for the treatment of Duchenne Muscular Dystrophy. Approval was limited to ambulatory patients aged 4–5 years. Elevidys utilizes an adeno-associated viral vector (AAVrh74) to deliver a portion of the dystrophin gene "microdystrophin.". Sarepta was approved under accelerated status by demonstrating that patients treated with Elevidys had increased microdystrophin expression. It was noted in a published FDA summary memo that the decision for approval went against the recommendations made by the Clinical, Clinical Pharmacology, and Statistics review teams, who did not feel the data submitted showed a definite clinical benefit. Elevidys was approved with the contingency that further clinical trial data would be submitted.

Hemgenix (etranacogene dezaparvovec-drlb, CSL Behring LLC) was submitted to the FDA on 24 March 2022 and approved on 22 November 2022 for the treatment of hemophilia B. Luxturna (voretigene neparvovec-rzyl, Spark Therapeutics Inc.) was submitted to the FDA on 16 May 2017 and approved on 18 December 2017 for the treatment of biallelic *RPE65* mutation-associated retinal dystrophy. Skysona (elivaldogene autotemcel, bluebird bio Inc.) was submitted to the FDA on 18 October 2021 and approved on 16 September 2022 to treat active cerebral adrenoleukodystrophy. Zynteglo (betibeglogene autotemcel, bluebird bio Inc.) was submitted to the FDA on 20 September 2021 and approved on 19 August 2022 to treat ß-Thalassemia. Roctavian (valoctocogene roxaparvovec-rvox) was submitted to the FDA on 23 December 2019 (resubmitted 29 September 2022) and approved on 29 June 2023 to treat severe hemophilia A only in the absence of AAV-5 preexisting antibodies. Vyjuvek (beremagene geperpavec) was submitted to the FDA on 20 June 2022 and approved on 19 May 2023 for the treatment of those >6 months of age with dystrophic epidermolysis bullosa due to COL7A1 variants. It should be noted that Vyjuvek is the first ever approved topical gene therapy and utilizes a herpes simplex virus type 1 (HSV-1) delivery system. HSV-1 is optimal for skin delivery as the virus naturally infects skin cells.

In the case of many of these FDA-approved therapies, their phase III trials continued after their authorizations, with an expectation of progression into phase IV studies.

While gene therapy in cystic fibrosis has had mixed results, it should be noted that small molecule regulators of the CFTR gene have proven that nucleotide delivery is not the only approach to modify gene expression in rare diseases. The FDA approved Elexacaftor–tezacaftor–ivacaftor, also known as triple therapy, which is recommended in patients with at least one copy of Phe508del CFTR variants [55,56]. Cystic fibrosis is an example where strategies outside of gene therapy should be continued in parallel, setting a critical mission that gene therapy trials do not overpower or result in underfunding small-molecule or other therapeutic approaches.

3. Biological Considerations

For effective gene therapy, one must confidently identify a causal gene, package that gene into a delivery system expressing the right amount in the right tissue/cell, and replace or repair the molecular mechanism with a measurable phenotype. This must be achieved while avoiding unforeseen biological challenges of viral vectors and overexpression of mRNA within cells. Below, we provide several areas of consideration for expanding gene therapy into additional clinical genetics.

3.1. Genetic Syndromes

The OMIM database (https://www.omim.org/) [57] represents a catalog of human genetic conditions. As of April 2023, the database contained >6000 gene-to-disease correlations. These correlations represent 4771 unique human genes on all human chromosomes (Figure 6A). Using the UniProt database of protein annotations [58], it is evident that only a few represent DNA binding factors or have annotated domains like a zinc finger or coiled-coil segment (Figure 6B). A significant portion of these proteins are transmembrane, suggesting they localize to the surface of a cell. Many proteins have catalytic activity, binding sites, and active sites. In some rare and genetic diseases, the active site becomes hyperactive, where inhibitors can ameliorate disease. Most diseases manifest from loss-of-function to protein biology and thus need correctors instead of inhibitors.

Using the Human Protein Atlas (HPA) database [59], it is observed that most of the genes are ubiquitously expressed in human tissues (Figure 6C). At the same time, they have more specificity when annotated based on cell types within each tissue (Figure 6D). This observation suggests that we should not address tissue specificity for each gene but rather cell type specificity, where emerging tools like single-cell transcriptomics are opening new doors for these insights. Of the OMIM genes, 2398 have been knocked out in a mouse model, can be purchased for lab use, and have undergone extensive phenotypic analysis based on the International Mouse Phenotyping Consortium (IMPC, Figure 6E) [60]. A total of 90% (2158/2398) of these genes show at least one observable phenotype altered by removing the gene, many matching the known human conditions, where these animals can serve as a pre-clinical gene therapy testing system.

It should be noted that 341 gene knockouts from the IMPC result in heterogeneous preweaning lethality (incomplete penetrance), and 131 are highly penetrant for lethality. The heterogeneity within phenotypes for genetic diseases represents one of the most considerable challenges in gene therapy; namely, how can one develop clinical trials to know success when phenotypes are not always predictable with our current state of knowledge.

It should be noted that the number of datasets showing gene expression within the HPA has little correlation to the number of altered phenotypes observed in the IMPC (R^2 of 2×10^{-5}, Figure 6F). This points to the need for further tools in genotype-to-phenotype predictions that will strengthen our ability to know when and how gene therapies may apply to an individual.

Many gene therapy delivery systems have a limited size of the genetic insert, with most of the OMIM genes within this window (Figure 6G). The largest database of human genetics, ClinVar [61], shows that of these OMIM genes, we have an array of known confident pathogenic variants (Figure 6G). While our pathogenic and likely pathogenic variants usually are significant changes to proteins (frameshift and nonsense variants), the current state of research is challenged by missense genetic changes and whether they confidently result in disease states (Figure 6H). Gene therapy can only be employed in high-confidence situations. Thus, the million plus variants of uncertain significance (VUSs) in OMIM genes would have a low probability of successful clinical trials, primarily if implemented based on newborn screening. This finding highlights that variant characterization remains a significant challenge in gene therapy expansion for genetic syndromes.

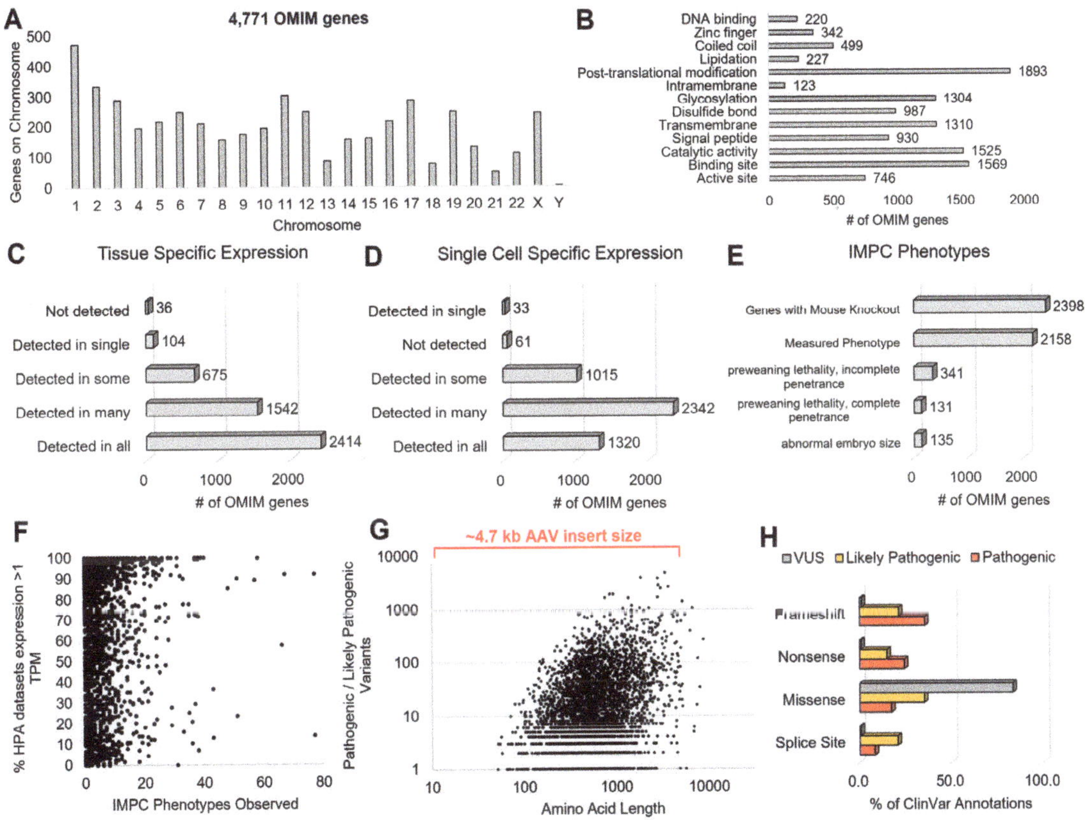

Figure 6. OMIM genes connecting human genotypes to phenotypes. (**A**) Number of OMIM genes per chromosome. (**B**) The number of OMIM genes with various human UniProt annotations. (**C**) Tissue- or (**D**) single-cell-specific expression annotation from the Human Protein Atlas for each of the OMIM genes. (**E**) The number of OMIM genes with various International Mouse Phenotyping Consortium (IMPC) annotations following knockout and phenotyping. (**F**) Each OMIM gene number of IMPC phenotypes altered in knockout (x-axis) relative to the % of datasets from the Human Protein Atlas where the gene is expressed >1 transcript per million (TPM). (**G**) The amino acid length of each OMIM gene (x-axis) relative to the number of ClinVar annotated pathogenic or likely pathogenic variants. (**H**) The percent of each variant class relative to variant alterations for the ClinVar database.

3.2. Cell and Promoter Specificity

Gene therapy is targeted to cell types based on the vector used to deliver the nucleic acids and sequences that can drive the expression of each gene only within that tissue/cell type, such as a cell-specific promoter element. The control of expression enables each gene to be made into mRNA and protein only in a specific cell type. To minimize the size of expression regulation sequences, promoters rather than enhancers are often used to achieve cell-type specificity [62]. Since the advent of RNA sequencing, there has been an expansion in defining tissue/cell-specific expression. Still, more recently, with techniques such as single-cell RNA sequencing, we are now resolving specificity in the different functional cell types within each tissue. This specificity of expression is critical to controlling many OMIM genes contributing to developmental pathways. The HPA annotation of cell specificity for 75 different cell types shows 1908 different human genes with highly specific expression within one of the cell types (Figure 7). More work is needed to determine which promoter elements may work, independent of cell-type-specific enhancers, for the desired tissue of an OMIM gene being nominated for gene therapy.

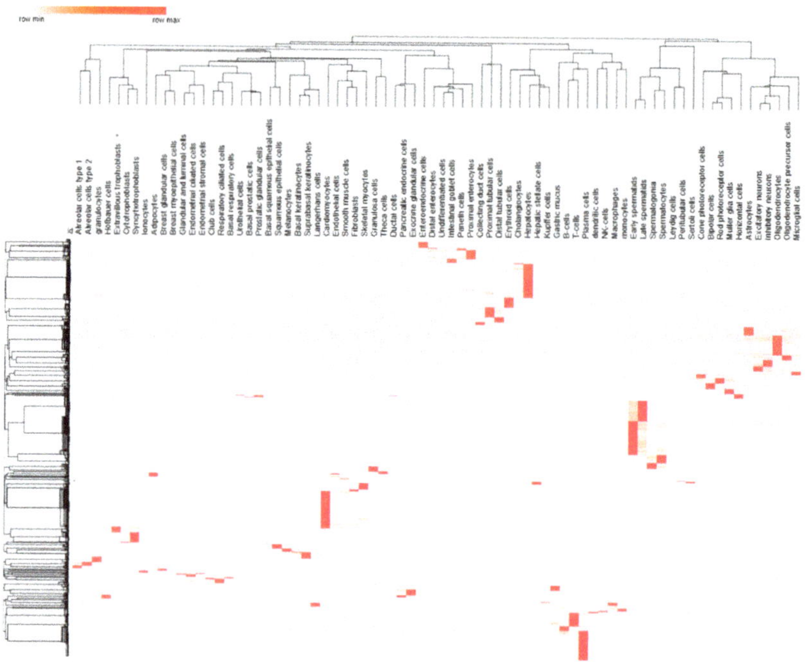

Figure 7. Heatmap of expression for cell-type-specific genes from the Human Protein Atlas. Red indicates the highest expression in the row. Dendrograms show one minus Spearman rank correlation with cell type on top and genes shown to the left.

It should be noted that the developmental trajectory of many genes makes it challenging to identify when gene therapy will be safe and effective. For example, variants that disrupt the complex developmental process of neural crest cells give rise to multiple, diverse peripheral cells [63] and require more critical reasoning on whether gene therapy can recover the developmental changes. Our work on LRP1-related syndrome [64] highlights the complex multi-phenotype traits associated with neural crest cells that will be difficult to advance gene therapy approaches within the developmental stages, often active in utero.

3.3. Variant Location within Proteins

As shown in Figure 6H, many clinically sequenced variants within genes that may benefit from gene therapy fall within sites that are difficult to annotate and thus result in an annotation as a VUS. These are often subtle missense variants within a gene and are the first observance of such variants. Most of these variants have only been identified in a single individual and never observed in the millions of sequenced human genomes completed to date, making it difficult to establish a causal nature of the missense variant [22]. Thus, it has become common that gene therapies are initiated only in individuals that have either a variant that occurs in multiple individuals (often autosomal recessive conditions) or the variant results in a frameshift or nonsense change that removes large chunks of protein observed to be removed in other patients with the disorder. There is a need for characterizing VUSs rapidly using existing data [23,64–68], high-throughput wet lab techniques used in NAA10 characterizations [69], knowledge from paralog proteins such as the work on SOX transcription factors [70], or through crowd-sourcing variant lists to identify matching variant locations and phenotypes as was the case for MED13 [71].

Unique variants within genes with early and penetrant phenotypes matched to other pathogenic cases with similar phenotypes are easier to diagnose and determine a missense variant as pathogenic. This relies on phenotype matching, even if variants are unique to a patient. However, in the case of most progressive disorders (such as neurodegeneration) that are detectable in newborn screening before the phenotype is observed, these missense variants cannot be mapped with confidence, preventing the initiation of gene therapy until a phenotype appears. Therefore, if we anticipate gene therapy to apply to every individual for a gene approved with therapy, we must build more robust tools for interpreting each amino acid within an observed gene.

3.4. Gene Isoforms and Common Variants

Among the OMIM genes, each gene has an average of 6.2 protein-coding isoforms. These isoforms represent changes in splicing or transcriptional start sites that can alter the sequence of each protein. It is important to remember that many genes have different isoforms within different tissues and that human variants can result in altered splicing [72]. Previously, we showed how variants could alter gene splicing, such as small GTPases [73], and how alternative transcriptional start sites can change the interpretation of common disease association variants, such as SHROOM3 for chronic kidney disease [36].

The *SMN1* and *SMN2* genes each contain multiple spliced isoforms variably expressed in different human datasets based on the GTEx database [72] (Figure 8A). Each of these different isoforms has splice differences that remove one of three exons, resulting in various-sized proteins of each (Figure 8B). New genomic tools such as GTEx have built correlations between genomic variants within genomes and expression (eQTLs) or splicing (sQTLs) for each gene. Both the *SMN1* and *SMN2* genes have eQTLs and sQTLs that modify the genes (Figure 8C). More importantly, these variants are found enriched within human populations such as Africans/African Americans and remain understudied. Interestingly, both the sQTLs in *SMN1* and *SMN2* are found at the C-terminal region of the genes in similar locations (Figure 8D).

While we highlight the role of variants of *SMN1* and *SMN2*, many human genes have variants that can modify expression levels or splicing [72]. However, most of these variants have remained understudied regarding how to incorporate them into gene therapy approaches. This represents a promising area for further exploration as we develop gene therapies for diverse human populations that are increasingly being studied using population-level genomics such as GTEx.

3.5. Risk of Overexpression

In gene therapy, determining and controlling the appropriate protein expression level in cells can be challenging, with uncertain outcomes if the expression is too high. Tools are available to help guide us to potential outcomes of gene overexpression, ranging from additional copies to overexpression in disease states. When determining a gene for therapy, it is critical to observe using data analysis tools if the overexpression could result in any measurable phenotypes. This can include the analysis of ClinGen [74] to determine if there are any known genetic events within humans for dosage sensitivity, specifically the genetic duplication of the gene that results in a measurable phenotype (triplosensitivity). As noted above, eQTLs can also tell us when subtle variants, often noncoding, can result in population-level increases in gene expression. These eQTL variants can be compared to Genome-Wide Association Studies (GWASs) or Phenome-Wide Association Studies (PheWASs) to find when these variants associated with elevated expression can also overlap with a measurable phenotype, taking care to determine the maximum peak overlap of colocalization of the expression and phenotype of the same variant [23].

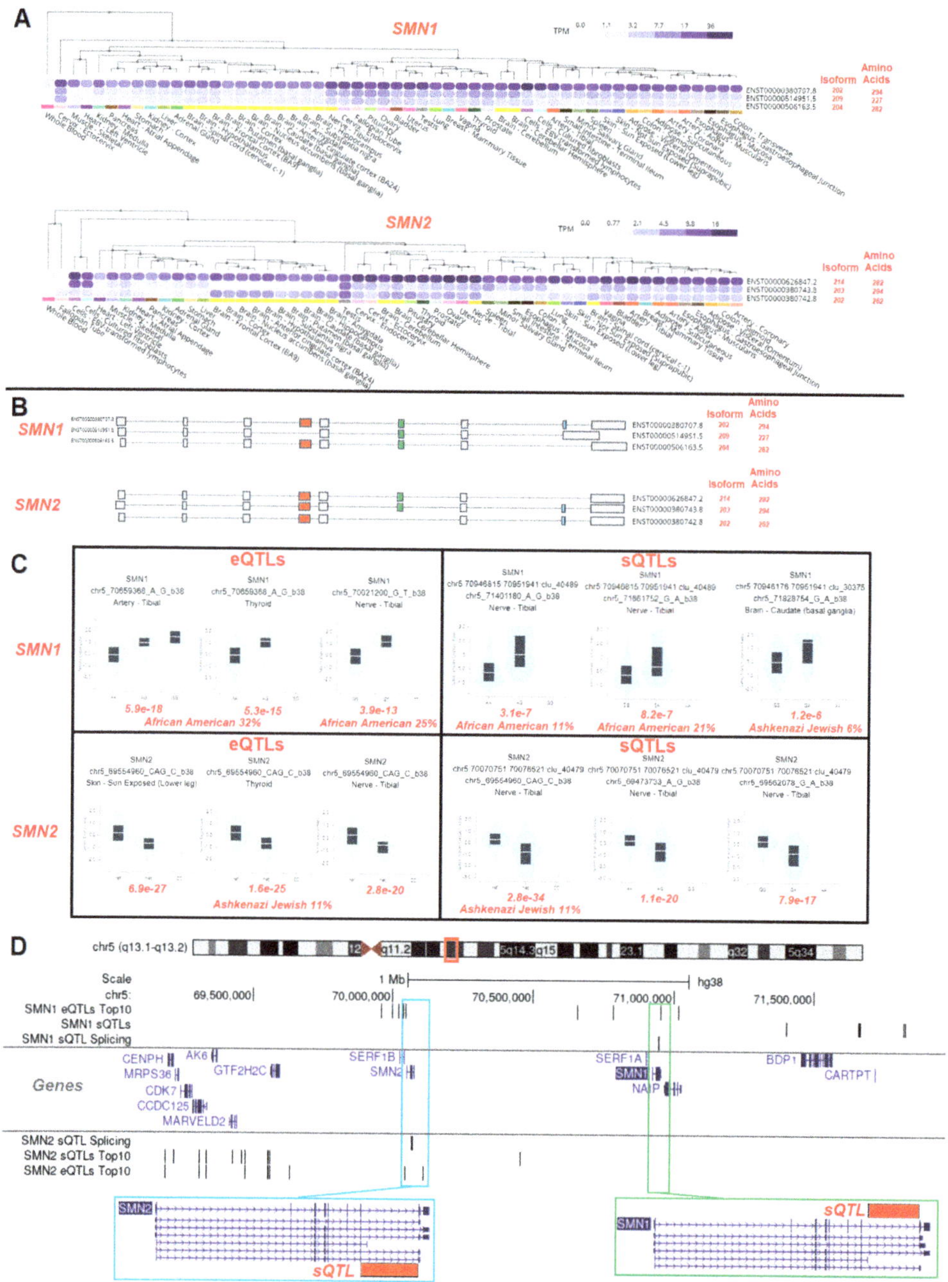

Figure 8. Isoforms and genetics of SMN1 and SMN2. (**A**) Top three protein-coding isoforms for SMN1 and SMN2 genes. (**B**) Exon map of isoforms within panel (**A**). (**C**) GTEx-measured eQTLs and sQTLs for the SMN1 and SMN2 genes. The significance and the population with the highest frequency of the variants are labeled in red below the violin plots. (**D**) Chromosome 5 map of the top eQTL and sQTL signals for SMN1 and SMN2.

An example of colocalized variants can be seen in the *NF1* gene, which is emerging as a new potential gene therapy target for Neurofibromatosis [75]. The variant chr17_31326275_T_C (rs9894648) is found in diverse populations with significant known *NF1* eQTLs over multiple tissues and a colocalized signal for the variant to traits such as sex-hormone-binding globulin protein (Figure 9). This suggests that modulation of *NF1* levels in gene therapy could have a resulting perturbation in hormone signaling that could be measured over gene therapy trials to determine if this has clinical utility. We must utilize our massive biological knowledgebases, such as eQTLs and GWASs/PheWASs, to determine non-biased traits that should be measured within clinical trials as a risk of overexpression of a chosen gene.

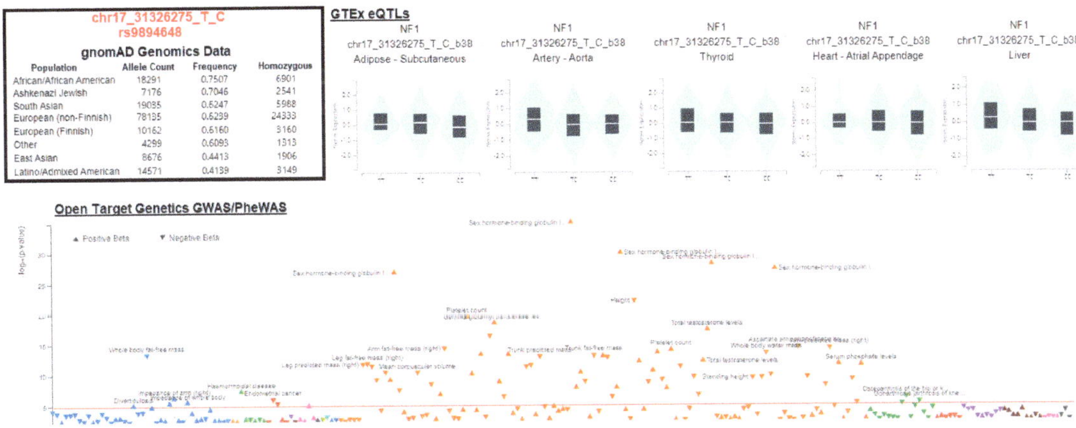

Figure 9. Representative analysis of a variant colocalized for expression and phenotypes. The first panel shows variant allele frequency data from gnomAD population genomics sequencing. The GTEx eQTL plots show five different tissues with significant eQTLs for the variant within the NF1 gene. The bottom plot shows the Open Target Genetics [76] data curation for significant traits associated with this variant.

3.6. Delivery Systems

A gene therapy delivery system must reach the targeted cells, evade immune system phagocytosis (depleting therapy), and make a functional protein once in the cell while avoiding lysosomal degradation [4]. Delivery strategies such as lipid-based systems and nanoparticles have little cell specificity for delivery, while viral strategies have more surface receptor specificity and higher risks of immune activation [5,77]. Non-viral delivery systems have seen a recent boost with use in SARS-CoV-2 and other mRNA vaccines, which has increased the hope of applying them to broader gene therapies [78]. Newer biological strategies, such as extracellular vesicles, are also emerging as ways to avoid immune activation [79]. Viral vectors such as adeno-associated viruses (AAVs) have lower immune activation and a limited 4.8 kilobase insert size. In contrast, larger viruses such as herpes simplex virus (HSV) have a larger insert capacity but higher immunogenicity with narrower cell targeting [80]. As many of these viruses are natural sources of infection, some individuals carry antibodies or T-cells that are responsive during gene therapy and must be monitored [81]. Substantial ongoing efforts are therefore aimed at reducing the immunogenicity of viral vectors and functionalizing non-viral vectors to enhance cell-type-specific targeting and effects.

Viral delivery systems are often matched to the cell/tissue type of natural infection, opening the door for engineering opportunities to enhance delivery to tissues without an optimal viral system. While there were significant investments in gene therapy approaches for cystic fibrosis, these therapies struggled to find therapeutic benefits due to difficulty in delivery to the progenitor cells of the lung. Hurdles to AAV gene transfer to airway epithelia for cystic fibrosis include (1) by-passing the mucus to reach the cell surface; (2) binding a receptor at the apical cell surface; (3) endocytosis for cell entry; (4) trafficking to the nucleus; (5) conversion of the single-stranded DNA core to double-stranded DNA followed by concatemerization and/or integration; and (6) achieving therapeutic levels of protein expression. As the current small molecule cystic fibrosis drugs are only recommended for individuals with a delta508 variant, gene therapy is still needed to treat individuals of diverse ancestry not having delta508 [82]. Over the past decade, improvement in the efficiency of AAV targeting of airway epithelia has been achieved by using different serotypes [83–88], site-directed mutagenesis modifications of viral capsids [89], and targeted evolution selection [90,91]. Currently, ongoing clinical trials using the AAV vector derived from directed evolutions demonstrate promising safety profiles for treating individuals who are ineligible for or unable to tolerate triple therapy (NCT05248230).

The prevailing hope throughout the gene therapy field is that viral delivery systems studied within each trial will be carried forward into the subsequent development to minimize the risks of gene therapy with delivery system human validation data [92]. Multiple AAV clinical trials have pointed towards hepatic injury risks [93], including cytokine/neutrophil-dependent mechanisms [94]. In animal studies, these risks are contributed to by environmental factors such as obesity and diabetes [95]. As gene therapy progresses in clinical trials and FDA-approved clinical use, we must document risk factors for adverse outcomes to each vector and determine environmental or genetic factors to help identify risks.

4. Immune Response

Currently, gene therapy is designed to deliver the desired effect in one dose. However, there is a lack of long-term data on the efficacy of these treatments as the FDA approvals have only been in the past few years [96,97]. As more data are obtained about these therapies, redosing may be necessary. The possibility of redosing poses a challenge to gene therapy vectors [98]. Viral vectors have most of their replication machinery removed to enable them to carry the desired gene. However, the vector still contains surface epitopes that elicit innate and adaptive responses against the virus as the wild-type immune response [99,100]. Usually, producing antibodies or T-cell adaptive responses to viral infections is advantageous to help clear infection and enables future viral detection to provide resistance. However, in the case of viral vectors of gene therapy, it is a significant roadblock, as the antibodies may already be present from similar natural infections, or the first dose may inhibit the efficacy of vector reutilization for future doses of gene therapy [101].

The presence of viral vector antibodies before treatment threatens the future accessibility of gene therapy and increases the risk of adverse events. In 1999, the University of Pennsylvania conducted a clinical trial for an adenovirus serotype 5 (Ad5)-based gene therapy for a rare metabolic disease known as ornithine transcarbamylase (OTC). One of the participants suffered from lethal systemic inflammation four days post-treatment [102]. A recent study by Somanathan et al. (2020) presents data suggesting that preexisting Ad5 antibodies may have contributed to the lethal inflammatory response [103]. Additionally, recent deaths in a pediatric high-dose adeno-associated virus (AAV) gene therapy trial for X-linked myotubular myopathy may have been caused by AAV antibodies and an exaggerated immune response similar to that observed in the OTC trial [104]. As a result of the risk of exaggerated immune response, made evident by these incidents, individuals with pre-existing immunity to specific viral vectors are to be excluded from viral-based gene therapy clinical trials [105].

Levels of pre-existing antibodies for AAVs have been noted to be high enough to reduce the patient inclusion population for clinical trials by almost 50% [106]. The prevalence of these antibodies (seroprevalence) can differ across populations. Some populations have been found to have over 90% pre-existing adenovirus immunity by age 2 [107]. The high prevalence of pre-existing antibodies can biologically limit the accessibility of gene therapies to specific populations and even perpetuate current racial disparities in healthcare accessibility. A recent study by Khatri et al. (2022) found seroprevalence was higher among U.S. racial minorities, specifically Hispanic and African American individuals [108]. Therefore, gene therapies utilizing viral vectors may have decreased efficacy in racial minorities.

Zolgensma highlights the gravity of this issue. Zolgensma uses the AAV9 vector. Khatri et al. (2022) found significantly higher AAV9 seroprevalence among black donors than white donors [108]. However, in their study of the differences in *SMN1* allele frequency in North America among different ethnic groups, Hendrickson et al. (2009) found black individuals to have five times the risk of being a carrier for SMA compared to white individuals [109]. The design of Zolgensma creates the potential for a lack of biological accessibility to one of the populations that could benefit the most from it.

To avoid this issue, gene therapy vectors must be chosen with their target population in mind. The vector utilized should be that which, along with being the most biologically functional and effective to deliver the gene of interest, is accessible to the broadest possible range of populations. Antibody titers can be used to measure pre-existing immunity. Two primary assays have been developed: binding assays that measure the total amount of antibodies (neutralizing and non-neutralizing) and neutralizing assays that only measure neutralizing antibodies [105]. Continued monitoring of global seroprevalence and continued prescreening of trial participants and potential gene therapy patients will be necessary to address the growing challenge of pre-existing immunity to viral vectors.

Research is needed to understand the immune response to viral vectors further. This enhanced understanding may allow for the targeted modulation of the immune response to improve vector efficacy and allow for possible redosing. Immune system modulation may involve antibody neutralization, as described in a review of recent research by Herzog and Biswas (2020) [110]. A specific strategy utilizes immunoglobulin-degrading enzymes from Streptococcus that can be administered prior to AAV treatment. The enzymes cut immunoglobulins at a specific site to make them unable to neutralize the vector. This strategy would prevent the development of an immune response, allowing for improved transduction and treatment efficacy [111].

Using viral vectors mandates the co-administration of steroids to prevent transaminitis, a broad immune modification [112]. Although initial study protocols suggested treatment for 30 days followed by a 30-day taper, most patients required steroids longer due to persistent transaminitis. Chand et al. summarized the initial studies with Onasemnogene abeparvovec (Zolgensma) for SMA and noted an average steroid usage of 83 days, ranging from 33 to 229 days [113]. In general, limited use of steroids is safe in infants and children. Steroids are frequently given to neonates with bronchopulmonary dysplasia, infants with infantile spasms, or children with nephrotic syndrome. Common short-term side effects include changes in appetite, mild immunosuppression, and gastrointestinal discomfort. Infants may exhibit changes in hunger or sleep patterns when started on steroids and often have a disrupted vaccination schedule. Stopping steroids after gene transfer becomes more difficult the longer the patient is on the steroids; careful tapering is required to avoid an adrenal crisis. Although common steroids, like prednisone and prednisolone, are relatively affordable compared to gene therapy, the potential side effects from longer-term steroid use could increase the overall cost burden, particularly if hospitalization is required.

5. Cost of Gene Therapy

While gene therapy brings significant benefits to patients, it also comes with incredible costs. Research and development have been estimated to cost between USD 318 million and USD 3 billion per gene therapy development [114]. Gene therapy for SMA consists of a one-time intravenous dose. The disease's rarity ensures a small number of patients receive the medication. The limited usage of the drug drives up the cost. More importantly, this suggests a needed international effort to identify all patients with these rare diseases to reduce cost per patient. Zolgensma, a gene therapy for SMA, costs USD 2.1 million for a one-time dose. The approved gene therapy for hemophilia B, Hemgenix, costs USD 3.5 million per treatment, making it the most expensive drug worldwide, highlighting the need to identify more patients with disease or drug competition to reduce pricing. The high cost of these treatments can be absorbed into the payer's system because the number of patients requiring treatment is relatively low. This may not be feasible when gene therapy is available for more diseases and a broader population of patients. A cost analysis of gene therapy versus other maintenance therapies for SMA shows that gene therapy is more cost-effective than lifelong intermittent doses of maintenance therapy [115]. This cost-effectiveness is not maintained when SMA patients suffer a relapse [116]. It is also likely to be less cost-effective in more mild diseases. As more data are obtained, cost-effectiveness may not be maintained.

With effective treatments that are more cost-effective for rare diseases, it will be imperative for payment systems to adapt and accommodate the high cost of the medications. It has been suggested that paying smaller amounts over time instead of one large payment before the administration could be an effective mechanism to share the cost between the payers and pharmaceutical companies [112]. It would also ensure the payment could be stopped if the therapy ceases to be effective, similar to stopping the medication if it is no longer effective. This model has already been used in national health plans [117]. Spain and France, for example, will only continue payments for hepatic C treatment if the patient is cured [114]. Novartis also utilizes this approach with Kymriah, a gene therapy for B-cell acute lymphoblastic leukemia. Novartis has an agreement with hospitals that they do not invoice for Kymriah until a 30-day outcome test is completed. No payment is required if the patient does not respond successfully to the treatment in this period [118]. This approach limits the financial burden on patients and hospital systems and increases the financial accessibility of these potentially curative treatments.

In the United States, the Orphan Drug Act (ODA) (1983) was developed to provide financial benefits to pharmaceutical companies for the development of drugs for rare diseases affecting fewer than 200,000 people in the U.S. Some of these benefits include market exclusivity, federal grants, and waivers of marketing application user fees [119]. However, there is a need to incentivize gene therapy development further and reduce the cost of this therapy. These reforms may include implementing a stratified benefit system in which incentives depend on the disease population size and decreasing exclusivity periods to ensure benefits are only utilized for drugs with small patient populations and limited economic potential [119].

6. Need for Increased Transparency

Gene therapy has a history of false hope and exaggerated hype. In the early 1990s, completing the first gene therapy clinical trial led to a wave of excitement perpetuated by the media. This enthusiasm spread to researchers and the public alike, leading to the initiation of numerous research projects and a push to advance gene therapy clinical trials. However, this excitement and rapid advancement proved to be self-destructive. In 1995, the NIH released a statement criticizing the field of gene therapy for rushed clinical trials, poor experimental design, and lack of rational scientific logic [120].

This pattern was seen again in 2008, with two reports in the *New England Journal of Medicine* describing a gene therapy to correct a form of congenital blindness. The media extrapolated the results of these reports to suggest the potential for curing eye conditions of all kinds. These statements were met with backlash from the scientific community, specifically about the pressure put on them to accelerate gene therapies [121].

These incidents illustrate how the revolutionary potential of gene therapy needs to be paired with humility. Gene therapy has the potential to do a lot of good, but there are risks and uncertainties. Improved multiway communication between all stakeholders—physicians, researchers, policymakers, companies, patients, and the public—about gene therapy's risks and benefits is necessary. The information conveyed to patients and the general public should be clear, relatable, concise, and reliable. This information may be paired with increased genetic education through genetic counseling for patients and their families, as knowledge of genetics is crucial to understanding gene therapy's risks and benefits [122].

The potential for side effects, the possibility that effectiveness may wane, and the plethora of new gene therapy drugs in the pipeline necessitate discussion between researchers, clinicians, and patients. This ongoing discussion will be essential to ensure side effects are noted swiftly, and changes to clinical practice can be made. Currently, rare disease advocacy groups have well-established registries collecting patient data across institutions, including groups serving multiple diagnoses like the Muscular Dystrophy Association and groups specific to one disease process like CureSMA, CureDuchenne, and Parent Project Muscular Dystrophy. These databases have years of patient information and already have the infrastructure to collect information on safety and patient outcomes as gene therapy is used and implemented in the future. These groups serve as a valuable resource for communication between patients, clinicians, and researchers.

Physicians from every specialty should know about the field to effectively communicate relevant information to their patients. Physicians and researchers should work together to ensure access to relevant information about current gene therapy developments to keep patients well informed about the current state of research. However, not all education is top-down. Researchers also need to hear from patients about their concerns and experiences to ensure research efforts align with the needs of the patient population for which they are developing treatments [120].

The high cost of gene therapy leads to a complicated pay structure. This requires clinicians, payers, and hospital systems to communicate to ensure timely patient drug delivery. Lastly, communication between policymakers, clinicians, patients, payers, and hospital systems must be prioritized to ensure safety and equitable distribution are established.

An increase in information sharing between companies and researchers, specifically about failed clinical trials, is also imperative to the informational accessibility of gene therapy. After a failed phase III clinical trial for gene therapy for epidermolysis bullosa, the company leading the study contacted other companies working on the disease and unpacked their data, presenting what they had learned from the failed study. As a result, one of the companies changed its inclusion endpoints [123]. This model of accountability and transparency is necessary for the future progression of gene therapy. The success of a gene therapy clinical trial hinges on multiple components, such as the vector selection, the gene delivered, and the promoter utilized. The accessibility of this information is essential to the analysis of both prior and present clinical trials to analyze current trends in trial design and common denominators for observed outcomes.

7. Ethical Considerations for Gene Therapy—Conclusions

The ethics of gene therapy are as multi-faceted as the field of medicine itself. We have laid out the biological, clinical, and public/patient-centric ethical considerations of gene therapy within this article (Figure 10). However, the ethical issues surrounding gene therapy are less about gene therapy itself and more about the medical, cultural, social, and political contexts in which it emerged. We cannot boil down these questions and issues to one-time decisions and solutions, which would disregard the relational and longitudinal nature of ethics [124]. Addison and Lassen unravel the concept of the ethics of gene therapy clinical trials as follows: "The ethical complexities of gene therapy are not confined to the consent process or the procedure, nor does the ethics review process resolve them. Rather, the treatment unfurls a multitude of ethical dilemmas, which manifest both in discrete moments of choice and the on-going endeavor of how to live well or care well in the aftermath of the event itself".

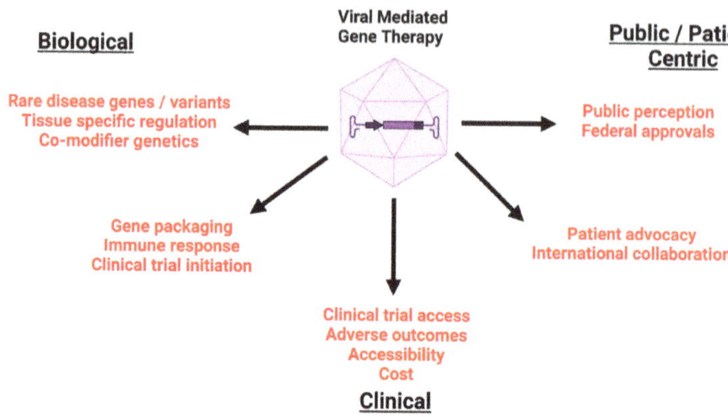

Figure 10. Summary of the ethical considerations of gene therapy. This figure was generated with BioRender.

The Hippocratic Oath [125], often referred to as the basis of ethical medical practice, presents the purpose of medicine as "to do away with suffering of the sick, to lessen the violence of their diseases." The purpose of medicine and the principle of ethical practice hinge on relieving patient suffering, which, at its core, is patient-centered [126]. Therefore, the ethical advancement of gene therapy hinges on developing patient-centered solutions to the present and emerging ethical dilemmas and issues faced within this field. With every decision and every advancement, we must remember the patient.

This patient-centered lens can serve as the basis for thinking about the ethics of many gene therapy topics we have discussed. As evident in our analysis of gene therapy clinical trials, gene therapy is still in its early stages of development, with most clinical trials falling into the early phase categories (phases I, I/II, and II). The lack of international partnerships has prevented the scale of gene therapy from matching the rarity of diseases it is being developed to treat, representing a significant ethical consideration for cross-border study designs [19].

Severe adverse events, even patient deaths, although they are to be actively avoided through proper monitoring and reporting, are not uncommon within early phase trials, especially phase I trials [127]. In 1999, 153,964 severe adverse events (17,399 of them patient deaths) were reported to the Center for Drug Evaluation and Research of the United States FDA [128]. That same year, the phase I gene therapy clinical trial for OTC deficiency resulting in death was highly publicized, with 22 *New York Times* articles [129]. The media focusses on gene therapy more than other disciplines, leading to an amplified perception of risk. We must be clear about who these risks fall upon. Ultimately, they fall upon the patients—those actively involved in trials, those who will receive these treatments in the future, and those directly and indirectly affected by the outcomes of these discussions and decisions. Therefore, we must actively involve patient populations in the discussions and decision-making processes about the acceptable level of risk.

One option discussed by Pattee in their commentary titled "Protections for Participants in Gene Therapy Trials: A Patient's Perspective" [130] is to consult patients who have participated in trials on trial design, development, and direction, such as ensuring the adequacy of informed consent materials and trial logistics. Doing so would increase trial transparency and public trust in gene therapy, even amid complex uncertainties within the field. Pattee also suggests further protecting patients participating in clinical trials through improved public education about clinical trials to clarify information and concerns presented in the media and including disease-specific experts within centralized IRBs to incorporate additional perspectives specific to the patient population during trial design and monitoring [130].

Accessibility is a crucial factor to be considered in the ethical advancement of gene therapy. Rare diseases affect a small number of individuals in distinct ways. No two patients are identical. Gene therapy reflects the patient population in this way—it is designed to be specialized. The needs are not equal; therefore, treatments cannot be equal. However, treatment equity is still needed, from costs to the type of rare disease to trial access that disproportionately benefits a few [118,131]. To think about equity and accessibility is to consider already present disparities in healthcare systems, patterns we see emerging from early research and clinical trials, and other potential barriers that could threaten the ethical advancement of gene therapy, the safety of patient populations, and the ability of patients to access these potentially curative treatments.

Over 50% of individuals with rare diseases report using their savings to cover medical costs, with one in ten filing for bankruptcy [123]. The high cost of gene therapies is thus likely to continue overwhelming patients with rare diseases and the funding agencies for medical care, thus limiting personal access. As shown in Tables 1–3, only a few rare diseases have authorized gene therapies, where the >5000 unique rare diseases represent a significant opportunity to reduce production costs through transparent design that enables the subsequent therapy to be developed at a lower cost. Further expansion of international collaborations will unite rare disease patients to present a more extensive base of therapies. No matter how effective or miraculous, a treatment inaccessible to patients has no real value. Thus, a balance of patient risk, education, and accessibility remains the ethical priority for gene therapy of rare diseases.

Author Contributions: Conceptualization, M.L.H., J.W.P. and J.M.K.; methodology, M.L.H., J.K.Z. and J.W.P.; formal analysis, M.L.H., J.K.Z., J.W.P. and J.M.K.; writing—original draft preparation, M.L.H., J.K.Z., X.L, D.B.C., M.R.W., D.L.V., C.P.B., Y.M.E., S.R., N.L.H., J.W.P. and J.M.K.; writing—review and editing, M.L.H., J.K.Z., X.L., D.B.C., M.R.W., C.P.B., Y.M.E., S.R., N.L.H., J.W.P. and J.M.K.; supervision, J.W.P. and J.M.K.; project administration, J.W.P. and J.M.K. All authors have read and agreed to the published version of the manuscript.

Funding: This research was partially supported by Helen DeVos Children's Hospital (J.M.K.), Michigan State University (X.L., D.B.C., M.R.W., D.L.V. and J.W.P.), and the Gerber Foundation (C.P.B., S.R., and J.W.P.). M.L.H. was an undergraduate fellow supported by the Gerber award.

Institutional Review Board Statement: Not applicable.

Informed Consent Statement: Not applicable.

Data Availability Statement: Not applicable.

Conflicts of Interest: The authors declare no conflicts of interest.

Abbreviations

FDA, Food and Drug Administration; SMA, Spinal Muscular Atrophy; DNA, deoxyribonucleic acid; RNA, ribonucleic acid; IRDiRC, International Rare Diseases Research Consortium; CRISPR, clustered regularly interspaced short palindromic repeats; Cas9, CRISPR-associated protein 9; TP53, tumor protein p53; siRNA, small interfering RNA; mRNA, messenger RNA; NIH, National Institutes of Health; NCI, National Cancer Institute; NIAID, National Institute of Allergy and Infectious Diseases; NHLBI, National Health Lung and Blood Institute; NIA, National Health Lung and Blood Institute; SARS-CoV-2, severe acute respiratory syndrome coronavirus 2; ARPA-H, Advanced Research Projects Agency for Health; AAV, adeno-associated virus; OMIM, Online Mendelian Inheritance in Man; HPA, Human Protein Atlas; IMPC, International Mouse Phenotyping Consortium; VUS, variant of uncertain significance; eQTL, expression quantitative trait loci; sQTL, splicing quantitative trait loci; GWAS, Genome-Wide Association Study; HSV, herpes simplex virus; Ad5, adenovirus serotype 5; OTC, ornithine transcarbamylase; ODA, Orphan Drug Act.

References

1. Wirth, T.; Parker, N.; Ylä-Herttuala, S. History of Gene Therapy. *Gene* **2013**, *525*, 162–169. [CrossRef]
2. Dunbar, C.E.; High, K.A.; Joung, J.K.; Kohn, D.B.; Ozawa, K.; Sadelain, M. Gene Therapy Comes of Age. *Science* **2018**, *359*, eaan4672. [CrossRef]
3. Hermonat, P.L.; Quirk, J.G.; Bishop, B.M.; Han, L. The Packaging Capacity of Adeno-Associated Virus (AAV) and the Potential for Wild-Type-Plus AAV Gene Therapy Vectors. *FEBS Lett.* **1997**, *407*, 78–84. [CrossRef]
4. Ibraheem, D.; Elaissari, A.; Fessi, H. Gene Therapy and DNA Delivery Systems. *Int. J. Pharm.* **2014**, *459*, 70–83. [CrossRef]
5. El-Aneed, A. An Overview of Current Delivery Systems in Cancer Gene Therapy. *J. Control. Release* **2004**, *94*, 1–14. [CrossRef]
6. Wang, D.; Tai, P.W.L.; Gao, G. Adeno-Associated Virus Vector as a Platform for Gene Therapy Delivery. *Nat. Rev. Drug Discov.* **2019**, *18*, 358–378. [CrossRef]
7. Phillips, A.J. The Challenge of Gene Therapy and DNA Delivery. *J. Pharm. Pharmacol.* **2001**, *53*, 1169–1174. [CrossRef]
8. Anderson, W.F. Prospects for Human Gene Therapy. *Science* **1984**, *226*, 401–409. [CrossRef]
9. Rosenberg, S.A.; Aebersold, P.; Cornetta, K.; Kasid, A.; Morgan, R.A.; Moen, R.; Karson, E.M.; Lotze, M.T.; Yang, J.C.; Topalian, S.L. Gene Transfer into Humans—Immunotherapy of Patients with Advanced Melanoma, Using Tumor-Infiltrating Lymphocytes Modified by Retroviral Gene Transduction. *N. Engl. J. Med.* **1990**, *323*, 570–578. [CrossRef]
10. Yang, G.; Cintina, I.; Pariser, A.; Oehrlein, E.; Sullivan, J.; Kennedy, A. The National Economic Burden of Rare Disease in the United States in 2019. *Orphanet J. Rare Dis.* **2022**, *17*, 163. [CrossRef]
11. Groft, S.C.; Posada, M.; Taruscio, D. Progress, Challenges and Global Approaches to Rare Diseases. *Acta Paediatr.* **2021**, *110*, 2711–2716. [CrossRef]
12. Schieppati, A.; Henter, J.-I.; Daina, E.; Aperia, A. Why Rare Diseases Are an Important Medical and Social Issue. *Lancet* **2008**, *371*, 2039–2041. [CrossRef]
13. Bean, L.J.H.; Hegde, M.R. Gene Variant Databases and Sharing: Creating a Global Genomic Variant Database for Personalized Medicine. *Hum. Mutat.* **2016**, *37*, 559–563. [CrossRef]
14. Boycott, K.M.; Rath, A.; Chong, J.X.; Hartley, T.; Alkuraya, F.S.; Baynam, G.; Brookes, A.J.; Brudno, M.; Carracedo, A.; den Dunnen, J.T.; et al. International Cooperation to Enable the Diagnosis of All Rare Genetic Diseases. *Am. J. Hum. Genet.* **2017**, *100*, 695–705. [CrossRef]
15. Wain, K.E.; Palen, E.; Savatt, J.M.; Shuman, D.; Finucane, B.; Seeley, A.; Challman, T.D.; Myers, S.M.; Martin, C.L. The Value of Genomic Variant ClinVar Submissions from Clinical Providers: Beyond the Addition of Novel Variants. *Hum. Mutat.* **2018**, *39*, 1660–1667. [CrossRef]
16. Austin, C.P.; Cutillo, C.M.; Lau, L.P.L.; Jonker, A.H.; Rath, A.; Julkowska, D.; Thomson, D.; Terry, S.F.; de Montleau, B.; Ardigò, D.; et al. Future of Rare Diseases Research 2017-2027: An IRDiRC Perspective. *Clin. Transl. Sci.* **2018**, *11*, 21–27. [CrossRef]
17. Lochmüller, H.; Torrent I Farnell, J.; Le Cam, Y.; Jonker, A.H.; Lau, L.P.; Baynam, G.; Kaufmann, P.; Dawkins, H.J.; Lasko, P.; Austin, C.P.; et al. The International Rare Diseases Research Consortium: Policies and Guidelines to Maximize Impact. *Eur. J. Hum. Genet.* **2017**, *25*, 1293–1302. [CrossRef]
18. Julkowska, D.; Austin, C.P.; Cutillo, C.M.; Gancberg, D.; Hager, C.; Halftermeyer, J.; Jonker, A.H.; Lau, L.P.L.; Norstedt, I.; Rath, A.; et al. The Importance of International Collaboration for Rare Diseases Research: A European Perspective. *Gene Ther.* **2017**, *24*, 562–571. [CrossRef]
19. Forman, J.; Taruscio, D.; Llera, V.A.; Barrera, L.A.; Coté, T.R.; Edfjäll, C.; Gavhed, D.; Haffner, M.E.; Nishimura, Y.; Posada, M.; et al. The Need for Worldwide Policy and Action Plans for Rare Diseases. *Acta Paediatr.* **2012**, *101*, 805–807. [CrossRef]
20. Bowling, K.M.; Thompson, M.L.; Finnila, C.R.; Hiatt, S.M.; Latner, D.R.; Amaral, M.D.; Lawlor, J.M.J.; East, K.M.; Cochran, M.E.; Greve, V.; et al. Genome Sequencing as a First-Line Diagnostic Test for Hospitalized Infants. *Genet. Med.* **2022**, *24*, 851–861. [CrossRef]
21. Bupp, C.P.; Ames, E.G.; Arenchild, M.K.; Caylor, S.; Dimmock, D.P.; Fakhoury, J.D.; Karna, P.; Lehman, A.; Meghea, C.I.; Misra, V.; et al. Breaking Barriers to Rapid Whole Genome Sequencing in Pediatrics: Michigan's Project Baby Deer. *Children* **2023**, *10*, 106. [CrossRef]
22. Prokop, J.W.; May, T.; Strong, K.; Bilinovich, S.M.; Bupp, C.; Rajasekaran, S.; Worthey, E.A.; Lazar, J. Genome Sequencing in the Clinic: The Past, Present, and Future of Genomic Medicine. *Physiol. Genom.* **2018**, *50*, 563–579. [CrossRef]
23. Prokop, J.W.; Jdanov, V.; Savage, L.; Morris, M.; Lamb, N.; VanSickle, E.; Stenger, C.L.; Rajasekaran, S.; Bupp, C.P. Computational and Experimental Analysis of Genetic Variants. *Compr. Physiol.* **2022**, *12*, 3303–3336. [CrossRef]
24. Prokop, J.W.; Lazar, J.; Crapitto, G.; Smith, D.C.; Worthey, E.A.; Jacob, H.J. Molecular Modeling in the Age of Clinical Genomics, the Enterprise of the next Generation. *J. Mol. Model.* **2017**, *23*, 75. [CrossRef]
25. Rajasekaran, S.; Bupp, C.P.; Leimanis-Laurens, M.; Shukla, A.; Russell, C.; Junewick, J.; Gleason, E.; VanSickle, E.A.; Edgerly, Y.; Wittmann, B.M.; et al. Repurposing Eflornithine to Treat a Patient with a Rare ODC1 Gain-of-Function Variant Disease. *Elife* **2021**, *10*, e67097. [CrossRef]
26. Stainier, D.Y.R.; Raz, E.; Lawson, N.D.; Ekker, S.C.; Burdine, R.D.; Eisen, J.S.; Ingham, P.W.; Schulte-Merker, S.; Yelon, D.; Weinstein, B.M.; et al. Guidelines for Morpholino Use in Zebrafish. *PLoS Genet.* **2017**, *13*, e1007000. [CrossRef]
27. Heasman, J.; Holwill, S.; Wylie, C.C. Fertilization of Cultured Xenopus Oocytes and Use in Studies of Maternally Inherited Molecules. *Methods Cell Biol.* **1991**, *36*, 213–230. [CrossRef]
28. Heasman, J. Morpholino Oligos: Making Sense of Antisense? *Dev. Biol.* **2002**, *243*, 209–214. [CrossRef]

29. Nasevicius, A.; Ekker, S.C. Effective Targeted Gene "knockdown" in Zebrafish. *Nat. Genet.* **2000**, *26*, 216–220. [CrossRef]
30. Bill, B.R.; Petzold, A.M.; Clark, K.J.; Schimmenti, L.A.; Ekker, S.C. A Primer for Morpholino Use in Zebrafish. *Zebrafish* **2009**, *6*, 69–77. [CrossRef]
31. Robu, M.E.; Larson, J.D.; Nasevicius, A.; Beiraghi, S.; Brenner, C.; Farber, S.A.; Ekker, S.C. P53 Activation by Knockdown Technologies. *PLoS Genet.* **2007**, *3*, e78. [CrossRef]
32. Scacheri, P.C.; Rozenblatt-Rosen, O.; Caplen, N.J.; Wolfsberg, T.G.; Umayam, L.; Lee, J.C.; Hughes, C.M.; Shanmugam, K.S.; Bhattacharjee, A.; Meyerson, M.; et al. Short Interfering RNAs Can Induce Unexpected and Divergent Changes in the Levels of Untargeted Proteins in Mammalian Cells. *Proc. Natl. Acad. Sci. USA* **2004**, *101*, 1892–1897. [CrossRef]
33. Summerton, J.E. Morpholino, siRNA, and S-DNA Compared: Impact of Structure and Mechanism of Action on off-Target Effects and Sequence Specificity. *Curr. Top. Med. Chem.* **2007**, *7*, 651–660. [CrossRef]
34. Eisen, J.S.; Smith, J.C. Controlling Morpholino Experiments: Don't Stop Making Antisense. *Development* **2008**, *135*, 1735–1743. [CrossRef]
35. Bedell, V.M.; Westcot, S.E.; Ekker, S.C. Lessons from Morpholino-Based Screening in Zebrafish. *Brief. Funct. Genom.* **2011**, *10*, 181–188. [CrossRef]
36. Prokop, J.W.; Yeo, N.C.; Ottmann, C.; Chhetri, S.B.; Florus, K.L.; Ross, E.J.; Sosonkina, N.; Link, B.A.; Freedman, B.I.; Coppola, C.J.; et al. Characterization of Coding/Noncoding Variants for SHROOM3 in Patients with CKD. *J. Am. Soc. Nephrol.* **2018**, *29*, 1525–1535. [CrossRef]
37. Schulte-Merker, S.; Stainier, D.Y.R. Out with the Old, in with the New: Reassessing Morpholino Knockdowns in Light of Genome Editing Technology. *Development* **2014**, *141*, 3103–3104. [CrossRef]
38. Orloff, J.; Douglas, F.; Pinheiro, J.; Levinson, S.; Branson, M.; Chaturvedi, P.; Ette, E.; Gallo, P.; Hirsch, G.; Mehta, C.; et al. The Future of Drug Development: Advancing Clinical Trial Design. *Nat. Rev. Drug Discov.* **2009**, *8*, 949–957. [CrossRef]
39. Shukla, V.; Seoane-Vazquez, E.; Fawaz, S.; Brown, L.; Rodriguez-Monguio, R. The Landscape of Cellular and Gene Therapy Products: Authorization, Discontinuations, and Cost. *Hum. Gene Ther. Clin. Dev.* **2019**, *30*, 102–113. [CrossRef]
40. Wirth, B. An Update of the Mutation Spectrum of the Survival Motor Neuron Gene (SMN1) in Autosomal Recessive Spinal Muscular Atrophy (SMA). *Hum. Mutat.* **2000**, *15*, 228–237. [CrossRef]
41. Kay, D.M.; Stevens, C.F.; Parker, A.; Saavedra-Matiz, C.A.; Sack, V.; Chung, W.K.; Chiriboga, C.A.; Engelstad, K.; Laureta, E.; Farooq, O.; et al. Implementation of Population-Based Newborn Screening Reveals Low Incidence of Spinal Muscular Atrophy. *Genet. Med.* **2020**, *22*, 1296–1302. [CrossRef]
42. Day, J.W.; Finkel, R.S.; Chiriboga, C.A.; Connolly, A.M.; Crawford, T.O.; Darras, B.T.; Iannaccone, S.T.; Kuntz, N.L.; Peña, L.D.M.; Shieh, P.B.; et al. Onasemnogene Abeparvovec Gene Therapy for Symptomatic Infantile-Onset Spinal Muscular Atrophy in Patients with Two Copies of SMN2 (STR1VE): An Open-Label, Single-Arm, Multicentre, Phase 3 Trial. *Lancet Neurol.* **2021**, *20*, 284–293. [CrossRef]
43. Strauss, K.A.; Farrar, M.A.; Muntoni, F.; Saito, K.; Mendell, J.R.; Servais, L.; McMillan, H.J.; Finkel, R.S.; Swoboda, K.J.; Kwon, J.M.; et al. Onasemnogene Abeparvovec for Presymptomatic Infants with Two Copies of SMN2 at Risk for Spinal Muscular Atrophy Type 1: The Phase III SPR1NT Trial. *Nat. Med.* **2022**, *28*, 1381–1389. [CrossRef]
44. Davis, J.L. The Blunt End: Surgical Challenges of Gene Therapy for Inherited Retinal Diseases. *Am. J. Ophthalmol.* **2018**, *196*, xxv–xxix. [CrossRef]
45. Eichler, F.; Duncan, C.; Musolino, P.L.; Orchard, P.J.; De Oliveira, S.; Thrasher, A.J.; Armant, M.; Dansereau, C.; Lund, T.C.; Miller, W.P.; et al. Hematopoietic Stem-Cell Gene Therapy for Cerebral Adrenoleukodystrophy. *N. Engl. J. Med.* **2017**, *377*, 1630–1638. [CrossRef]
46. Locatelli, F.; Thompson, A.A.; Kwiatkowski, J.L.; Porter, J.B.; Thrasher, A.J.; Hongeng, S.; Sauer, M.G.; Thuret, I.; Lal, A.; Algeri, M.; et al. Betibeglogene Autotemcel Gene Therapy for Non-B0/B0 Genotype β-Thalassemia. *N. Engl. J. Med.* **2022**, *386*, 415–427. [CrossRef]
47. Newman, N.J.; Yu-Wai-Man, P.; Carelli, V.; Biousse, V.; Moster, M.L.; Vignal-Clermont, C.; Sergott, R.C.; Klopstock, T.; Sadun, A.A.; Girmens, J.-F.; et al. Intravitreal Gene Therapy vs. Natural History in Patients With Leber Hereditary Optic Neuropathy Carrying the m.11778G>A ND4 Mutation: Systematic Review and Indirect Comparison. *Front. Neurol.* **2021**, *12*, 662838. [CrossRef]
48. Aitken, M.L.; Moss, R.B.; Waltz, D.A.; Dovey, M.E.; Tonelli, M.R.; McNamara, S.C.; Gibson, R.L.; Ramsey, B.W.; Carter, B.J.; Reynolds, T.C. A Phase I Study of Aerosolized Administration of tgAAVCF to Cystic Fibrosis Subjects with Mild Lung Disease. *Hum. Gene Ther.* **2001**, *12*, 1907–1916. [CrossRef]
49. Moss, R.B.; Rodman, D.; Spencer, L.T.; Aitken, M.L.; Zeitlin, P.L.; Waltz, D.; Milla, C.; Brody, A.S.; Clancy, J.P.; Ramsey, B.; et al. Repeated Adeno-Associated Virus Serotype 2 Aerosol-Mediated Cystic Fibrosis Transmembrane Regulator Gene Transfer to the Lungs of Patients with Cystic Fibrosis: A Multicenter, Double-Blind, Placebo-Controlled Trial. *Chest* **2004**, *125*, 509–521. [CrossRef]
50. Moss, R.B.; Milla, C.; Colombo, J.; Accurso, F.; Zeitlin, P.L.; Clancy, J.P.; Spencer, L.T.; Pilewski, J.; Waltz, D.A.; Dorkin, H.L.; et al. Repeated Aerosolized AAV-CFTR for Treatment of Cystic Fibrosis: A Randomized Placebo-Controlled Phase 2B Trial. *Hum. Gene Ther.* **2007**, *18*, 726–732. [CrossRef]
51. Russell, S.; Bennett, J.; Wellman, J.A.; Chung, D.C.; Yu, Z.-F.; Tillman, A.; Wittes, J.; Pappas, J.; Elci, O.; McCague, S.; et al. Efficacy and Safety of Voretigene Neparvovec (AAV2-hRPE65v2) in Patients with RPE65-Mediated Inherited Retinal Dystrophy: A Randomised, Controlled, Open-Label, Phase 3 Trial. *Lancet* **2017**, *390*, 849–860. [CrossRef] [PubMed]

52. Ozelo, M.C.; Mahlangu, J.; Pasi, K.J.; Giermasz, A.; Leavitt, A.D.; Laffan, M.; Symington, E.; Quon, D.V.; Wang, J.-D.; Peerlinck, K.; et al. Valoctocogene Roxaparvovec Gene Therapy for Hemophilia A. *N. Engl. J. Med.* **2022**, *386*, 1013–1025. [CrossRef] [PubMed]
53. Prakash, V. Spinraza-a Rare Disease Success Story. *Gene Ther.* **2017**, *24*, 497. [CrossRef] [PubMed]
54. Mercuri, E.; Darras, B.T.; Chiriboga, C.A.; Day, J.W.; Campbell, C.; Connolly, A.M.; Iannaccone, S.T.; Kirschner, J.; Kuntz, N.L.; Saito, K.; et al. Nusinersen versus Sham Control in Later-Onset Spinal Muscular Atrophy. *N. Engl. J. Med.* **2018**, *378*, 625–635. [CrossRef] [PubMed]
55. Middleton, P.G.; Mall, M.A.; Dřevínek, P.; Lands, L.C.; McKone, E.F.; Polineni, D.; Ramsey, B.W.; Taylor-Cousar, J.L.; Tullis, E.; Vermeulen, F.; et al. Elexacaftor-Tezacaftor-Ivacaftor for Cystic Fibrosis with a Single Phe508del Allele. *N. Engl. J. Med.* **2019**, *381*, 1809–1819. [CrossRef] [PubMed]
56. Barry, P.J.; Mall, M.A.; Álvarez, A.; Colombo, C.; de Winter-de Groot, K.M.; Fajac, I.; McBennett, K.A.; McKone, E.F.; Ramsey, B.W.; Sutharsan, S.; et al. Triple Therapy for Cystic Fibrosis Phe508del-Gating and -Residual Function Genotypes. *N. Engl. J. Med.* **2021**, *385*, 815–825. [CrossRef]
57. Amberger, J.S.; Bocchini, C.A.; Schiettecatte, F.; Scott, A.F.; Hamosh, A. OMIM.Org: Online Mendelian Inheritance in Man (OMIM®), an Online Catalog of Human Genes and Genetic Disorders. *Nucleic Acids Res.* **2015**, *43*, D789–D798. [CrossRef]
58. UniProt Consortium UniProt: A Hub for Protein Information. *Nucleic Acids Res.* **2015**, *43*, D204–D212. [CrossRef]
59. Uhlen, M.; Oksvold, P.; Fagerberg, L.; Lundberg, E.; Jonasson, K.; Forsberg, M.; Zwahlen, M.; Kampf, C.; Wester, K.; Hober, S.; et al. Towards a Knowledge-Based Human Protein Atlas. *Nat. Biotechnol.* **2010**, *28*, 1248–1250. [CrossRef]
60. Meehan, T.F.; Conte, N.; West, D.B.; Jacobsen, J.O.; Mason, J.; Warren, J.; Chen, C.-K.; Tudose, I.; Relac, M.; Matthews, P.; et al. Disease Model Discovery from 3,328 Gene Knockouts by The International Mouse Phenotyping Consortium. *Nat. Genet.* **2017**, *49*, 1231–1238. [CrossRef]
61. Landrum, M.J.; Lee, J.M.; Benson, M.; Brown, G.; Chao, C.; Chitipiralla, S.; Gu, B.; Hart, J.; Hoffman, D.; Hoover, J.; et al. ClinVar: Public Archive of Interpretations of Clinically Relevant Variants. *Nucleic Acids Res.* **2016**, *44*, D862–D868. [CrossRef] [PubMed]
62. Walther, W.; Stein, U. Cell Type Specific and Inducible Promoters for Vectors in Gene Therapy as an Approach for Cell Targeting. *J. Mol. Med.* **1996**, *74*, 379–392. [CrossRef] [PubMed]
63. Le Douarin, N.M.; Creuzet, S.; Couly, G.; Dupin, E. Neural Crest Cell Plasticity and Its Limits. *Development* **2004**, *131*, 4637–4650. [CrossRef] [PubMed]
64. Mark, P.R.; Murray, S.A.; Yang, T.; Eby, A.; Lai, A.; Lu, D.; Zieba, J.; Rajasekaran, S.; VanSickle, E.A.; Rossetti, L.Z.; et al. Autosomal Recessive LRP1-Related Syndrome Featuring Cardiopulmonary Dysfunction, Bone Dysmorphology, and Corneal Clouding. *Cold Spring Harb. Mol. Case Stud.* **2022**, *8*, a006169. [PubMed]
65. Møller, R.S.; Weckhuysen, S.; Chipaux, M.; Marsan, E.; Taly, V.; Bebin, E.M.; Hiatt, S.M.; Prokop, J.W.; Bowling, K.M.; Mei, D.; et al. Germline and Somatic Mutations in the MTOR Gene in Focal Cortical Dysplasia and Epilepsy. *Neurol. Genet.* **2016**, *2*, e118. [CrossRef]
66. Holtz, A.M.; VanCoillie, R.; Vansickle, E.A.; Carere, D.A.; Withrow, K.; Torti, E.; Juusola, J.; Millan, F.; Person, R.; Guillen Sacoto, M.J.; et al. Heterozygous Variants in MYH10 Associated with Neurodevelopmental Disorders and Congenital Anomalies with Evidence for Primary Cilia-Dependent Defects in Hedgehog Signaling. *Genet. Med.* **2022**, *24*, 2065–2078. [CrossRef] [PubMed]
67. Savage, L.; Adams, S.D.; James, K.; Chowdhury, S.; Rajasekaran, S.; Prokop, J.W.; Bupp, C. Rapid Whole-Genome Sequencing Identifies a Homozygous Novel Variant, His540Arg, in HSD17B4 Resulting in D-Bifunctional Protein Deficiency Disorder Diagnosis. *Cold Spring Harb. Mol. Case Stud.* **2020**, *6*, a005496. [CrossRef] [PubMed]
68. Cook, T.W.; Wilstermann, A.M.; Mitchell, J.T.; Arnold, N.E.; Rajasekaran, S.; Bupp, C.P.; Prokop, J.W. Understanding Insulin in the Age of Precision Medicine and Big Data: Under-Explored Nature of Genomics. *Biomolecules* **2023**, *13*, 257. [CrossRef]
69. Afrin, A.; Prokop, J.W.; Underwood, A.; Uhl, K.L.; VanSickle, E.A.; Baruwal, R.; Wajda, M.; Rajasekaran, S.; Bupp, C. NAA10 Variant in 38-Week-Gestation Male Patient: A Case Study. *Cold Spring Harb. Mol. Case Stud.* **2020**, *6*, a005868. [CrossRef]
70. Underwood, A.; Rasicci, D.T.; Hinds, D.; Mitchell, J.T.; Zieba, J.K.; Mills, J.; Arnold, N.E.; Cook, T.W.; Moustaqil, M.; Gambin, Y.; et al. Evolutionary Landscape of SOX Genes to Inform Genotype-to-Phenotype Relationships. *Genes* **2023**, *14*, 222. [CrossRef]
71. Snijders Blok, L.; Hiatt, S.M.; Bowling, K.M.; Prokop, J.W.; Engel, K.L.; Cochran, J.N.; Bebin, E.M.; Bijlsma, E.K.; Ruivenkamp, C.A.L.; Terhal, P.; et al. De Novo Mutations in MED13, a Component of the Mediator Complex, Are Associated with a Novel Neurodevelopmental Disorder. *Hum. Genet.* **2018**, *137*, 375–388. [CrossRef] [PubMed]
72. GTEx Consortium. The GTEx Consortium Atlas of Genetic Regulatory Effects across Human Tissues. *Science* **2020**, *369*, 1318–1330. [CrossRef] [PubMed]
73. Das, A.S.; Sherry, E.C.; Vaughan, R.M.; Henderson, M.L.; Zieba, J.; Uhl, K.L.; Koehn, O.; Bupp, C.P.; Rajasekaran, S.; Li, X.; et al. The Complex, Dynamic SpliceOme of the Small GTPase Transcripts Altered by Technique, Sex, Genetics, Tissue Specificity, and RNA Base Editing. *Front. Cell Dev. Biol.* **2022**, *10*, 1033695. [CrossRef] [PubMed]
74. Rehm, H.L.; Berg, J.S.; Brooks, L.D.; Bustamante, C.D.; Evans, J.P.; Landrum, M.J.; Ledbetter, D.H.; Maglott, D.R.; Martin, C.L.; Nussbaum, R.L.; et al. ClinGen—The Clinical Genome Resource. *N. Engl. J. Med.* **2015**, *372*, 2235–2242. [CrossRef] [PubMed]
75. Bai, R.-Y.; Esposito, D.; Tam, A.J.; McCormick, F.; Riggins, G.J.; Wade Clapp, D.; Staedtke, V. Feasibility of Using NF1-GRD and AAV for Gene Replacement Therapy in NF1-Associated Tumors. *Gene Ther.* **2019**, *26*, 277–286. [CrossRef]
76. Carvalho-Silva, D.; Pierleoni, A.; Pignatelli, M.; Ong, C.; Fumis, L.; Karamanis, N.; Carmona, M.; Faulconbridge, A.; Hercules, A.; McAuley, E.; et al. Open Targets Platform: New Developments and Updates Two Years On. *Nucleic Acids Res.* **2019**, *47*, D1056–D1065. [CrossRef]

77. Nayerossadat, N.; Maedeh, T.; Ali, P.A. Viral and Nonviral Delivery Systems for Gene Delivery. *Adv. Biomed. Res.* **2012**, *1*, 27. [CrossRef]
78. Wang, Y.; Zhang, R.; Tang, L.; Yang, L. Nonviral Delivery Systems of mRNA Vaccines for Cancer Gene Therapy. *Pharmaceutics* **2022**, *14*, 512. [CrossRef]
79. Cecchin, R.; Troyer, Z.; Witwer, K.; Morris, K.V. Extracellular Vesicles: The next Generation in Gene Therapy Delivery. *Mol. Ther.* **2023**, *31*, 1225–1230. [CrossRef]
80. Sayed, N.; Allawadhi, P.; Khurana, A.; Singh, V.; Navik, U.; Pasumarthi, S.K.; Khurana, I.; Banothu, A.K.; Weiskirchen, R.; Bharani, K.K. Gene Therapy: Comprehensive Overview and Therapeutic Applications. *Life Sci.* **2022**, *294*, 120375. [CrossRef]
81. Cucchiarini, M. Human Gene Therapy: Novel Approaches to Improve the Current Gene Delivery Systems. *Discov. Med.* **2016**, *21*, 495–506. [PubMed]
82. Sanders, M.; Lawlor, J.M.J.; Li, X.; Schuen, J.N.; Millard, S.L.; Zhang, X.; Buck, L.; Grysko, B.; Uhl, K.L.; Hinds, D.; et al. Genomic, Transcriptomic, and Protein Landscape Profile of CFTR and Cystic Fibrosis. *Hum. Genet.* **2021**, *140*, 423–439. [CrossRef] [PubMed]
83. Keswani, S.G.; Balaji, S.; Le, L.; Leung, A.; Katz, A.B.; Lim, F.-Y.; Habli, M.; Jones, H.N.; Wilson, J.M.; Crombleholme, T.M. Pseudotyped AAV Vector-Mediated Gene Transfer in a Human Fetal Trachea Xenograft Model: Implications for in Utero Gene Therapy for Cystic Fibrosis. *PLoS ONE* **2012**, *7*, e43633. [CrossRef] [PubMed]
84. Limberis, M.P.; Vandenberghe, L.H.; Zhang, L.; Pickles, R.J.; Wilson, J.M. Transduction Efficiencies of Novel AAV Vectors in Mouse Airway Epithelium In Vivo and Human Ciliated Airway Epithelium In Vitro. *Mol. Ther.* **2009**, *17*, 294–301. [CrossRef] [PubMed]
85. Bals, R.; Xiao, W.; Sang, N.; Weiner, D.J.; Meegalla, R.L.; Wilson, J.M. Transduction of Well-Differentiated Airway Epithelium by Recombinant Adeno-Associated Virus Is Limited by Vector Entry. *J. Virol.* **1999**, *73*, 6085–6088. [CrossRef] [PubMed]
86. Sirninger, J.; Muller, C.; Braag, S.; Tang, Q.; Yue, H.; Detrisac, C.; Ferkol, T.; Guggino, W.B.; Flotte, T.R. Functional Characterization of a Recombinant Adeno-Associated Virus 5-Pseudotyped Cystic Fibrosis Transmembrane Conductance Regulator Vector. *Hum. Gene Ther.* **2004**, *15*, 832–841. [CrossRef] [PubMed]
87. Zabner, J.; Seiler, M.; Walters, R.; Kotin, R.M.; Fulgeras, W.; Davidson, B.L.; Chiorini, J.A. Adeno-Associated Virus Type 5 (AAV5) but Not AAV2 Binds to the Apical Surfaces of Airway Epithelia and Facilitates Gene Transfer. *J. Virol.* **2000**, *74*, 3852–3858. [CrossRef]
88. Fischer, A.C.; Smith, C.I.; Cebotaru, L.; Zhang, X.; Askin, F.B.; Wright, J.; Guggino, S.E.; Adams, R.J.; Flotte, T.; Guggino, W.B. Expression of a Truncated Cystic Fibrosis Transmembrane Conductance Regulator with an AAV5-Pseudotyped Vector in Primates. *Mol. Ther.* **2007**, *15*, 756–763. [CrossRef]
89. Song, Y.; Lou, H.H.; Boyer, J.L.; Limberis, M.P.; Vandenberghe, L.H.; Hackett, N.R.; Leopold, P.L.; Wilson, J.M.; Crystal, R.G. Functional Cystic Fibrosis Transmembrane Conductance Regulator Expression in Cystic Fibrosis Airway Epithelial Cells by AAV6.2-Mediated Segmental Trans-Splicing. *Hum. Gene Ther.* **2009**, *20*, 267–281. [CrossRef]
90. Excoffon, K.J.D.A.; Koerber, J.T.; Dickey, D.D.; Murtha, M.; Keshavjee, S.; Kaspar, B.K.; Zabner, J.; Schaffer, D.V. Directed Evolution of Adeno-Associated Virus to an Infectious Respiratory Virus. *Proc. Natl. Acad. Sci. USA* **2009**, *106*, 3865–3870. [CrossRef]
91. Li, W.; Zhang, L.; Johnson, J.S.; Zhijian, W.; Grieger, J.C.; Ping-Jie, X.; Drouin, L.M.; Agbandje-McKenna, M.; Pickles, R.J.; Samulski, R.J. Generation of Novel AAV Variants by Directed Evolution for Improved CFTR Delivery to Human Ciliated Airway Epithelium. *Mol. Ther.* **2009**, *17*, 2067–2077. [CrossRef] [PubMed]
92. Paunovska, K.; Loughrey, D.; Dahlman, J.E. Drug Delivery Systems for RNA Therapeutics. *Nat. Rev. Genet.* **2022**, *23*, 265–280. [CrossRef]
93. Hasbrouck, N.C.; High, K.A. AAV-Mediated Gene Transfer for the Treatment of Hemophilia B: Problems and Prospects. *Gene Ther.* **2008**, *15*, 870–875. [CrossRef] [PubMed]
94. Muruve, D.A.; Barnes, M.J.; Stillman, I.E.; Libermann, T.A. Adenoviral Gene Therapy Leads to Rapid Induction of Multiple Chemokines and Acute Neutrophil-Dependent Hepatic Injury In Vivo. *Hum. Gene Ther.* **1999**, *10*, 965–976. [CrossRef] [PubMed]
95. Cheng, Y.; Zhang, Z.; Gao, P.; Lai, H.; Zhong, W.; Feng, N.; Yang, Y.; Yu, H.; Zhang, Y.; Han, Y.; et al. AAV Induces Hepatic Necroptosis and Carcinoma in Diabetic and Obese Mice Dependent on Pebp1 Pathway. *EMBO Mol. Med.* **2023**, *15*, e17230. [CrossRef]
96. Deverman, B.E.; Ravina, B.M.; Bankiewicz, K.S.; Paul, S.M.; Sah, D.W.Y. Gene Therapy for Neurological Disorders: Progress and Prospects. *Nat. Rev. Drug Discov.* **2018**, *17*, 767. [CrossRef]
97. Kumar, S.R.; Markusic, D.M.; Biswas, M.; High, K.A.; Herzog, R.W. Clinical Development of Gene Therapy: Results and Lessons from Recent Successes. *Mol. Ther. Methods Clin. Dev.* **2016**, *3*, 16034. [CrossRef]
98. Gupta, V.; Lourenço, S.P.; Hidalgo, I.J. Development of Gene Therapy Vectors: Remaining Challenges. *J. Pharm. Sci.* **2021**, *110*, 1915–1920. [CrossRef]
99. Thomas, C.E.; Ehrhardt, A.; Kay, M.A. Progress and Problems with the Use of Viral Vectors for Gene Therapy. *Nat. Rev. Genet.* **2003**, *4*, 346–358. [CrossRef]
100. Shirley, J.L.; de Jong, Y.P.; Terhorst, C.; Herzog, R.W. Immune Responses to Viral Gene Therapy Vectors. *Mol. Ther.* **2020**, *28*, 709–722. [CrossRef]
101. Kishimoto, T.K.; Samulski, R.J. Addressing High Dose AAV Toxicity—"One and Done" or "Slower and Lower"? *Expert. Opin. Biol. Ther.* **2022**, *22*, 1067–1071. [CrossRef] [PubMed]
102. Lehrman, S. Virus Treatment Questioned after Gene Therapy Death. *Nature* **1999**, *401*, 517–518. [CrossRef] [PubMed]

103. Somanathan, S.; Calcedo, R.; Wilson, J.M. Adenovirus-Antibody Complexes Contributed to Lethal Systemic Inflammation in a Gene Therapy Trial. *Mol. Ther.* **2020**, *28*, 784–793. [CrossRef] [PubMed]
104. Wilson, J.M.; Flotte, T.R. Moving Forward After Two Deaths in a Gene Therapy Trial of Myotubular Myopathy. *Hum. Gene Ther.* **2020**, *31*, 695–696. [CrossRef] [PubMed]
105. Mendell, J.R.; Connolly, A.M.; Lehman, K.J.; Griffin, D.A.; Khan, S.Z.; Dharia, S.D.; Quintana-Gallardo, L.; Rodino-Klapac, L.R. Testing Preexisting Antibodies Prior to AAV Gene Transfer Therapy: Rationale, Lessons and Future Considerations. *Mol. Ther. Methods Clin. Dev.* **2022**, *25*, 74–83. [CrossRef] [PubMed]
106. Rabinowitz, J.; Chan, Y.K.; Samulski, R.J. Adeno-Associated Virus (AAV) versus Immune Response. *Viruses* **2019**, *11*, 102. [CrossRef] [PubMed]
107. Mennechet, F.J.D.; Paris, O.; Ouoba, A.R.; Salazar Arenas, S.; Sirima, S.B.; Takoudjou Dzomo, G.R.; Diarra, A.; Traore, I.T.; Kania, D.; Eichholz, K.; et al. A Review of 65 Years of Human Adenovirus Seroprevalence. *Expert. Rev. Vaccines* **2019**, *18*, 597–613. [CrossRef] [PubMed]
108. Khatri, A.; Shelke, R.; Guan, S.; Somanathan, S. Higher Seroprevalence of Anti-Adeno-Associated Viral Vector Neutralizing Antibodies Among Racial Minorities in the United States. *Hum. Gene Ther.* **2022**, *33*, 442–450. [CrossRef]
109. Hendrickson, B.C.; Donohoe, C.; Akmaev, V.R.; Sugarman, E.A.; Labrousse, P.; Boguslavskiy, L.; Flynn, K.; Rohlfs, E.M.; Walker, A.; Allitto, B.; et al. Differences in SMN1 Allele Frequencies among Ethnic Groups within North America. *J. Med. Genet.* **2009**, *46*, 641–644. [CrossRef]
110. Herzog, R.W.; Biswas, M. Neutralizing the Neutralizers in AAV Gene Therapy. *Mol. Ther.* **2020**, *28*, 1741–1742. [CrossRef]
111. Leborgne, C.; Barbon, E.; Alexander, J.M.; Hanby, H.; Delignat, S.; Cohen, D.M.; Collaud, F.; Muraleetharan, S.; Lupo, D.; Silverberg, J.; et al. IgG-Cleaving Endopeptidase Enables In Vivo Gene Therapy in the Presence of Anti-AAV Neutralizing Antibodies. *Nat. Med.* **2020**, *26*, 1096–1101. [CrossRef] [PubMed]
112. Hampson, G.; Towse, A.; Pearson, S.D.; Dreitlein, W.B.; Henshall, C. Gene Therapy: Evidence, Value and Affordability in the US Health Care System. *J. Comp. Eff. Res.* **2018**, *7*, 15–28. [CrossRef] [PubMed]
113. Chand, D.; Mohr, F.; McMillan, H.; Tukov, F.F.; Montgomery, K.; Kleyn, A.; Sun, R.; Tauscher-Wisniewski, S.; Kaufmann, P.; Kullak-Ublick, G. Hepatotoxicity Following Administration of Onasemnogene Abeparvovec (AVXS-101) for the Treatment of Spinal Muscular Atrophy. *J. Hepatol.* **2021**, *74*, 560–566. [CrossRef] [PubMed]
114. Landfeldt, E. Gene Therapy for Neuromuscular Diseases: Health Economic Challenges and Future Perspectives. *J. Neuromuscul. Dis.* **2022**, *9*, 675–688. [CrossRef] [PubMed]
115. Dean, R.; Jensen, I.; Cyr, P.; Miller, B.; Maru, B.; Sproule, D.M.; Feltner, D.E.; Wiesner, T.; Malone, D.C.; Bischof, M.; et al. An Updated Cost-Utility Model for Onasemnogene Abeparvovec (Zolgensma®) in Spinal Muscular Atrophy Type 1 Patients and Comparison with Evaluation by the Institute for Clinical and Effectiveness Review (ICER). *J. Mark. Access Health Policy* **2021**, *9*, 1889841. [CrossRef] [PubMed]
116. Broekhoff, T.F.; Sweegers, C.C.G.; Krijkamp, E.M.; Mantel-Teeuwisse, A.K.; Leufkens, H.G.M.; Goettsch, W.G.; Vreman, R.A. Early Cost-Effectiveness of Onasemnogene Abeparvovec-Xioi (Zolgensma) and Nusinersen (Spinraza) Treatment for Spinal Muscular Atrophy I in The Netherlands With Relapse Scenarios. *Value Health* **2021**, *24*, 759–769. [CrossRef]
117. Ryan, M.M. Gene Therapy for Neuromuscular Disorders: Prospects and Ethics. *Arch. Dis. Child.* **2022**, *107*, 421–426. [CrossRef]
118. Salzman, R.; Cook, F.; Hunt, T.; Malech, H.L.; Reilly, P.; Foss-Campbell, B.; Barrett, D. Addressing the Value of Gene Therapy and Enhancing Patient Access to Transformative Treatments. *Mol. Ther.* **2018**, *26*, 2717–2726. [CrossRef]
119. Daniel, M.G.; Pawlik, T.M.; Fader, A.N.; Esnaola, N.F.; Makary, M.A. The Orphan Drug Act: Restoring the Mission to Rare Diseases. *Am. J. Clin. Oncol.* **2016**, *39*, 210–213. [CrossRef]
120. Stockdale, A. Waiting for the Cure: Mapping the Social Relations of Human Gene Therapy Research. *Sociol. Health Illn.* **1999**, *21*, 579–596. [CrossRef]
121. Watts, G. Gene Therapy Is in Danger of Being Overhyped, Expert Says. *BMJ* **2008**, *336*, 977. [CrossRef]
122. Delhove, J.; Osenk, I.; Prichard, I.; Donnelley, M. Public Acceptability of Gene Therapy and Gene Editing for Human Use: A Systematic Review. *Hum. Gene Ther.* **2020**, *31*, 20–46. [CrossRef] [PubMed]
123. White, W. A Rare Disease Patient/Caregiver Perspective on Fair Pricing and Access to Gene-Based Therapies. *Gene Ther.* **2019**, *27*, 474–481. [CrossRef] [PubMed]
124. Addison, C.; Lassen, J. "My Whole Life Is Ethics!" Ordinary Ethics and Gene Therapy Clinical Trials. *Med. Anthropol.* **2017**, *36*, 672–684. [CrossRef]
125. Sioutis, S.; Reppas, L.; Bekos, A.; Limneos, P.; Saranteas, T.; Mavrogenis, A.F. The Hippocratic Oath: Analysis and Contemporary Meaning. *Orthopedics* **2021**, *44*, 264–272. [CrossRef] [PubMed]
126. Sharrer, G.T. Personalized Medicine: Ethical Aspects. *Methods Mol. Biol.* **2017**, *1606*, 37–50. [CrossRef]
127. Deakin, C.T.; Alexander, I.E.; Kerridge, I. Accepting Risk in Clinical Research: Is the Gene Therapy Field Becoming Too Risk-Averse? *Mol. Ther.* **2009**, *17*, 1842–1848. [CrossRef]
128. *FAERS Reporting by Patient Outcomes by Year*; FDA: Silver Spring, MD, USA, 2019. Available online: https://www.fda.gov/drugs/questions-and-answers-fdas-adverse-event-reporting-system-faers/faers-reporting-patient-outcomes-year. (accessed on 10 December 2023).
129. The New York Times. Available online: https://www.nytimes.com/topic/person/jesse-gelsinger. (accessed on 10 December 2023).

130. Pattee, S.R. Protections for Participants in Gene Therapy Trials: A Patient's Perspective. *Hum. Gene Ther.* **2008**, *19*, 9–10. [CrossRef]
131. Braveman, P. Health Disparities and Health Equity: Concepts and Measurement. *Annu. Rev. Public. Health* **2006**, *27*, 167–194. [CrossRef]

BioTech

Article

Evolved Eugenics and Reinforcement of "Othering": Renewed Ethico-Legal Perspectives of Genome Editing in Reproduction

Pin Lean Lau

Brunel Law School, Brunel University London, Uxbridge UB8 3PH, UK; pinlean.lau@brunel.ac.uk

Abstract: This article extends an exploration into renewed ethico-legal perspectives of genome editing technologies, examined from an evolved conceptualization of eugenics in contemporary human reproduction. Whilst the ethico-legal conundrums presented by genome-editing technologies in various aspects of modern medicine have thus far inspired a comprehensive trove of academic scholarship—and notwithstanding the World Health Organization's (WHO) publication of guidelines on human genome editing in 2021—the legislative landscape for these technologies remain relatively unchanged. Accordingly, this paper presents the unresolved problematic questions that still require significant reflection. First, the paper highlights these questions, which primarily center around the tension between reproductive autonomy and the legal governance of reproductive/genome editing technologies by a democratic state. Secondly, the paper interrogates the evolved conceptualization of eugenics, exercised on the part of prospective parents as part of reproductive autonomy. By this, the paper predicates that it indirectly reinforces societal and systemic problems of discrimination and "othering", increasing reproductive inequalities in excluded communities. Thirdly, the paper attempts to offer narratives of intersectionality as a facilitating tool in a continuing dialogue to build belonging, foster a healthy and balanced exercise of reproductive autonomy, and increase reproductive equalities.

Keywords: human genome editing; germline editing; eugenics; biomedical technologies; autonomy; right to privacy; hereditary; Crispr/Cas9; reproduction; reproductive technologies

Key Contribution: This paper interrogates the breadth of reproductive autonomy in human genome editing, making claims that it can indirectly contribute to discrimination and "othering". It offers intersectionality narratives as an approach to reflect on how reproductive autonomy can be exercised in a balanced manner.

Citation: Lau, P.L. Evolved Eugenics and Reinforcement of "Othering": Renewed Ethico-Legal Perspectives of Genome Editing in Reproduction. *BioTech* **2023**, *12*, 51. https://doi.org/10.3390/biotech12030051

Academic Editor: Vasiliki Mollaki

Received: 2 May 2023
Revised: 7 June 2023
Accepted: 15 June 2023
Published: 11 July 2023

1. Introduction

The Third International Summit on Human Genome Editing recently took place in March 2023 in London, England—and as international experts on human genome editing congregated at the Francis Crick Institute, what must surely be recalled in the mind was the shocking events that had unfurled at the Second International Summit on Human Genome Editing in Hong Kong in 2018. This shocking event was none other than the announcement made by Chinese biophysics scientist and researcher, Dr. He Jiankui at the second summit, that he had conducted highly secretive and allegedly successful experiments using the genome editing technology known as Crispr/Cas9, on twin embryos (effectively performing heritable human gene editing), removing the CCR5 gene in said embryos to make them resistant to HIV [1]. This immediately prompted an international outcry over what would become known as the "He Jiankui Affair", earning He the moniker of "China's Dr. Frankenstein". Five years on, the He Jiankui Affair still raises antipathetic feelings, reminding us that the generational sanctity of human life continues to be vigorously safeguarded when it comes to human germline genome editing. The problems with this safeguarding, even now, are its non-legally binding nature, its reliance on the good faith of an international scientific community to uphold a consensus on moratorium [2], and most critically, its lack of mettle due to an absent international regulatory framework convention.

Whilst the He Jiankui Affair may be a disturbing true story, inspiring the streaming giant Netflix to launch a documentary titled "Make People Better" [3] and prompting the WHO to issue three reports on human genome editing, the profound consequences of the use of genome editing for human germline modification or alteration is still debated today. Indeed, in the Third International Summit on Human Genome Editing, the organizing committee of the summit issued a statement reiterating that "heritable human genome editing remains unacceptable at this time" [4]. As "governance frameworks and ethical principles for the responsible use of heritable human genome editing are not in place," it is therefore still incumbent upon us to continue to ensure the protection of individuals from "unproven interventions in the guide of therapies" and that the international dialogues on proper governance frameworks, safety and efficacy standards, ethical approvals, and legitimate research in this field need to continue.

It would be remiss not to consider how we have arrived at this impasse. In 2020, the Nobel Prize in Chemistry was awarded to Emmanuelle Charpentier and Jennifer Doudna "for the development of a method of genome editing" [5], a revolutionary innovation known as CRISPR/Cas9 [6]. CRISPR/Cas9 is a genome editing tool that allows scientists to "edit the human genome with unprecedented precision, efficiency and flexibility" [7]. Although CRISPR had been hailed as a ground-breaking invention that could potentially transform the future of humankind by curing genetic and heritable diseases, an international scientific community at the International Summit on Human Gene Editing in Washington DC [8] in 2015 agreed that a global moratorium be imposed on human germ-line (heritable) gene editing. For the many stakeholders in the ethical, legal, social, and scientific community, germ-line gene editing is controversial for various legal and ethical reasons, amongst which, it includes the recollection of eugenic policies of various autocratic governments and a blatant disregard for human rights protections.

It is therefore unsurprising that the He Jiankui Affair was greeted with such shock and trepidation. Besides the fact that the secret experiment was highly unethical and problematic [1], it was apparent that global standards on gene editing needed to be established. After two years since the establishment of the WHO expert committee, on 12 July 2021, the WHO Expert Advisory Committee on Developing Global Standards for Governance and Oversight of Human Genome Editing (Committee) published two reports: Human Genome Editing: A Framework for Governance [9], and Human Genome Editing: Recommendations [10]. An accompanying Position Paper [11] was also published, summarizing the key points in the reports. Although other reports have been published prior to this, such as the Nuffield Council on Bioethics' Genome Editing and Human Reproduction [12], the Committee's reports are comprehensively unique, in that its recommendations are premised on "systems-level improvements needed to build capacity in all countries" [13]. The Committee also presented a new governance framework that builds on identifiable tools, organizations, and situations that integrate the practical difficulties of regulating human genome editing.

The Herculean task of formulating the governance framework and recommendations do not escape our admiration and is a long-awaited welcome in this field. However, it would be remiss not to question the way considerations of human rights may be factored into these recommendations. Whilst the Committee's Recommendations incorporate hypothetical scenarios involving somatic and heritable human genome editing and proposes key ethical values and principles for use, the intrinsic human rights protections (articulated, for example, in the European Convention on Human Rights [14] or the Oviedo Convention [15]) appear to be left to the devices of institutions engaged in active governance. In LMICs (low-to-middle-income-countries) where the regulation of genome editing is not a priority or where regulation would not be in its economic interest (for example, where medical or reproductive tourism represent a lucrative commodified means of income), it would be challenging to compel compliance with the governance framework and recommendations, absent of true sanctions.

It is emphasized that the Committee's Recommendations and framework deal with governance and that the WHO does not have the authority to regulate genome editing in individual countries. However, it also cannot be the intention that the absence of a legally positive genome editing regulation may render these Recommendations and framework unworkable in some countries due to incompatibility and hesitancy. A continuance to guarantee human rights protections in a constitutional space must be reiterated as a means of sustaining equitable governance. The key ethical values in the Recommendations can be an effective springboard to consider practical human rights questions, such as equitable access to therapies, respect for privacy and autonomy, genetic non-discrimination, and issues of disability, amongst others. Alongside adapting national systems with the Committee's Recommendations, introducing a mechanism of "entry points of regulation" [16] relative to the role that human rights play in different constitutional systems, could be tailored by different countries to demonstrate their concerns, the "entry points" in which legally positive regulation must then be implemented.

However, these are early days yet, as the Committee continues its important work in the forthcoming months to assist the WHO in implementing the Recommendations, including building "an inclusive global dialogue on frontier technologies" [10]. As this chapter continues to unfold in the saga of human genome editing, we should continue to aspire towards achieving a truly contemporary legal application of human rights in different constitutional settings for human genome editing.

Hence, this article presents the unresolved problematic questions that still require significant reflection. First, the article highlights these questions, which primarily center around the tension between reproductive autonomy and legal governance of reproductive and genome editing technologies in reproduction by a democratic state. Secondly, the article interrogates the evolved conceptualization of eugenics, exercised on the part of prospective parents as part of reproductive autonomy. Thirdly, the article offers narratives of intersectionality as a facilitating tool in a continuing dialogue to build belonging, foster a healthy and balanced exercise of reproductive autonomy, and increase reproductive equalities.

2. Re-Making 'Perfect' Babies: Between Reproductive Autonomy and Legitimate Governance

In an earlier piece of work [7] (p. 285), this author juggled arguments that straddled Mill's concept of liberty [14] (as applied to children) and the natural dénouement in determining the welfare of a child as being exercised by parents. Such position is that if we align with J.S. Mill's concept of human liberty, it suggests that children, as individuals, lack the necessary capacity to exercise personal freedoms [17]. While there are criticisms of Mill's exclusion of children from discussions about self-development and the importance of liberty and autonomy in that process, the lack of in-depth analysis in this area supports Mill's stance on liberty [18]. Other scholarly viewpoints have accused Mill of promoting moral and legal paternalism, rejecting the idea of "adult autonomy" as a legitimate way to impose one's choices on another, particularly on children [19]. If we accept these critiques of Mill's stance, it would logically extend to parental decisions over their own children, going beyond the exploration of accepted parental responsibilities in natural and societal contexts [16] (p. 303).

In "normal" circumstances of child-rearing, it is challenging enough to demonstrate the development of independence in children and future generations. In matters concerning reproductive technologies and the exercise of reproductive autonomy, for instance, over the use of a preimplantation genetic diagnosis (PGD) [7], it is more complicated. If reproductive autonomy is equated to parental guidance towards a certain future plan for a child, how does one determine if this is a result of natural parenting or might be a hindrance to autonomy [16] (p. 303)? Divergent beliefs about what constitutes autonomy and who it applies to will likely lead to different responses to this question. Some parents may argue that their decisions for their children's well-being are based on what they believe is best. In the case of being able to grant only the best human traits to children, could the desire for the "best" lead to eugenics? These questions challenge the fundamental principles of autonomy, a concept well-known in moral and legal philosophy, a prevalent topic in debates about medical treatment and individual decision-making processes. While it is easy to recognize that autonomy is needed for certain decisions, it is harder to understand its broad range in various aspects of daily life, particularly when it comes to children or future generations. Its importance is often elevated to a "supreme status", which can shut down opposing views [7].

2.1. *Preimplantation Genetic Diagnosis: A Gateway to Re-Making Babies?*

In terms of reproductive technologies, the conceptual reproductive autonomy of parents versus legitimate state governance had already been tested earlier: when PGD emerged as a diagnostic tool that would be able to screen if embryos used in in-vitro fertilization treatments are healthy and free from genetic or other known abnormalities [16] (p. 303). PGD, which is used to screen for chromosomal abnormalities, can be more accurately targeted when specific genetic abnormalities have been identified in one or both potential parents and when couples want to prevent passing on hereditary genetic conditions to their future children. This is why PGD has been widely used in clinical settings to select healthy embryos for implantation. Single-gene disorders, such as sickle-cell anemia, cystic fibrosis, and Huntington's disease, are examples of genetic anomalies that can be detected [20]. In these cases, PGD can be useful since it allows pre-implantation embryos to be examined in order to determine whether or not they contain the genetic material that is related to these disorders. However, more controversially, the effect of PGD is that embryos that are found to be "unhealthy" are ultimately discarded, thereby engaging questions of ethics and legality of embryo selection in this manner [21].

While PGD is becoming more popular across the globe, it is noted that it is subject to varying levels of regulation and sometimes no regulation at all in some countries. Science and technology advancements, such as CRISPR/Cas9 genome editing tools, are expected to further alter the landscape of medical and scientific treatments in the near future [7] (p. 86). It is noted that if the genome editing of embryos is a future viable option (where unhealthy embryos could potentially be fixed using technologies, such as CRISPR/Cas9), it will need to be conducted alongside PGD. This does not preclude the fact that unsuccessful attempts to repair the genetic mutations in the embryo will also still result in such embryos being discarded [22]. Hence, this could potentially impact how PGD, together with genome editing, is marketed and offered as part of fertility treatment services. This may force us to confront the difficult and highly debated ethical questions related to germline gene therapy and genetic enhancements or interventions and the possible ideation of creating designer babies [7] (p. 3).

Since the regulatory landscape for PGD is also somewhat fragmented across the globe [6], it is not surprising that there have been intense debates regarding its use. The concerns around embryo selection and the subsequent disposal of unhealthy embryos are some of the key ethical issues it raises, with prominent scientists, such as Tania Simoncelli, warning that it provides a gateway to a "new era of eugenics" [23]. Similar to the present debates surrounding human germline genome editing, PGD in its development and deployment, have been subject to the "designer babies" narrative [24].

Whilst CRISPR/Cas9 is not presently suited for commercial applications in the manner of existing fertility treatments and services and it is not likely that "designer babies" in the dystopian sense so feared by society are a possibility in the near future, the potential promise of CRISPR/Cas9 in eradicating serious genetic conditions throughout the germline [25] would hold some hope for those who suffer from such conditions. It is difficult to generate justifications for an argument that promotes gene editing for the purpose of improving a child's chances of success in the world, versus a necessity to treat a very serious genetic condition. Any decision regarding gene editing should place the welfare and autonomy of the individual above external pressures to conform to societal success standards [26]. Additionally, gene editing does not guarantee a child's chances of success, as success is a multifaceted concept that depends on a multitude of factors, including social and economic opportunities, personal values and aspirations, and individual abilities and abilities [27].

2.2. Genome Editing: Dark History, Unintended Consequences, and Reproductive Commodification

Although genome editing is presented as a panacea for many genetic ills, tinkering with our blueprint of existence raises profound moral questions that challenge our idea of what it means to be human.

This conundrum is further dominated by the specter of eugenics, when the ideology of improving humanity through selective breeding led to grave injustices and atrocities [28]. The manipulation of the human genome, even with benevolent intentions, risks resurrecting the ghosts of eugenics, as it invites the possibility of creating a genetically superior or "designer" human race [29]. This has the potential to exacerbate existing social inequalities, create a division between the genetically enhanced and the unmodified [30], and perpetuate discrimination and prejudice based on genetic makeup. The ethical implications of such a future, where access to genome editing becomes a privilege of the few, while the rest of humanity is left behind, are nothing short of dystopian [31].

Another ethical concern stems from the inherent uncertainty and potential unintended consequences of tampering with the complex web of genetic interactions. The human genome is a marvel of nature's design [32], intricately woven together with countless genes, regulatory elements, and epigenetic modifications that influence our development, health, and identity. Editing even a single gene could have unforeseen ripple effects on the entire genome, leading to unintended consequences that may manifest in future generations [33]. The long-term effects of such alterations are largely unknown, and the potential for irreversible harm to individuals, families, and entire populations raises profound ethical dilemmas about the risks we are willing to take with the genetic heritage of humanity [34].

Furthermore, the commodification of genome editing raises troubling ethical questions about the commercialization of life itself [35]. As gene editing technologies become more accessible and market-driven, there is a risk of prioritizing profits over ethics. With the commercialization of genome editing, genetic enhancements will be available only to those who can afford them, exacerbating social inequalities and perpetuating genetic divides [36]. As technology advances, the ethical implications of turning human genes into products that can be bought and sold and the potential for exploitation and abuse raise acute concerns about the erosion of our moral compass.

In the context of reproduction, especially where the possibilities of human germline manipulation are possible, the problematic concerns surrounding genome editing are incredibly complicated and multi-factorial, harking back to Jurgen Habermas' discourse on the future of human nature [37]. Reproduction, unfortunately, has been subject to commodification concerns throughout the course of women's history, from reproductive tourism [38], wombs for 'rent' via commercial surrogacy [39], to renewed questions of making perfect babies [40] with PGD coupled with genome editing. The commodification of reproduction has emerged as a complex and contentious issue, giving rise to significant concerns with respect to its human rights implications. Central among these concerns is the potential for the exploitation of vulnerable individuals, particularly women who engage as conduit providers in reproductive services, such as egg donation or surrogacy out of financial necessity [41]. If we consider genome editing possibilities as potentially transforming the core narratives in reproductive commodification, the chasm between inequalities in reproduction will only serve to be magnified. For one, there is the disconcerting possibility that vulnerable women from socioeconomically disadvantaged backgrounds may further be exploited to take on the risks of carrying a genetically modified embryo as surrogates.

The potential commodification of human life, a similar concern (to the commodification of genome editing), raises ethical questions about the moral worth and dignity of human beings when it comes to buying and selling reproductive materials, such as gametes (eggs and sperm), embryos, or whole surrogacy arrangements [42]. When reproductive processes are reduced to commodities, genetic material and reproductive services are treated as commodities, the intrinsic value of human life and relationships become threatened [43], and widely held ethical and philosophical notions of the sanctity and inherent dignity of human beings are called into question.

In addition, the rights and welfare of children born through reproductive technologies or surrogacy also raise concerns in the context of commodification. Children conceived through these methods may face unique challenges related to their identity, origins, and relationships [44]. Questions about the genetic lineage, legal status, and nature of their relationships with the individuals involved in their conception and birth may arise, with potential implications for their human rights, including the right to know and have a relationship with their biological parents [44]. Legal frameworks governing reproductive technologies and surrogacy vary across jurisdictions and may not always adequately protect the rights and interests of these children [45]. This highlights the need for comprehensive and robust legal protections to safeguard the rights of children born through reproductive commodification.

Ultimately, the commodification of reproduction, vis-à-vis human germline genome editing, can exacerbate existing disparities and inequalities in society, as access to reproductive services may be contingent upon financial resources. This can result in a greater reproductive divide than already exists, where individuals and couples with economic means have greater access to advanced reproductive technologies, while others are left without viable options, leading to further reproductive injustice and inequality. This raises concerns about equitable access to reproductive services as a fundamental human right [46] and underscores the need to address socioeconomic disparities and ensure that all individuals have equal opportunities to exercise their reproductive choices, irrespective of their financial status [47].

2.3. *Regulating Reproductive Autonomy in Genome Editing for Reproduction*

Whilst the WHO has provided its guidance vis-à-vis the reports on standards and governance, as well as recommendations for human genome editing, leading scholars in the field have recognized that the WHO recommendation "has shifted global considerations of governing human genome editing to more pragmatic ends" [48]. Instead of recommending an outright ban on human genome editing, the WHO instead recommends that the technology be properly evaluated and "handled with care" [48]. Besides the fact that these recommendations are markedly different from the self-imposed global moratorium by the international scientific community, it also does not escape recognition that WHO recommendations do not have the force of law. Hence, considered on a global basis, it may be true to state that there is no one, unified, harmonized international law on human genome editing.

Nevertheless, it may be inferred that prior to the recommendations, there is a variety of international human rights laws [49] that either directly or indirectly have the capacity to govern genome editing [50]. For example, in the 1997 Convention for the Protection of Human Rights and Dignity of the Human Being with regard to the Application of Biology and Medicine: Convention on Human Rights and Biomedicine (the Oviedo Convention), Article 13 has usually been interpreted to mean that human genome editing is not allowed. In other soft law instruments, such as the UNESCO Universal Declaration on the Human Genome and Human Rights, Articles 1 and 10 have commonly been interpreted to emphasize that "human rights, fundamental freedoms and liberties, and human dignity, must always prevail over any research or applications that pertain to the human genome. This illustrates the respect given to key values such as personal autonomy, integrity and informed choice, especially where biology, genetics and medicine are concerned" [50].

The 2005 UNESCO Universal Declaration on Bioethics and Human Rights, in Article 2 sub-sections (d) and (f), highlights respectively, the importance of freedom of scientific research that must consider human rights and fundamental freedoms and liberties and equitable access to medical, scientific, and technological developments [50].

Verily, insofar as the domain of governance frameworks is concerned, antecedent to the WHO recommendations, some degree of apprehension and prognostication have been demonstrated regarding the path that biomedical technologies, such as genome editing tools, may traverse. Nevertheless, the actuality is that such regulations have a restricted scope, primarily when these technologies progress rapidly, and legal systems endeavor to keep pace with such developments. It becomes therefore incumbent upon us to modify the global human rights framework concurrently with the novel WHO recommendations and to work towards constructing an all-encompassing worldwide discourse on cutting-edge technologies.

In doing so, however, careful attention must be weighed between reproductive autonomy and state governance. As ethical and legal conundrums of unprecedented proportions, it is complicated, and practically impossible, to strike a balance between the sacred autonomy of parents in deciding when and how to edit their progeny's genes and the state's legitimate right to regulate such profound alterations of the human genome.

While parental autonomy is an essential cornerstone of personal freedom, it cannot be absolute when it comes to the manipulation of the human genome, notwithstanding that it may be for the parents' own offspring. A legitimate interest of the state is to ensure genetic modifications do not violate fundamental ethical and human rights principles, jeopardize public health, or foster or even exacerbate existing inequalities and discrimination. It is therefore paramount that we carefully calibrate the delicate balance between parental autonomy and the state regulation of gene editing in order to preserve the sanctity of life, dignity of the human person, and the well-being of our species.

3. The Specter of Ghosts Past: Evolved Eugenics

The term "eugenics" is considered an almost pejorative one. Considering its association with some of the most horrific terrors that have been inflicted in human history, it is not surprising why this is the case. In any narrative that serves the improvement of human genetics, the specter of the past eugenics movement continues to haunt in several ways. First, it concerns the fear of state control over human reproduction [51]. In many ways, in contemporary democratic societies, state control already exists over reproduction. Take, for example, the United States' Supreme Court decision in Dobbs v Jackson Women's Health Organization [52], which effectively overturned a 1973 ruling in Roe v Wade [53] that guaranteed a constitutional right to bodily autonomy vis-à-vis the right to abortions. In many countries, women still do not have the power to realize the full extent of their sexual and reproductive rights under international law. Secondly, the fear is that genome editing could be deployed in instances "that merely deviate from a debatable genetic norm, rather than inevitably causing serious suffering" [51], and thirdly, the fear is the non-medical, non-therapeutic, genetic enhancement of characteristics, such as height, eye color, or intelligence [51]. This trio of fears is well-founded, and when viewed in context of the capabilities of genome editing, what becomes amplified is the struggle to contain the use of technologies without infringing on personal autonomy and human rights.

3.1. *Evolved Eugenics: A Palatable Version of Its Predecessor?*

Enter evolved eugenics, or as it has come to be known, "liberal eugenics" [54], where one of its strongest proponents is a prominent Professor of Ethics, Nicholas Agar. Whilst it has not been widely received, the concept of this evolved form of eugenics seeks to remove state control over reproductive choices, in favor of parental autonomy, prefaced always by the notion that the future life plan of individuals must be respected [7] (p. 54). The author of this paper states the following [7] (p. 56):

> The contemporary movement of liberal eugenics, in itself, is premised on the fact that should technological advancements progress to the point of safety and availability, then parents should be at liberty to use at their disposal, the full

> spectrum of these technologies for the purposes of enhancement of their future offspring. The allure of liberal eugenics pivots on the centrality of this choice: the shift in autonomy from state to individual, and the freedom from state interference in its subsequent exercise by individuals. As a firm supporter of scientific and technological developments seeking to improve the quality of human life, Agar contends for the benefits that may be reaped from genetic treatments and engineering tools. Agar would be quick to argue that, should we focus on the veritable sustenance and orientation of a variety of "life plans", the 'new' eugenics foothold vis-à-vis tools of genetic engineering technology, is capable of presenting adequate constrains built into the exercise of autonomy (in this regard, bearing upon the parents of the future offspring), which will not interfere into this varied projected plan of the offspring's future, and will not be capable of directing the offspring only into the direction of one life plan.

Following the arguments of evolved eugenics, then should it not appear, that since the offensive and deplorable aspects of state-sponsored or state-sanctioned eugenics have been removed, that eugenics as we knew of, should no longer be objectionable [7] (p. 57) [19]? Be that as it may, the concept may still be extremely vertiginous to most. It also ignores the reality that, notwithstanding the purported rein of choice and freedom imbued on parents, the so-called benefits of human genome editing are not exercised by the intended beneficiary of such technology—the future offspring [7] (p. 58).

Additionally, whilst it has always been an important point that an individual's life plan not be directed into only a limited direction, the reality is that some parental choices and actions can, and do, steer their children into specific life plans. Take the example of Harvard Girl [55], whose sole purpose of education was apparently to be accepted into the top Ivy League schools in the United States. Amy Chua's Battle Hymn of the Tiger Mother [56] provoked controversy when it was published, revealing a list of child-rearing edicts that indirectly steered her daughters, Sophia and Lulu, into only Ivy League schools, and both achieved virtuoso pianist and violinist status. These are the realities of parental choices and actions, and even if they may not begin with the intention of limiting their children's life plans, the consequential happenings are difficult to ignore. Hence, by which benchmark are we to determine that an individual's life plan is suitably safeguarded? This is, in this author's opinion, one key failing of evolved eugenics. Cloaking something deplorable with a shiny overcoat does not cease to eradicate the darkness of its history and the insurmountable limitations on life that it can bring.

Therefore, parental autonomy, choice, and actions on their own form part of parental child-rearing, which does not change the fact that future children's life plans may already be limited. With the possibilities of a genetic supermarket being offered as enticement for human enhancement in genome editing, so too remains the limitation of a future child's life plan; in fact, it is entirely humanly possible that the limitation of this life plan leads to further isolation and separation and perhaps objectionably, also reinforces the notion of such offspring's "othering"—an "othering" interpreted to displace such child, guide him/her/them into a specific acceptable future life plan, all for the purpose of doing the bidding of the invisible hand of the state [7] (p. 62).

3.2. *Contemporary Interpretations of Evolved Eugenics and "Othering"*

It is the premise of this chapter to highlight a renewed angle of viewing the positive arguments towards human genome editing. Notwithstanding the allegedly more positive aspects of evolved eugenics, as used in the context here, and whilst this has somehow been equated to future offspring being better off due to the possible choices made by their parents, this author counters otherwise.

An alternative interpretation of liberal, or evolved, eugenics offered in this chapter is that the surrender of autonomy to parents is insufficient regardless, because it cannot be completely value-free of the parents' own desires and wishes. More importantly, although bleak, as individuals existing as part of democratic societies, the existence of power relations in human interactions, vis-à-vis Foucault's theory, is "subject to negotiation, each individual having his place in the hierarchy, no matter how flexible it would be" [57]. The purported individual control by state is otherwise wielded through "bio-power and politicization of the human body via subjugation through social and covertly political controls [58].

Foucault offers the following: "we should admit rather that power produces knowledge ... ; that power and knowledge directly imply one another; that there is no power relation without the correlative constitution of a field of knowledge, nor any knowledge that does not presuppose and constitute at the same time power relations; and the body" [58] (p. 25). As such, this author opines that this upholds the "politicization" of human corporeality, as postulated by Foucault, and indirectly constitutes an insidious "invisible hand" that remains under the sway of the state. Likewise, the interplay of power dynamics within the precincts of familial relations is rife, and the quest for parity between parties is unavoidably askew towards the stronger party, as evidenced by the fragmentation of authority, knowledge, and command. However, this is not to suggest that this "invisible hand" is universally deleterious. On the contrary, the author contends that some degree of state intervention is indispensable, since the discrete realm of liberal eugenics and genome editing transcends the boundaries of human existence and necessitates regulation. The thesis posited is simply that the exercise of parental autonomy is not entirely autonomous and cannot be entirely apprehended as depicted by the tenets of liberal eugenics [7] (p. 66).

In the meantime, much of the existing literature on the possible consequences of human genome editing has focused on access to technologies, inequalities, and an inevitable genetic divided [12]. Whilst this genetic divide will, no doubt, contribute to an additional layer of systematic discrimination and inequalities in society, another consequence of a genetic divide is to further magnify the problem of "othering", a problem that, in the 21st century, we are fighting very dexterously to eradicate. It is entirely plausible that a future offspring may also experience "othering" as a consequence of being a product of genome editing. Much of existing literature has focused on the privilege of the potentially enhanced, without adequately considering the possibility that such enhancement may also create ostracization, viewing the genetically enhanced as alien to human nature. Whilst others may conject that comparisons of a genetic elite as "other" versus the systemic oppression of marginalized groups throughout history is an unfair and unbalanced rendering, our present realities of "othering" groups of individuals cannot be denied. One example of this "othering" that can be illustrated was from the recent vaccination programs for COVID-19, where anti-vaccination groups proclaimed (incorrectly) that the mRNA vaccines altered the genetic make-up of those who took said vaccines—and that this "alleged" alteration of our fundamental DNA is viewed as highly problematic and negative. Whilst this allegation proved to be untrue, what is undeniable is the way those who received the mRNA vaccines were "judged", for willfully agreeing to the alleged tampering with the genetic make-up.

Throughout the course of history, as well, the "otherness" of being a woman, being gay, being a person with disabilities, being Roma, and being, essentially, a member of key populations [59] has been acutely felt, and in the epoch of the 21st century, "othering" continues to be a problem. Described as "a set of dynamics, processes and structures that engender marginality and persistent inequality across any of the full range of human differences based on groups identities" [60], "othering" is an unfortunate consequence of systemic discrimination and prejudice. In most cases, "othering" manifests through different ways, such as essentializing explanations [61], culturalist explanations [61] (p. 262), and racializing explanations [61] (p. 263).

Whilst "othering" can appear in many forms, including outward expressions of prejudice, it is also embedded in "institutionalization and structural features" [61] (p. 262), where "individual acts of discrimination have a cumulative and magnifying effect that may help explain many group–based inequalities" [61] (p. 263). The author posits that the genetic divide, vis-à-vis genome editing, feeds auxiliary negativity towards "othering" narratives, rendering those who cannot or do not have access to technologies, voiceless, invisible, and deviant when medicine is unable to cure them.

It is difficult to sustain the alleged benefits of evolved eugenics, even if the life plan of an individual is varied and even if parental reproductive autonomy is assumed to be the gospel truth as to what amounts to the best interest of the child [62]. At the very least, genome editing that leads to evolved eugenics in any form, will have profound implications on society, law, and policy, as Susan Stabile stipulates in the following [63]:

> The contention of this Article is that an underlying attitude of "othering" pervades current discussions about what the law should and should not do to address the conditions and needs of various categories of persons. Although we do not necessarily acknowledge it, the fact that our discussions proceed from a view of the people whose situations or problems being discussed as "other" makes a difference in how we evaluate various legal and public policy initiatives. The corollary is that if, instead of proceeding from a view of others as fundamentally "not us," we possessed an attitude of solidarity, of valuing others and seeing them as not separate or other, our views on any number of issues of public policy might be very different.

4. Intersectionality: Balancing the Exercise of Parental Reproductive Autonomy

In situating experiences and narratives of privilege and oppression within reproduction and, indeed, in the many facets of medicine and health, generally, this chapter recommends deeper reflections and insights into intersectionality to influence, embed, and allow for an expansion of the considerations regarding human genome editing.

The word "intersectionality" is often credited to Kimberle Crenshaw, who coined the term in 1989 [64], although it should be acknowledged that claims about the interconnectedness of race, class, gender, sexuality, and other social identities have always functioned as part of the everyday life experiences of many marginalized groups' activities even before the term came into being. Intersectionality, added to the Oxford dictionary in 2015 is defined as "the interconnected nature of social categorizations such as race, class, and gender, regarded as creating overlapping and interdependent systems of discrimination or disadvantage". It is a powerful analytical framework and tool for academic scholarship and a compelling driver for societal, policy, and legislative movement, change, and development. In this chapter, the author posits that the role of intersectionality goes beyond a call for equalities [65]. This chapter recommends that intersectionality, in addressing the myriad of ways genome editing technologies are made available, is critical in ways that will make us rethink how oppressive power structures are placed, how structural and systemic inequalities can permeate many aspects of just "being" and "existing", and how we might be able to use this knowledge to reorient and center voices and experiences of marginalized communities [66].

Consistent with narratives of "othering" offered earlier, the twin diametric of privilege versus oppression plays a critical role in the under-represented picture of all communities in healthcare systems, management, quality of services, and available data. In intersectionality theory, it is critical to acknowledge that oppression does not occur in a vacuum and all types of oppression are interconnected to each other. Some of the examples of social markers, such as race, class, gender, sex, identity, socio-economic situatedness, and the like, are factors that are linked to how one experiences privilege and/or oppression. Intersectionality activists explain that in order for us to truly comprehend how oppression in society works, it means that we must always consider any type of social marker that could potentially be negatively used by oppressors to marginalize others in a community [67].

How do we do this in practice? How can we impart the reality that parental autonomy is inextricably linked to intersectionality and how it is experienced by different population groups? A starting point is education, awareness, and the openness to expand critical scientific knowledge beyond existing boundaries. This begins with the necessary acknowledgement that differences in different groups can combine and create inequalities and contribute to new movements of understanding [68]. Rascouet-Paz further states the following:

> For scholars and activists, intersectionality underscores the social and political implications of categories of difference and processes of differentiation ... In turn, this creates not only new avenues of inquiry but also crucial opportunities for the creation of 'alliances, framings, and policies to address multiple inequalities.

Amidst the realm of sciences, there has been a rising clamor to integrate the concept of intersectionality as a theoretical framework in the generation of research inquiries and in the methodologies adopted. The quintessential query that comes to mind is not whether quantitative fields are capable of methodologically assimilating intersectionality, but rather if these fields are ready to broaden their definitions of epistemological methodologies so as to accommodate the intersectional inquiry in the STEM domains [69]. In essence, this necessitates a more reflected scientific inquiry, and in the context of genome editing, a conscious goal towards the equanimity of serving populations that have a necessity for such technology. Multi-stakeholder dialogues are necessitated between institutions, such as the European Medicines Agency (EMA), industry, academia, patients, and members of key population groups, in order to bolster and support the generation of data through genome editing development plans. The potential for using Health Technology Assessment (HTA) to increase financing and affordability for intersectional population groups in accessing genome editing technologies could also be explored [70].

Incorporating intersectionality into governance and regulatory frameworks for human genome editing may not provide the answers that we seek but may assist in determining how to balance parental reproductive autonomy against such governance. Though the application of genome editing for the prevention or treatment of life-threatening illnesses in unborn children seems to be an unassailable practice, it is common knowledge that distinguishing between healing and enhancement, as we travel the continuum that extends from the treatment of grave pathologies to interventions aimed at physical or cognitive refinement, is an intricate task that does not meet with unanimity among experts.

5. Conclusions

Genome editing technologies, and indeed, human genome editing, have rewritten the legal and ethical debates in this field [71]. Many scientists and scholars have provided compelling justification of why the highly transformative technology should be reasonably reined in to protect communities, whilst pursuing responsible and innovative research. Renewed understandings of procreative liberties and intersectionality must be suffused into the dialogue when making allowances for legal and regulatory interventions, ensuring that a healthy environment can support the thriving genome editing technologies. Simultaneously, the applications of genome editing technologies should be adequately based on proper risk and assessment, paying keen attention to international global standards of safety that have been developed, and ensuring the protection of all population groups of patients in society.

Funding: This research received no external funding.

Institutional Review Board Statement: Not applicable.

Informed Consent Statement: Not applicable.

Data Availability Statement: No new data were created or analyzed in this study. Data sharing is not applicable to this article.

Conflicts of Interest: The author declares no conflict of interest.

References

1. Sandor, J. The Ethics of Genome Editing. *SRHM Sex. Reprod. Health Matters* **2018**. Available online: http://www.srhm.org/news/the-ethics-of-genome-editing/ (accessed on 13 October 2021).
2. Wade, N. Scientists Seek Moratorium on Edits to Human Genome That Could Be Inherited. *The New York Times*, 19 January 2018; Volume 3. Available online: https://www.nytimes.com/2015/12/04/science/crispr-cas9-human-genome-editing-moratorium.html (accessed on 30 May 2018).

3. Schaefer, G.O. Did He Jiankui "Make People Better"? Documentary Spurs a New Look at the Case of the First Gene-Edited Babies. The Conversation. 20 December 2022. Available online: http://theconversation.com/did-he-jiankui-make-people-better-documentary-spurs-a-new-look-at-the-case-of-the-first-gene-edited-babies-196714 (accessed on 24 March 2023).
4. Statement from the Organising Committee of the Third International Summit on Human Genome Editing. 2023. Available online: https://www.theglob-alfund.org/en/key-populations/ (accessed on 14 June 2023).
5. Charpentier, E.; Doudna, J.A. *The Nobel Prize in Chemistry 2020*; Press Release; The Royal Swedish Academy of Sciences: Stockholm, Sweden, 2020.
6. Hsu, P.D.; Lander, E.S.; Zhang, F. Development and Applications of CRISPR-Cas9 for Genome Engineering. *Cell* **2014**, *157*, 1262. [CrossRef] [PubMed]
7. Lau, P.L. *Comparative Legal Frameworks for Pre-Implantation Embryonic Genetic Interventions*; Springer International Publishing: New York, NY, USA, 2019. Available online: http://link.springer.com/10.1007/978-3-030-22308-3 (accessed on 19 November 2019).
8. Committee on Science, Technology, and Law, Policy and Global Affairs, and National Academies of Sciences, Engineering, and Medicine. *International Summit on Human Gene Editing: A Global Discussion*; Olson, S., Ed.; National Academies Press: Cambridge, MA, USA, 2016. Available online: http://www.nap.edu/catalog/21913 (accessed on 19 June 2018).
9. World Health Organization. *Human Genome Editing: A Framework for Governance*; World Health Organization: Geneva, Switzerland, 2021. Available online: https://apps.who.int/iris/handle/10665/342484 (accessed on 4 October 2021).
10. World Health Organization. *Human Genome Editing: Recommendations*; World Health Organization: Geneva, Switzerland, 2021. Available online: https://apps.who.int/iris/handle/10665/342486 (accessed on 4 October 2021).
11. World Health Organization. *Human Genome Editing: Position Paper*; World Health Organization: Geneva, Switzerland, 2021. Available online: https://apps.who.int/iris/handle/10665/342485 (accessed on 4 October 2021).
12. Nuffield Council on Bioethics. *Genome Editing and Human Reproduction: Social and Ethical Issues*; Nuffield Council on Bioethics: London, UK, 2018.
13. World Health Organization. *WHO Issues New Recommendations on Human Genome Editing for the Advancement of Public Health*; World Health Organization: Geneva, Switzerland, 2021. Available online: https://www.who.int/news/item/12-07-2021-who-issues-new-recommendations-on-human-genome-editing-for-the-advancement-of-public-health (accessed on 13 October 2021).
14. Conseil de l'Europe. Convention for the Protection of Human Rights and Fundamental Freedoms: European Human Rights Convention (Editions du Conseil de l'Europe 1950). Available online: https://www.echr.coe.int/european-convention-on-human-rights (accessed on 16 June 2016).
15. Conseil de l'Europe. Convention for the Protection of Human Rights and Dignity of the Human Being with Regard to the Application of Biology and Medicine: Convention on Human Rights and Biomedicine (Editions du Conseil de l'Europe 1997). Available online: http://193.205.211.30/lawtech/images/lawtech/law/convenzioneoviedo.pdf (accessed on 17 February 2017).
16. Lau, P.L. The Genius & The Imbecile: Disentangling the "Legal" Framework of Autonomy in Modern Liberal Eugenics, From Non-Therapeutic Gene Enhancement Use in Gene Editing Technologies. In *Current Debates in International Relations and Law*; IJOPEC: London, UK, 2018; Volume 4.
17. Mill, J.S. *On Liberty*; John W Parker and Son, West Strand: Hoboken, NJ, USA, 1859.
18. Stanley, S.; Mill, J.S. Children's Liberty, and the Unraveling of Autonomy. *Rev. Politics* **2017**, *79*, 49–72. Available online: https://www.cambridge.org/core/product/identifier/S0034670516000723/type/journal_article (accessed on 25 October 2017). [CrossRef]
19. Simões, M.C. Paternalism and Antipaternalism. *Int. J. Moral Philos.* **2011**, *10*, 65. Available online: https://periodicos.ufsc.br/index.php/ethic/article/view/22549 (accessed on 13 October 2017).
20. Coggon, J.; Miola, J. Autonomy, Liberty, and Medical Decision-Making. *Camb. Law J.* **2011**, *70*, 523. Available online: http://www.journals.cambridge.org/abstract_S0008197311000845 (accessed on 25 October 2017). [CrossRef] [PubMed]
21. Basille, C.; Frydman, R.; Aly, A.E.; Lelorch, M.; Frydman, N.A. Preimplantation Genetic Diagnosis: State of the Art. *Eur. J. Obstet. Gynecol. Reprod. Biol.* **2009**, *145*, 9. Available online: http://linkinghub.elsevier.com/retrieve/pii/S0301211509002449 (accessed on 23 November 2015). [CrossRef]
22. Chen, H.F.; Chen, S.U.; Ma, G.C.; Hsieh, S.T.; Tsai, H.D.; Yang, Y.S.; Chen, M. Preimplantation Genetic Diagnosis and Screening: Current Status and Future Challenges. *J. Formos. Med. Assoc.* **2018**, *117*, 94. Available online: http://linkinghub.elsevier.com/retrieve/pii/S092966461730579X (accessed on 14 March 2018). [CrossRef]
23. Simoncelli, T. *Pre-Implantation Genetic Diagnosis and Selection: From Disease Prevention to Customized Conception*; Population and Development Program; Hampshire College: Amherst, MA, USA, 2003.
24. Franklin, S.; Roberts, C. *Born and Made: An Ethnography of Preimplantation Genetic Diagnosis*; Princeton University Press: Princeton, NJ, USA, 2006.
25. Belluck, P. Gene Editing for "Designer Babies"? Highly Unlikely, Scientists Say. *The New York Times*, 4 August 2017. Available online: https://www.nytimes.com/2017/08/04/science/gene-editing-embryos-designer-babies.html(accessed on 6 June 2018).
26. Liao, S.; Savulescu, J.; Sheehan, M. The Ashley Treatment: Best Interests, Convenience, and Parental Decision-Making. *Hastings Cent. Rep.* **2007**, *37*, 16. [CrossRef]
27. Sandel, M. The Case against Perfection. *Atl. Mon.* **2004**, *293*, 51. Available online: http://jrichardstevens.com/articles/sandel-genetics.pdf (accessed on 9 January 2017).

28. Galton, F. *Inquiries into Human Faculty and Its Development*; Macmillan: Stuttgart, Germany, 1883. Available online: http://galton.org/books/human-faculty/text/human-faculty.pdf (accessed on 26 October 2017).
29. Saetz, S.B.; Court, M.V.; Henshaw, M.W. *Eugenics and the Third Reich*; The Eugenics Bulletin: Long Island, NY, USA, 1985.
30. Silver, L. *Remaking Eden: How Genetic Engineering and Cloning Will Transform the American Family*; Avon Books Inc.: New York, NY, USA, 1997.
31. Gaskell, G.; Bard, I.; Allansdottir, A.; da Cunha, R.V.; Eduard, P.; Hampel, J.; Hildt, E.; Hofmaier, C.; Kronberger, N.; Lausen, S.; et al. Public Views on Gene Editing and Its Uses. *Nat. Biotechnol.* **2017**, *35*, 1021–1023. Available online: https://www.nature.com/articles/nbt.3958 (accessed on 2 January 2020). [CrossRef]
32. An Overview of the Human Genome Project (National Human Genome Research Institute (NHGRI)). Available online: https://www.genome.gov/12011238/an-overview-of-the-human-genome-project/ (accessed on 16 May 2018).
33. Ormond, K.E.; Mortlock, D.P.; Scholes, D.T.; Shriner, D.; Virani, A.; Young, C.E. Human Germline Genome Editing. *Am. J. Hum. Genet.* **2017**, *101*, 167–169. Available online: http://linkinghub.elsevier.com/retrieve/pii/S0002929717302471 (accessed on 25 May 2018). [CrossRef] [PubMed]
34. Cribbs, A.P.; Perera, S.M.W. Science and Bioethics of CRISPR-Cas9 Gene Editing: An Analysis Towards Separating Facts and Fiction. *Yale J. Biol. Med.* **2017**, *90*, 625–629. [PubMed]
35. Maloney, L. The Commodification of Human Beings. *Extra Leg. Northeast. Univ. Law J.* **2015**, *15*, 1–15.
36. Rao, R. Coercion, Commercialization, and Commodification: The Ethics of Compensation for Egg Donors in Stem Cell Research. *Berkeley Technol. Law J.* **2006**, *21*, 1055.
37. Habermas, J. (Ed.) *The Future of Human Nature*; Polity Press: Cambridge, UK, 2003. Available online: https://philpapers.org/rec/HABTFO-2 (accessed on 13 September 2017).
38. Voigt, C.; Laing, J.H. Journey into Parenthood: Commodification of Reproduction as a New Tourism Niche Market. *J. Travel Tour. Mark.* **2010**, *27*, 252. [CrossRef]
39. Scott, E.S. Surrogacy and the Politics of Commodification. *Law Contemp. Probl.* **2009**, *72*, 109.
40. Rothschild, J. *The Dream of the Perfect Child*; Indiana University Press: Bloomington, IN, USA, 2005.
41. Rozée, V.; Sayeed Unisa, S.; de La Rochebrochard, E. The Social Paradoxes of Commercial Surrogacy in Developing Countries: India before the New Law of 2018. *BMC Women's Health* **2020**, *20*, 234. [CrossRef]
42. Barroso, L.R. Here, There, and Everywhere: Human Dignity in Contemporary Law and in the Transnational Discourse. *Comp. Law Rev.* **2012**, *35*, 331.
43. Hurlbut, J.B.; Jasanoff, S.; Saha, K. Constitutionalism at the Nexus of Life and Law. *Sci. Technol. Hum. Values* **2020**, *45*, 979. [CrossRef]
44. Zillen, K.; Garland, J.; Slokenberga, S. *The Rights of Children in Biomedicine: Challenges Posed by Scientific Advances and Uncertainties*; Committee on Bioethics of the Council of Europe: Strasbourg, France, 2017.
45. Lau, P.L. Genetic Testing or Screening at Pre-Birth Stage. In *Children's Rights in Biomedicine: Protection from Scientific Risk and Uncertainty in Pursuit of the Highest Attainable Standard of Health*; in press; Slokenberga, S., Garland, J., Eds.; Uppsala University: Uppsala, Sweden, 2023.
46. Galloway, K. Assisted Reproductive Technologies and Human Rights. 11 Right Now. 2014. Available online: https://rightnow.org.au/opinion/assisted-reproductive-technologies-and-human-rights/ (accessed on 26 April 2023).
47. Kollodge, R.; Nationen, V. (Eds.) *Reproductive Health and Rights in an Age of Inequality*; United Nations Population Fund: New York, NY, USA, 2017.
48. Cohen, I.G.; Sherkow, J.S.; Adashi, E.Y. Handle with Care: The WHO Report on Human Genome Editing. *Hastings Cent. Rep.* **2022**, *52*, 10. Available online: https://onlinelibrary.wiley.com/doi/10.1002/hast.1350 (accessed on 26 April 2023). [CrossRef]
49. Yotova, R. Regulating Genome Editing under International Human Rights Law. *Int. Comp. Law Q.* **2020**, *69*, 653. Available online: https://www.cambridge.org/core/product/identifier/S0020589320000184/type/journal_article (accessed on 14 November 2021). [CrossRef]
50. Lau, P.L. Addressing Cognitive Vulnerabilities through Genome and Epigenome Editing: Techno-Legal Adaptations for Persons with Intellectual Disabilities. *Eur. J. Health Law* **2022**, *29*, 409–434. Available online: https://brill.com/view/journals/ejhl/aop/article-10.1163-15718093-bja10085/article-10.1163-15718093-bja10085.xml (accessed on 24 July 2022). [CrossRef]
51. Coghlan, N. *If the EU Picks Baby Genes*; Verfassungsblog: Berlin, Germany, 2023. Available online: https://verfassungsblog.de/if-the-eu-picks-baby-genes/ (accessed on 27 April 2023).
52. Supreme Court Case: Dobbs v. Jackson Women's Health Organization (*Center for Reproductive Rights*). Available online: https://reproductiverights.org/case/scotus-mississippi-abortion-ban/ (accessed on 8 January 2022).
53. Wade, V.R. 410 U.S. *Justia Law* **1973**, *113*, 17–26. Available online: https://supreme.justia.com/cases/federal/us/410/113/ (accessed on 2 May 2018).
54. Agar, N. Liberal Eugenics. *Public Aff. Q.* **1998**, *12*, 137. Available online: http://www.jstor.org/stable/40441188 (accessed on 29 December 2016).
55. Weihua, L.; Zhang Xinwu, Z. *Harvard Girl Liu Yiting: A Character Training Record*; Writers Publishing House: Beijing, China, 2000.
56. Chua, A. *Battle Hymn of the Tiger Mother*; Penguin Group: New York, NY, USA, 2011.
57. Foucault, M. Naissance de La Clinique Une Archéologie Du Regard Médical. Available online: https://philpapers.org/rec/FOUNDL (accessed on 10 March 2017).

58. Foucault, M. *Discipline and Punish: The Birth of The Prison*; Vintage Books Random House: New York, NY, USA, 1977. Available online: https://monoskop.org/images/4/43/Foucault_Michel_Discipline_and_Punish_The_Birth_of_the_Prison_1977_1995.pdf (accessed on 14 March 2023).
59. The Global Fund. Key Populations. The Global Fund: Geneva, Switzerland. Available online: https://www.theglobalfund.org/en/key-populations/ (accessed on 10 July 2023).
60. Powell, J.A.; Menendian, S. The Problem of Othering: Towards Inclusiveness and Belonging; Othering and Belonging: 2017. Available online: http://www.otheringandbelonging.org/the-problem-of-othering/ (accessed on 14 March 2023).
61. Johnson, J.L.; Bottorff, J.L.; Browne, A.J.; Grewal, S.; Hilton, B.A.; Clarke, H. Othering and Being Othered in the Context of Health Care Services. *Health Commun.* **2004**, *16*, 255–260. Available online: http://www.tandfonline.com/doi/abs/10.1207/S15327027HC1602_7 (accessed on 30 April 2023). [CrossRef]
62. Savulescu, J. Procreative Beneficence: Why We Should Select the Best Children. *Bioethics* **2001**, *15*, 413. [CrossRef]
63. Stabile, S.J. Othering and the Law. *St. Thomas LJ* **2009**, *12*, 381. Available online: http://www.ssrn.com/abstract=1301720 (accessed on 30 April 2023). [CrossRef]
64. Crenshaw, K. *On Intersectionality: Essential Writings*; The New Press: New York, NY, USA, 2017.
65. Lau, P.L. Reflections on Intersectionality: Artificial Intelligence in Women's Healthcare—Betwixt Privilege and Oppression. In *IV Yearbook on Socio-Economic Constitutions: Law and the Governance of Artificial Intelligence*; in press; The New Press: New York, NY, USA, 2023.
66. Kelly, C.; Kasperavicius, D.; Duncan, D.; Etherington, C.; Giangregorio, L.; Presseau, J.; Sibley, K.M.; Straus, S. 'Doing' or 'Using' Intersectionality? Opportunities and Challenges in Incorporating Intersectionality into Knowledge Translation Theory and Practice. *Int. J. Equity Health* **2021**, *20*, 187. Available online: https://equityhealthj.biomedcentral.com/articles/10.1186/s12939-021-01509-z (accessed on 20 August 2022). [CrossRef] [PubMed]
67. Taylor, B. *Intersectionality 101: What Is It and Why Is It Important?* Womankind Worldwide: London, UK, 2019. Available online: https://www.womankind.org.uk/intersectionality-101-what-is-it-and-why-is-it-important/ (accessed on 17 March 2023).
68. Paz, R. *The Indispensable Work of Understanding Intersectionality*; Annual Reviews: San Mateo, CA, USA, 2020. Available online: https://www.annualreviews.org/shot-of-science/story/indispensable-work-understanding-intersectionality (accessed on 1 May 2023).
69. Shattuck-Heidorn, H.; Boulicault, M.; Rushovich, T.; Richardson, S.S. Intersectionality as Live Theory and Practice in Biomedical Sciences. In *The Routledge Companion to Intersectionalities*; Routledge: London, UK, 2023.
70. European Association of Health Law Interest Group on Supranational BioLaw. *Health as a Fundamental Value; Towards an Inclusive and Equitable Pharmaceutical Strategy for the European Union'*; European Health Policy Platform: Brussels, Belgium, 2022; Volume 45.
71. Sandor, J. Genome Editing: Learning from Its Past and Envisioning Its Future. In *Governing, Protecting, and Regulating the Future of Genome Editing*; Slokenberga, S., Minssen, T., Nordberg, A., Eds.; Brill Nijhoff: Boston, MA, USA, 2023. Available online: https://brill.com/view/book/9789004526136/BP000008.xml (accessed on 1 May 2023).

BioTech

MDPI

Article

Artificial Intelligence in Biomedicine: A Legal Insight

Takis Vidalis

Hellenic National Commission for Bioethics and Technoethics, 10674 Athens, Greece; t.vidalis@bioethics.gr

Abstract: The involvement of artificial intelligence in biomedicine promises better support for decision-making both in conventional and research medical practice. Yet two important issues emerge in relation to personal data handling, and the influence of AI on patient/doctor relationships. The development of AI algorithms presupposes extensive processing of big data in biobanks, for which procedures of compliance with data protection need to be ensured. This article addresses this problem in the framework of the EU legislation (GDPR) and explains the legal prerequisites pertinent to various categories of health data. Furthermore, the self-learning systems of AI may affect the fulfillment of medical duties, particularly if the attending physicians rely on unsupervised applications operating beyond their direct control. The article argues that the patient informed consent prerequisite plays a key role here, not only in conventional medical acts but also in clinical research procedures.

Keywords: artificial intelligence; biomedicine; data protection; medical duty; informed consent; unsupervised systems

Citation: Vidalis, T. Artificial Intelligence in Biomedicine: A Legal Insight. *BioTech* **2021**, *10*, 15. https://doi.org/10.3390/biotech10030015

Academic Editor: Maestri Enrico

Received: 12 April 2021
Accepted: 29 June 2021
Published: 14 July 2021

1. Introduction

Developments in contemporary biomedicine raise ethical and legal questions relevant to the extensive use of artificial intelligence (AI) applications both in conventional medical practice and in research activities [1] (p. 5). With no doubt, the introduction of algorithms promises better results in the evaluation of specific cases, if these algorithms are formed and constantly updated on the basis of appropriate statistical information deriving from clinical studies with similar characteristics. On the other hand, AI applications as substitutes of individual physicians, namely human decision-makers, do not always ensure the best option is followed for a particular patient, even if decisions they recommend are evidence-based [2] (p. 400). Indeed, statistical evidence does not necessarily capture the complex nature of specific clinical cases; medical practice cannot be reduced to pure mathematical models. That is why the involvement of AI systems and the extent of their use by attending physicians are topics that influence the patient/physician relationship in terms of ethics and law.

We can distinguish two central questions concerning the use of AI in biomedicine from a legal standpoint.

First, we encounter a question referring to the formation of algorithms suitable for supporting medical decision-making. This work presupposes extensive processing of massive information, including scientific information, statistical data, and personal data of health importance (genetic, clinical, and lifestyle data) [1]. The collection and processing of personal data in particular are subject to the data protection legal framework.

The second question is relevant to the influence of the AI automated decisions on the attending physicians' legal liability, or even in ethical terms, their role regarding fulfillment of medical duty. We will explore these questions in conventional medical practice, and in clinical research, with reference to the basic instruments of the common European legislation that also determines the general framework for specific national regulation in the European countries.

2. Data Collection and Processing

Over the last decades, progress in biomedicine has been closely associated with health data management thanks to continuously enhanced technological abilities that we dispose for data collection and processing. Current applications based on extensive personal data use that include e-prescription systems and e-health records characterize the regular performance of diagnostic, preventive, and therapeutic medical acts. These applications indicate the importance of AI components in data handling, providing immediate and accurate responses to the physician's input [3] (pp. 33–37).

With the progress of Medical Genetics and the opening of a new era towards Personalized Medicine [2] (p. 409), [4] (pp. 21 et seq, 41 et seq), the role of data collection becomes crucial. As the current expression of that new era, Precision Medicine intends to develop tailor-made health services and therapeutic means pertinent to specific profiles of patient groups or even individual patients [5–7]. In this regard, AI applications will ensure feasibility since the need for accurate and rapid data processing at this scale is obvious and cannot be met by conventional human-guided methods.

In this data-centered context, the role of ethical and legal norms is pivotal. Personal data nowadays represent a distinct value in modern societies, particularly when the subject's identity is known or may be revealed. This is because, following the fundamental principles of a democratic society, every person enjoys a space of self-determination, which also includes elements characterizing the personality's very essence. Thus, all information related to elements of the person's identification and privacy, forming the distinct space of "informational self-determination" [8] (pp. 398 et seq) must remain protected from any intervention of the state or thirds if unauthorized by the person concerned. Simple data of identification such as the name, the address, the phone number, the social security number, etc., belongs to this protected space.

Most importantly, special data categories are referring to the person's intimate thoughts or private activity. Here, protection is stricter in legal terms, as any unauthorized disclosure of these data to thirds may severely damage the data subject in various social situations. In this category of "sensitive" data belong the person's biological characteristics (genetic, etc.), personal health information, as well as philosophical or political or religious beliefs, information on friendly or sexual relationships, etc. (GDPR, art. 9).

Informational autonomy illustrates the ethical ground for personal data protection in general terms, justifying specific legal measures in relevance. Nowadays, all democratic countries have adopted laws that govern this area with detailed provisions setting up specific control mechanisms for preventing or sanctioning violations. In Europe, "guardians" of the system are the data protection authorities (GDPR, Chapter VI) enjoying an independent administrative status and the courts. The European legal framework is embedded in the General Data Protection Regulation (GDPR), an instrument that binds all EU member states and also governs data transfer and handling in non-EU countries (GDPR, Chapter V). This means that a non-EU country (including countries outside Europe, such as the USA, Canada, China, Australia, etc.) needs to demonstrate compliance with the standards of the GDPR for receiving and processing data deriving from the EU (GDPR, art. 44). Therefore, the legal relevance of the GDPR is broader in geographical terms, which makes it really influential when the issue is to promote health data collection and processing at a global scale.

On the other hand, the GDPR does not regulate data protection exhaustively. As a product of states' negotiations and compromising, it leaves considerable discretion of regulation to national laws in EU member states, which sometimes leads to diverse modes of implementation in each separate national legal system. Thus, even if the form of an EU's "Regulation" represents binding legislation directly enforced in the member-states' legal systems, in the example of GDPR, national decision-making in relevance continues to hold a substantial normative role (GDPR, art. 9 (para 3, 4), 23, 46, 49, etc.).

Given this regulatory context in Europe, it is essential to distinguish categories of information relevant to health that may be accumulated at a scale of databases promising the formation of AI algorithms suitable for supporting clinical decisions. This is because the data protection regulation focuses on identifiable (GDPR, art. 4 (1)) health data exclusively, not on mere statistical data, which remain anonymous. Statistical data deriving from epidemiological studies cover a significant part of the databases' content, and their processing is vital for the formation of AI algorithms. Still, that information remains indifferent for the law, since, in principle, there is no possibility of detecting the data subjects.

Under the GDPR's regime, data may be identifiable in to two categories: either data with known subjects, when the identity matters in processing given its purposes, or "pseudonymized" data, after codification, when the identity is in principle irrelevant to the processing purposes, but still may be detected if the code of anonymization is accessible [9] (pp. 663–664). Thus, personal data are equated only to identifiable data in the strict legal terminology, and data protection refers to the above two categories exclusively.

The collection of personal data raises specific issues. Data sources are either an original collection based on direct contact with the data subjects (healthy persons or patients) or an already existing database, available for further use with different purposes than the original ones. For example, databases in hospitals comprising medical health records of patients or in insurance facilities or workplaces may be of interest for further use, particularly research use.

It is evident that the existing databases of health data are of crucial importance for forming collections on the scale of big data in order to achieve a statistically valid multifactorial volume for testing AI applications. On the other hand, new data collections from a particular group of persons ensure that new research topics will be addressed that data already stored for other purposes cannot cover. Thus, a big comprehensive database promising the design of AI algorithms suitable for medical decision-making needs to exploit the massive material of existing databases, and also run new research to accumulate information responding to new questions of clinical importance [1] (p. 2).

Bearing in mind the above classification, the GDPR establishes a critical differentiation in data protection, focusing mostly on the issue of the subject's informed consent as a prerequisite for ensuring personal control over any possible data use (GDPR, art. 7, 8, 9 (a)).

First, for new collections of health-related data, the subject's informed consent is always necessary since new research objectives involve direct contact with investigators asking for such data. Still, in contrast to the previous regime governing data protection in the EU (Directive 95/46) the GDPR does not consider specific consent as a strict requirement. Following the recital 33 of its explanatory part, a consent of "generic" nature may be sufficient if determining a broader framework for the data's secondary use [10] (p. 660), namely for future research purposes, on the evident condition that this does not mean a general permission of any research use, a "*carte blanche*" granted to investigators. Furthermore, the option that is given by recital 33 always presupposes that this "generic" consent fulfills the conditions of freedom, which is not the case when there is a "clear imbalance between the data subject and the controller" (meaning an unequal position of them, due to relationships of dependence, etc., according to recital 43 of the explanatory part). On the other hand, the original consent is required even if investigators apply data pseudonymization, and processing excludes the possibility of access to subjects' identities, as far as the link between data and identities exists and may be known to one or more persons of the research team.

Second, regarding collections of already stored data, initially gathered for other reasons (clinical or not), the law allows further processing for new research purposes, even without the data subjects' fresh consent, on the condition that the purposes of the secondary use of data are compatible or relevant to the research purpose that justified the original collection of data, following art. 6 para 4 (a) of the GDPR. In that case, informed consent is not considered a necessary mechanism of control for data protection. This provision facilitates research activities significantly, since to repeat communication with subjects that consented initially to the data use in other settings is practically impossible. Nevertheless, the GDPR does not leave the data protection uncontrolled. Substitute safeguards need to be in place necessarily, after specific national legislative measures (GDPR, art. 9 para 2 j) which indicatively may require pseudonymization or other technical methods to ensure confidential processing (installing firewalls, etc.). Most EU member states have already enacted such specific legislation for the implementation of the GDPR's provision.

Third, when it comes to the use of anonymous (or "anonymized") data, that is, data with unknown or untraceable identity, any research use is allowed with no engagement of data protection control mechanisms. Indeed, this information is not conceptualized as "personal data" by the law, similarly to what happens with statistical data. This is also important, as it covers collections of stored data that may be transferred to research facilities after anonymization at their source, with no involvement of the research team whatsoever. For example, suppose a big data collection supporting Precision Medicine's objectives that includes partial collections of health data from private insurance companies: if these companies have performed the data anonymization in situ before transferring the collections to the research facilities, no data protection issue occurs, as researchers of the latter have no access to the anonymization procedure.

Nevertheless, in the context of big data, we must admit that neither pseudonymization nor even anonymization at the source of data secures protection of the data subjects. Indeed, the massive amount of multifactorial information from multiple sources makes possible the development of specific algorithms that may lead to findings detecting the subjects' identity even in these data categories, following a methodology of "deep mining" analysis in which the role of AI is of course critical [10] (p. 661). This fact challenges the efficiency of the legal provisions mentioned above, which means that, eventually, the most reliable preventive mechanism for data protection remains the subjects' informed consent prerequisite. At least for new data collections, the generic model of informed consent, as acknowledged by the GDPR, could ensure the development of big databases without compromising the data safety or the research potential.

As a last means of protection, the GDPR recognizes specific rights for the data subjects (GDPR, Chapter III) that are fully enforceable before the courts, representing the "coercive" dimension of data protection in case of violation. Any unauthorized identification of anonymized data through "deep mining" analysis in the context of big data or other methods is, therefore, subject to administrative or judicial control under the light of these specific rights. Amongst them, the "right to erasure," namely the subject's legal option to ask for complete removal of his/her personal data from a database, is the most crucial here (GDPR, art. 17). Although the GDPR mentions significant exceptions regarding this right exercise, based on public interest reasons (such as public health or safety reasons), the data controller is in principle fully responsible for complying when the data subject files a relevant application. Exceptions can be considered only if their reason is specifically justified and documented. In this strict context, a potential identification of originally anonymized data in a big database would be legally unacceptable if not associated directly with evident priorities in public health.

3. Artificial Intelligence and the Medical Duty

Besides the issues related to data handling, questions concerning AI applications in medical decision-making should also be considered. To what extent can a physician's decision regarding a specific patient rely on automatically yielded guidance after AI data processing?

This is a problem relevant to the "interpretability" of AI systems [11] (pp. 3 et seq), particularly when self-learning (unsupervised) systems are engaged in conventional clinical practice or clinical research. Indeed, self-learning systems cannot be addressed as conventional medical instruments that support the physicians' practice so far, or even as supervised AI systems, where close dependence on the human initiative (and responsibility) of the system's expected outcomes still exists [2] (p. 399), [12] (p. 419). Self-learning ability means a certain degree of machines' self-programming after evaluating massive information deriving from a big data biobank, which includes the relevance of existing data to specific clinical contexts. Compared to conventional medical instruments, here we have a process of data appraisal beyond direct human control. Although the algorithms that are developed for such systems are evidence-based, their automatic outcomes for supporting medical decision-making escape by default from the area of knowledge not only of ordinary medical practitioners but also of these intelligent systems' developers raising questions on transparency regarding their functional characteristics [4] (p. 27), [13] (pp. 6 et seq). An appropriate legal methodology for addressing cases of AI developers' professional liability should be adopted here [14] (pp. 393 et seq).

There is a clear ethical question here on whether the use of such systems meets the principles of the essential medical duty in the patient/doctor relationship, that is, the "beneficence, non-maleficence" and the informed consent (as expression of personal autonomy) requirements [15] (pp. 118 et seq, 155 et seq, 217 et seq). From a legal point of view, this question also refers to the extent of medical liability, especially when medical malpractice occurs. In any sense, accountability is a general problem related to the use of AI systems that influences professional liability, and not only in Medicine [4] (pp. 29–30, 236 et seq). Is it possible, then, to accuse a physician for medical malpractice based upon guidance from unsupervised self-learning AI systems that resulted in the patient's harm?

To answer this question, we need, first, to highlight some elements of conventional clinical practice. Conventional medical acts should be based on two conditions: (a) the physician's performance *lege artis*, namely according to the standard of care [16] (p. 6), which also includes compliance with relevant protocols, and (b) the patient's informed consent (or choice), which involves patients in decision-making. On the one hand, these two prerequisites reflect the two ethical principles already mentioned; on the other, they determine the framework within which the liability of doctors should be judged in concrete legal terms. The current legislation in Europe (at the level of international instruments and mostly of national laws) contains specific provisions referring to these prerequisites, making their content legally binding.

(a) Medical performance *lege artis* means that we admit as an axiom the existence of objective scientific norms in the framework of which doctors may exercise their activity. This does not contravene the doctors' scientific independence and freedom of thought; it only excludes absurd practices with no scientific evidence, contrary to "professional standards" (art. 4 of the Oviedo Convention).

There is no doubt that often the evidence issue is vague, as diverging scientific opinions cannot be excluded; therefore, opinions expressing minorities in the scientific community cannot be considered by definition absurd. Still, the axiom requires that, at least, we need firm scientific justification for accepting a certain medical art as compliant to the *leges artis*. The era of evidence-based medicine contributed to the clarification of these problems. Protocols containing specific and detailed guidelines are now developed based on the substantial progress of clinical research and the statistical reliability of research findings. These normative instruments significantly facilitate doctors' good practice, and prevent the occurrence of severe malpractice incidents. Moreover, in the context of evidence-based medicine, the role of data processing, statistics, and mathematics became crucial several decades before the emergence of AI systems. This is a crucial point in our approach.

(b) On the other hand, the patients' informed consent or choice holds a key role in medical practice (Oviedo Convention, art. 5, 6), even if the physician's performance relies on machine support and guidance based on complex calculations with the use of advanced technology. This means that the physician always needs to provide appropriate information to the patient and obtain relevant consent before acting. The use of AI systems and their expected benefit or risks following evidence-based criteria definitely belongs to the content of information and possibly influences the consent, particularly of an expert patient. Nevertheless, there is no reason to exclude from this general rule even self-learning AI systems, on the condition that the patient has consented to this involvement of a "substitute" medical knowledge, and been assured that the final decision for the medical act in relevance lies on the attending physician's direct control. Under the medical liability's point of view, this latter element is the only decisive. Indeed, supposing that the attending physician has minimal or no specific technical expertise about the precise details of a medical instrument's structure and function (which is the usual case), it is sufficient to demonstrate awareness of potential benefits and risks from its use to fulfill the law's conditions on liability. The quality of patient information is the legal guarantee for this.

Certainly, AI unsupervised, self-learning applications are characterized by an "opaque" element that remains uncontrolled by human users [4] (p. 27), [11] (p. 15), [12] (pp. 420,421). Still, in the end, what matters is the final decision of physicians about the medical act in relevance. Physicians should take the risk even for this uncontrolled element of AI systems if they believe that the benefits are more important than the potential negative implications from the use of these systems in a particular case. It is worth noting here that, in terms of medical liability, what we expect from physicians is a *lege artis* performance only, even if the final result could be non-beneficial for the patient. Medical liability concerns only criteria of good practice; therefore, if the use of AI self-learning systems is evidence-based in similar cases, no differences exist comparing to the use of conventional medical devices.

Yet, this is true for conventional medical practice when evidence-based rules are in place. Can we suggest the same for practice in clinical research [2] (pp. 409 et seq, 413 et seq)? How appropriate is the experimentation in clinical trials with AI self-learning systems when no evidence-based criteria exist, and the question is precisely to identify such criteria? Under the medical liability view, this is a difficult problem to the extent that the "opaque" element of AI remains uncontrolled even by experts as mentioned above. An ethical question arises as well: Are we allowed to involve volunteers in experimental procedures when part of these remains beyond the investigators' direct control?

Again, the informed consent prerequisite is the only guarantee, here, if we assume that the information provided to the volunteers clearly includes the involvement of self-learning AI applications in the clinical trial's development, mentioning potential risks and specific measures to be taken for preventing them. The difference that may arise compared to conventional clinical acts is that, in clinical research, we have to cope with a great deal of uncertainty by definition; therefore, the degree of risks may be unacceptable with the use of such systems.

Nevertheless, risk acceptance is still a matter of the volunteer's free decision. Certainly, in clinical trials, the informed consent prerequisite has limited impact compared to conventional medical acts since the law requires previous approval of the research protocol's scientific and ethical appropriateness. This means that volunteers are invited to consent only on the condition that minimal evidence on safety and risk/benefit assessment has been obtained and confirmed by the approval mentioned above (Oviedo Convention, art. 16, 17, Directive 2001/20, art. 3, Regulation 536/2014, art. 28). In our example, minimal evidence needs to refer to the AI algorithms' specific characteristics and self-learning operation as manifested in previous pre-clinical tests. As it happens with the new molecules' in vivo testing in pre-clinical studies demonstrating the expected influence on animal organisms, this step seems both necessary and sufficient to ensure the minimal evidence that allows the protocol's ethical approval; moreover, it justifies seeking the volunteer's informed consent. This analogy is defensible because, in terms of safety, the impact of an experimental substance on a living organism's vital functions is not less risky than the AI's self-learning guidance of clinical decision-making since both are based on a rational assessment of scientific data. In this comparison, the expected guarantees for a positive outcome have the same degree of reliability. In other words, the degree of uncertainty is comparable, particularly if no option of return to the condition before the intervention is ensured.

4. Conclusions

The novel element that AI applications bring to biomedicine is the mobilization of machine-controlled inputs in decision-making regarding either conventional or experimental medical acts. Relying on AI systems' self-learning operations, this technological development facilitates immensely the accurate appraisal of data relevant to specific clinical situations based on robust medical evidence. There is no doubt that machine self-learning guarantees what the human medical practice, even of highly experienced experts, cannot provide, namely to yield practical guidance timely from a work of massive data processing. Yet, the cost that we need to accept for that is not trivial.

First, there is a cost regarding the need to handle big health data, which refers to risks occurring for the protection of identifiable personal data. The latter's collection and processing involve procedures that, in principle, may guarantee protection, but still the risk is persistent at that scale, since nothing is "automatically" in place, and specific responsibilities of many people acting in that field need to be considered.

In Europe, following the GDPR's regulation, data controllers, data processors, and data protection officers are the main responsible persons, here (GDPR, art. 24, 28, 37) Since the development of more advanced AI systems is embedded in the permanent accumulation of massive information, a particular problem of data transfer emerges, given that no unified binding legislation and controls exist at the global scale, and additional procedures for ensuring the data subjects' rights need to be observed.

Second, a further cost is related to the medical performance as such, that is, the extent of medical acts' dependence on machine-controlled guidance. Inevitably, in unsupervised, self-learning AI medical applications, we have to cope with an "opaque" element that escapes the attending physician's direct control, although it still affects medical liability.

We argued that in conventional clinical practice, the attending physician remains responsible (a) for using such systems only if they are evidence-based, and (b) for providing appropriate information to the patient that includes necessarily a risk/benefit appraisal for these systems; if the patient consents on the basis of that information, the essential legal requirements for assuming good medical practice are fulfilled.

In the clinical research context, evidence on the use of experimental self-learning AI applications is under investigation by definition; therefore, the above model needs to be reconsidered since we have to deal with an essential element of uncertainty that may entail risks for the volunteers' health. Here, we propose an analogy between the AI application's uncertainty and the uncertainty deriving from the use of experimental molecules in interventional clinical studies. We may assume that the levels of potential risks are similar. Guarantees for both acts' suitability remain, on the one hand, the successful results that pre-clinical trials demonstrate and, on the other, the information provided to the clinical trial's volunteers for the use of such experimental methods.

Under this view, we can conclude that legally speaking at least, there is already a rationale framework for appraising the issue of medical liability, even when the use of self-learning AI systems cannot be equated to that of conventional medical instruments, where usually no "opaque" characteristics escaping from the physician's direct control exist.

Funding: This research received no external funding.

Acknowledgments: I would like to thank G. Yannopoulos, A. Varveris and my postgraduate students at the Law School of the University of Athens for our fruitful discussions on the topic that inspired me to develop my arguments substantially.

Conflicts of Interest: The author declares no conflict of interest.

References

1. Oliveira, A.L. Biotechnology, Big Data and Artificial Intelligence. *Biotechnol. J.* **2019**, *14*. [CrossRef] [PubMed]
2. Sahner, D.; Spellmeyer, D.C. Artificial Intelligence: Emerging Applications in Biotechnology and Pharma. In *Biotechnology Entrepreneurship: Leading, Managing, and Commercializing Innovative Technologies*; Academic Press: Cambridge, MA, USA, 2020; pp. 399–417. [CrossRef]
3. Weiss, J.; Natarajan, S.; Paissig, P.; McCarthy, C.; Page, D. Machine learning for personalized medicine: Predicting primary MI from electronic medical records. *AI Mag.* **2012**, *33*, 33–45.

4. Institute of Electrical and Electronics Engineers. Ethically Aligned Design: A Vision for Prioritizing Human Well-being with Autonomous and Intelligent Systems. Version 2. 2017. Available online: https://standards.ieee.org/content/dam/ieee-standards/standards/web/documents/other/ead_v2.pdf (accessed on 1 July 2021).
5. EU Council. Council Conclusions on Personalised Medicine for Patients. Available online: https://eur-lex.europa.eu/legal-content/EN/TXT/PDF/?uri=OJ:C:2015:421:FULL&from=EN (accessed on 1 July 2021).
6. National Institutes of Health, The All of US Research Program. Available online: https://allofus.nih.gov/ (accessed on 1 July 2021).
7. National Research Council for the National Academies. Toward Precision Medicine: Building a Knowledge Network for Biomedical Research and a New Taxonomy of Disease. Available online: https://www.plengegen.com/wpcontent/uploads/4_Toward-Precision-Medicine.pdf (accessed on 1 July 2021).
8. Simitis, S. Die informationelle Selbstbestimmung–Grundbedingung einer verfassungskonformen Informationsordnung. *Neue Juristische Wochenschrift* **1984**, *37*, 398–405.
9. Elger, B.S.; Caplan, A.L. Consent and Anonymization in Research Involving Biobanks. *EMBO Rep.* **2006**, *7*, 663–666. [CrossRef] [PubMed]
10. Townend, D. Conclusion: Harmonization in genomic and health data sharing for research: An impossible dream? *Hum. Genet.* **2018**, *137*, 657–664. [CrossRef] [PubMed]
11. Ordish, J.; Murfet, H.; Mitchell, C.; Hall, A. Black Box Medicine and Transparency: Interpretability by Design Framework. *PHG Foundation*. 2020. Available online: https://www.phgfoundation.org/documents/black-box-interpetability-framework.pdf (accessed on 1 July 2021).
12. Wanerman, R.E.; Javitt, G.H.; Shah, A.B. Artificial Intelligence in Biotechnology: A Framework for Commercialization. In *Biotechnology Entrepreneurship: Leading, Managing, and Commercializing Innovative Technologies*; Shimasaki, C., Ed.; Academic Press: Cambridge, MA, USA, 2020; pp. 419–427. [CrossRef]
13. Ordish, J.; Brigden, T.; Hall, A. Black Box Medicine and Transparency: The Ethics of Transparency and Explanation. *PHG Foundation*. 2020. Available online: https://www.phgfoundation.org/documents/black-box-ethics-transparency-explanation.pdf (accessed on 1 July 2021).
14. Sherer, M.U. Regulating Artificial Intelligence Systems: Risks, Challenges, Competencies, and Strategies. *Harvard J. Law Technol.* **2016**, *29*, 353–400. [CrossRef]
15. Beauchamp, T.L.; Childress, J.F. *Principles of Biomedical Ethics*, 8th ed.; Oxford U.P.: Oxford, UK, 2019.
16. Nys, H. *Report on Medical Liability in Council of Europe Member States*; European Committee on Legal Co-Operation, Council of Europe: Strasbourg, France, 2005; Available online: https://rm.coe.int/1680700281 (accessed on 1 July 2021).

BioTech

MDPI

Review

Review of the Oscillation of Research Regulations for Bioethics in the Republic of Korea: Comparison with Japan

Seung-Hyo Hyeon [1], Juyoung An [2], Hwa-Shin Ryoo [3] and Min-Kyu Lee [4,*]

1 Department of Public Administration, Graduate School, Chungbuk National University, 1 Chungdae-ro, Seowon-gu, Cheongju-si 28644, Chungcheongbuk-do, Republic of Korea; po@chungbuk.ac.kr
2 Faculty of Policy Science, Ryukoku University, 67 Tsukamoto-cho, Fukakusa Fushimi-ku, Kyoto 612-8577, Japan; juyoung@policy.ryukoku.ac.jp
3 Law School, Chungbuk National University, 1 Chungdae-ro, Seowon-gu, Cheongju-si 28644, Chungcheongbuk-do, Republic of Korea; lawdeo@chungbuk.ac.kr
4 Department of Public Administration, College of Social Sciences, Chungbuk National University, Chungdae-ro, Seowon-gu, Cheongju-si 28644, Chungcheongbuk-do, Republic of Korea
* Correspondence: baroo@chungbuk.ac.kr; Tel.: +82-43-261-3613

Abstract: The Bioethics Act in the Republic of Korea has undergone great fluctuations akin to the pendulum of a clock. Since Professor Hwang's research ethics issue, domestic embryonic stem cell research has lost its vitality. This study argues that the Republic of Korea needs a reference point that does not waiver. This study examined the characteristics of life science- and ethics-related systems in the Republic of Korea and Japan. It also examined the pendulum-like policy changes in the Republic of Korea. It then compared the strengths and weaknesses between the Republic of Korea and Japan. Finally, we proposed a system improvement strategy for the development of bioethics research in Asian countries. In particular, this study argues that the advantages of Japan's slow but stable system should be introduced.

Keywords: Bioethics Act; Woo-seok Hwang; Shinya Yamanaka; stem cell

Key Contribution: This study conducted a comparative analysis of the fluctuating regulatory system in life science research in the Republic of Korea and the stable; albeit slower system in Japan. The study highlights the stability of Japan's system as an advantageous model that can be emulated by other Asian countries with similar cultural backgrounds.

Citation: Hyeon, S.-H.; An, J.; Ryoo, H.-S.; Lee, M.-K. Review of the Oscillation of Research Regulations for Bioethics in the Republic of Korea: Comparison with Japan. *BioTech* **2023**, *12*, 47. https://doi.org/10.3390/biotech12020047

Academic Editor: Vasiliki Mollaki

Received: 19 April 2023
Revised: 8 June 2023
Accepted: 9 June 2023
Published: 15 June 2023

1. Introduction

The Japanese government has been active in resolving ethical, legal, and social issues regarding human embryonic stem cell and embryonic research, in what has been classified as a research-friendly policy [1]. However, in Japan, there is also a view that government regulations could hinder various areas of human stem cell research. In particular, as an Asian country, Japan is criticized for its inability to make quick decisions, even though it has a centralized government. The development of stem cell research policies and regulations in Japan has involved lengthy periods of discussion, preparation, and review, taking five to ten years for each case. These regulatory delays have presented challenges to Japanese researchers, hindering their progress and competitiveness. Japan has had limited involvement in human embryonic stem cell (hESC) research, compared to other countries, due to regulatory delays and a lack of guidelines for the international distribution of hESC lines. Regulatory developments have also hindered Japan's participation in somatic cell nuclear transfer (SCNT) and germline differentiation studies, limiting researchers to animal studies [2].

Although Japan is a country without religious or political confrontation regarding bioethics, it has been criticized for slow decision making compared to other countries, such as Singapore, due to bureaucracy [3]. Japan's bioethics system is slow and stuffy. Japan has achieved a successful case of research with the development of groundbreaking technologies such as iPS (induced Pluripotent Stem) cells [4]. The use of iPS cell technology raises ethical and legal concerns regarding the informed consent of tissue donors, but it is considered to raise fewer concerns compared to the use of embryonic stem (ES) cells [5].

In contrast, the Republic of Korea's bioethics legislation has experienced great fluctuations akin to the swinging of a pendulum. The Bioethics Act passed by the National Assembly (the congress) in 2003 reflected the opinions of the government and members of the National Assembly, who insisted that life science and technology should be developed. In July 2002, after announcing that the Korean branch of Clonade was conducting research on human cloning, the Ministry of Health and Welfare of the Republic of Korea made a pre-announcement of the bioethics bill. The bill prohibited the creation of embryos for purposes other than pregnancy and allowed research on embryos older than five years after in vitro fertilization. At a public hearing held on October 9th of the same year, the scientific community generally agreed, but civic groups objected [6–8]. It was evaluated that the Korean government listened to the stance of civic groups in the early stage, but it sided with the scientific community in the final stage [6].

In 2004, Dr. Woo-seok Hwang succeeded in obtaining ES cells through SCNT technology in human eggs, and in 2005 he reported that he had created "customized cloned human embryonic stem cells". However, the journal Nature pointed out problems in relation to the research, such as the provision of eggs by female researchers and the review by the Hanyang University Clinical Ethics Committee in May 2004. The Korean Society for Bioethics sent an open inquiry requesting the sources of 242 eggs for Dr. Woo-seok Hwang's research [9].

After Woo-seok Hwang's research ethics issue was highlighted, the opinion that the social atmosphere should strengthen bioethics has gained strength. Since bioethics was emphasized in the revision of the Bioethics Act in 2018, ES cell research in the Republic of Korea lost vitality. In the revision of the Bioethics Act in 2020, requirements for acceptance were eased by reflecting the opinions of the scientific community again [9].

We compare the regulations related to life science research in the Republic of Korea and Japan. In particular, an issue arose in the Republic of Korea because its regulations were insufficient to ensure ethics and safety. We argue that the Republic of Korea needs to take advantage of Japan's slow but stable system, which we will introduce later. We also review the process that has hindered the development and discuss the desired direction for the development of life science research.

2. Review of Research-Related Systems for Life Sciences in Japan

2.1. *Background on the Establishment of Laws Related to Human Embryonic Stem Cells in Japan*

In 2000, the Japanese National Diet (the congress) enacted the "Act on the Regulation of Human Cloning Technology and Other Technologies" and prohibited human cloning. Regarding human embryonic research, in September 2001 the "Guidelines for the Establishment and Use of Human Embryonic Stem Cells" was announced, allowing human embryonic research under certain restrictions. In June 2004, the Bioethics Committee under the Ministry of Education, Culture, Sports, Science, and Technology allowed human embryonic research only for basic science research, but not for clinical application. In July 2006, the Bioethics Committee published the "Guidelines for Clinical Research Using Human Stem Cells" and banned clinical research [10].

2.2. *Research Trends and Achievements in Japan*

In Japan, there was research on introduced pluripotent stem (iPS) cells, which are relatively free from ethical issues related to the use of eggs and embryos [10]. In 2006, Shinya Yamanaka Shinya's team succeeded in generating iPS cells from mouse embryonic or adult fibroblasts [4]. In 2007, they succeeded in generating iPS cells from adult humans [11]. Yamanaka was awarded the Nobel Prize in Physiology or Medicine for this achievement in 2012. The Japanese government actively supports research and development using iPS cells. In June 2013, clinical trials using iPS cells were approved in Japan for the first time in the world [10]. In 2013, researchers in Japan succeeded in generating iPS cells from adults using a combination of plasmids encoding OCT3/4, SOX2, KLF4, L-MYC, LIN28, and shRNA for TP53, which are easily accessible. It is expected that making iPS cells from less invasive tissues would facilitate disease treatment [12].

2.3. *Japan's Slow but Stable System for Life Science Research*

In May 2014, Japan renamed the Council for Science and Technology (CST), which was established during the reorganization of the government organization, to the Council for Science, Technology and Innovation (CSTI), strengthening the regulatory function over science and technology policy [10]. The CSTI is chaired by the Prime Minister under the control of the Cabinet Office. In principle, the CSTI meets at least once a month. The characteristics of the CSTI are "strategic and timely", "comprehensive", and "voluntary". "Strategic and timely" means that a comprehensive strategy related to science and technology should be established to respond to national and social challenges in a timely manner. "Comprehensive" emphasizes the relationship between society and humans, such as ethical issues including humanities and social sciences. "Voluntary" means not only responding to the advice of the Prime Minister and others but also expressing one's own opinion. The prime minister, as well as related ministers, researchers, and lawmakers, actively participate in the CSTI meeting, and the detailed minutes of each meeting are made public. Materials referenced by members are made public on the Home Office website [13].

The Bioethics Professional Investigation Society (BPIS) was established under the CSTI. The BPIS reviews the guidelines for the establishment and use of human ES cells. The BPIS held its first meeting in 2001 and the 136th meeting on 27 Feb 2023. Fifteen meetings were held over a period of about one year and nine months to discuss how to amend guidelines allowing clinical research on human ES cells. At the 75th meeting held in September 2013, trends in gamete generation research were reviewed. At two meetings held in October and November of the same year, opinions on the latest research trends were presented by researchers. For about one year and six months from December 2013 to June 2015, whether to allow research on human ES cells was discussed (Table 1) [14,15].

Table 1. List of Bioethics Professional Investigation Society (BPIS) conferences related to human ES cell research.

No.	Date	Title
89–78	3 June 2015 (Heisei 27) - 20 December 2013 (Heisei 25)	▪ Regarding research on the production of human embryos by germ cells generated from human ES cells, etc. ▪ Regarding the status of the reexamination of relevant guidelines for human ES cells ▪ Regarding the review status of the revision of guidelines for human ES cells ▪ Other matters
77	27 November 2013 (Heisei 25)	▪ Listening to trends in germ cell generation research, such as ES cells: Atsuo Ogura (Director, Bioresource Center, Institute of Physical and Chemical Research) and one other person
76	18 October 2013 (Heisei 25)	▪ Listening to trends in germ cell generation research, such as ES cells: Takehiko Ogawa (Professor, Department of Molecular Biomedical Sciences, Department of Medicine, Yokohama City University)
75	20 September 2013 (Heisei 25)	▪ Regarding the trend in germ cell generation research, such as ES cells

Source: [14,15].

3. Review of Research-Related Systems for the Life Sciences in the Republic of Korea

3.1. *Review of Life Science Technology and Bioethics-Related Systems in the Republic of Korea*

The Ministry of Health and Welfare and the Ministry of Science and Technology each prepared a bill to enact the Bioethics Act. The Ministry of Health and Welfare announced the draft in December 2000 to collect the opinions of civic groups that were emphasizing bioethics [16] (pp. 45–47). In May 2001, the Ministry of Science and Technology produced the basic framework of the Basic Act on Bioethics, which was different from the Ministry of Health and Welfare's plan in that it prohibited the cloning of human embryos [6] (pp. 56–57). The announcement of this basic framework caused an organized backlash from the scientific community [16] (p. 56).

In 2001, the Citizen Science Center of the People's Solidarity for Participatory Democracy formed a network with religious, women's, environmental, and animal rights groups that judged that the bioethics bills would be difficult to pass due to opposition from scientists. On 19 July 2001, they officially launched the "joint campaign group for the prompt enactment of the Basic Act on Bioethics" [16] (pp. 56–60). In December 2002, the American company Clonade claimed to have created a cloned baby. At this time, members of the National Assembly submitted bills to ban human cloning [6] (pp. 61–62).

Eventually, the government's final draft was passed in the plenary session of the National Assembly on 29 December 2003. The government finally sided with the scientific community and put more emphasis on fostering biotechnology [6] (p. 45), [17] (p. 167).

In the process of legislating the Bioethics Act, opinions in favor of the ethics community were discussed first. However, it ended with the scientific community and the ethics community confronting each other. Due to this confrontation, various actors in the policy network contributed strongly by quickly adjusting their interests. However, by focusing only on solving the problem quickly, a debate within the scientific community about how to perform specific technology in accordance with bioethics was ignored. The fact that the process of thinking and discussing was omitted remains a problem.

3.2. *Discussions on the Bioethics Act in the Republic of Korea*

3.2.1. Discussion of the Moral Status of the Human Embryo

The author of a law thesis divided a human embryo's status into personalism and impersonalism. They critiqued impersonalism from a personalist perspective, arguing that an embryo should be protected like a human since it can never transition from non-human to human [18,19].

It was also argued that a human embryo should be considered equal in moral status to an adult, even before being implanted in the womb. Thus, using cloned embryos for experimentation created through in vitro fertilization and SCNT was criticized as an act that undermines the dignity of human life. This argument advocated for the cessation of such experiments [20].

Human life extension has become a reality through medical advancements, but issues with organism cloning have emerged. It has been argued that treatment with adult stem cells poses minimal ethical concerns, while using ES cells raises ethical dilemmas due to harm inflicted on the embryo. Furthermore, considering the continuity and potential of life, there are no justifiable reasons to prioritize human life over embryonic life [21].

3.2.2. Discussion from a Feminist Perspective

The feminist point of view argued that the existing concept of life did not deviate from the patriarchal and male-centered point of view and that women's voices and experiences were ignored in biotechnology. [22].

Human eggs can be obtained only through a women's donation, as artificial production is not yet possible. However, the process of superovulation using ovulation injection can lead to physical discomfort and even life-threatening symptoms for women. Therefore, the argument highlights the importance of handling egg usage in biotechnology research with caution and respect for women's well-being [23].

The media's coverage of Woo-seok Hwang incident was criticized from a feminist perspective. The feminist media focused on human rights-based bioethics and criticized the nationalist approach that treated women's bodies as tools for life science. In contrast, the mainstream media prioritized a utilitarian discourse highlighting national interests and creating a divide between "advanced science" and "outdated ethics", and marginalizing women's perspectives [24].

3.2.3. Discussions from a Legal Perspective

The law governing life sciences and biotechnology was criticized for its broad and abstract provisions. The focus was on the use of oocytes, which are cells involved in oogenesis. Concerns were raised about the potential exploitation of oocyte donors by researchers. It was argued that women donating oocytes for medical or reproductive purposes should be afforded extra protections. Additionally, during the revision of the Bioethics Act, there were calls for provisions regulating stem cell research and cross-species transplantation [25].

The institutionalization of bioethics in the Republic of Korea was criticized as inadequate. It was argued that participation in bioethics discussions should extend beyond bioethicists, scientists, and lawyers to include scholars from other fields. Furthermore, it was emphasized that a rationalist model should be pursued to establish public ethics [26].

3.3. *Reinforcing Life Science Research Regulations after the Woo-seok Hwang Incident*

3.3.1. Research Misconduct by Woo-seok Hwang's Team

The "Woo-seok Hwang Incident" occurred after the enactment of the Bioethics Act [7]. In 2004, Dr. Woo-seok Hwang reported that his team had succeeded in obtaining ES cells through SCNT technology in human eggs. In 2005, he reported that he had created "customized cloned human embryonic stem cells" [8,27]. In a May 2004 special article in *Nature* revealed that eggs were provided by a doctoral student in Dr. Woo-seok Hwang's team and another female researcher. Researchers are inevitably vulnerable to pressure from research directors. Thus, it was believed that egg donation by the researchers was inappropriate [28]. After raising these issues, on 22 November 2005, MBC PD Notebook aired with the theme of "Suspicion of Woo-seok Hwang's myth" [27].

It was pointed out that Dr. Woo-Seok Hwang's team violated the guidelines prohibiting the creation of human embryos for research purposes while receiving eggs from female researchers. The Institutional Bioethics Board (IRB) of Hanyang University took responsibility for reviewing and approving the research protocol. Questions were also raised as to whether this was conducted properly. This pointed out that the IRB system and organization, which had left bioethics to the conscience of the researchers was also responsible [29].

3.3.2. Various Opinions after Woo-seok Hwang Incident

As a result of the apology for the incident, Deputy Prime Minister Myung Oh, who served as the Minister of Science and Technology, resigned and appointed Deputy Prime Minister Woo-shik Kim, while Kim acknowledged the need for human embryo cloning and stem cell research, saying, "First of all, the problem is that the focus is on performance, and then I think that the problem of research ethics, integrity, and insufficient verification systems have worked in combination". It became an issue in local elections in 2006, as well as the presidential election in 2007. The position of the Grand National Party candidate Myung-bak Lee, Uri Party, Democratic Party, and the People First Party were in the position to allow an exception for the purpose of treating rare and incurable diseases, while the position of the Democratic Labor Party candidate Young-gil Kwon was to ban it completely [9].

In the investigation into the Woo-seok Hwang incident, it was found that somatic ES cells could not be produced even after using about 2000 eggs [27]. Regarding this, in July 2006, a "Discussion on the Reevaluation of Somatic Cell Cloning Embryo Research" was held at Ewha Womans University, where stakeholders such as domestic stem cell researchers and bioethicists gathered and discussed. Discussions were focused on the issue of stem cells and the possibility of research on somatic cell cloning of embryos. At this forum, the bioethics community took the position that concerns about bioethics had increased after the incident. Participants expressed concerns that female eggs might be indiscriminately donated for somatic cell cloning. In particular, in Woo-seok Hwang's case, most egg donors were family members of patients with incurable diseases and 15 to 20% of them developed hyperovulation syndrome. Ra-geum Huh, a professor at Ewha Womans University, argued that this practice should be corrected [30]. Protestants, Catholics, women's groups, and civic groups opposed somatic ES cell research from the perspective of damaging human dignity [9].

In contrast, the position of embryo cloning researchers was that there was no need to reconsider the decision to allow somatic cell-cloning embryo research from two to three years ago. Hyeong-min Jeong, a professor at CHA University argued that only the Republic of Korea was regressing at a time when foreign scientists has started research on somatic ES cells. Professor Dong-wook Kim of Yonsei University also took the position that "now it is more important to discuss the scope of permission rather than whether or not to permit research". However, although some scientists agreed with the position of emphasizing bioethics, they were aware of the concern that human eggs should not be used indiscriminately. Professor Hyeong-min Jeong said that it was right to apply it to humans after conducting sufficient animal research. Professor Dong-wook Kim and Professor Yong-man Han of the Republic of Korea Institute of Science and Technology (KAIST) also said that bioethics education and publicity were necessary for researchers. It was the position that consciousness needed to be strengthened [30]. In a situation where the possibility of technological success was slim, there was a coexisting position that it was difficult to allow embryo cloning research without any safety measures (Table 2) [9].

Table 2. Conflicts of positions in the 2008 revision of the Bioethics Act.

Division	Expansion of Regulations	Reduction of Regulations
Participants	Protestants/Catholics, civic groups, women's groups, Democratic Labor Party	Life scientists, Woo-seok Hwang support group, Buddhists
Faith	Bioethics, prohibition of embryo research	Improve national competitiveness, permission to study embryos for research and therapeutic purposes
Policy preference	- Agree with the revision of the Bioethics Act - Residual embryo research and the production and research of somatic cell cloning of embryos are prohibited - Expansion of adult stem cell transplantation - Prohibition of xenogeneic nuclear transfer - Genetic testing is prohibited in principle	- Opposition to the revision of the Bioethics Act - Elimination of restrictions on the type of eggs used for research - Preparation of grounds for allowing oocyte donation for treatment and research purposes and compensation for actual expenses - Allow cross-species experiments - Withdrawal of free stem cell provision

Source: [9].

3.3.3. Revision of the Bioethics Act in 2008

In the midst of such conflicting opinions, an amendment to the Bioethics and Safety Act was passed by the National Assembly on 16 May 2008. This bill was a combination of the main contents of the Grand National Party lawmaker Jae-Wan Park and the government amendment bill. It was aimed at protecting the health of egg donors by conducting health examinations and limiting the frequency of egg collection [31].

The revision of the Bioethics Act in 2008 after the Woo-seok Hwang incident appeared to be strengthening the act. Regarding research on somatic cell cloning of embryos, which was an issue, the existing limited permission was maintained, while the range of eggs that could be used for research was limited, and the health protection of egg donors was further strengthened [8].

The revision of the Bioethics Act in 2008 ensured the safety of egg donors, expanded the scope of the prohibition on interspecies SCNT research, and established the Institutional Bioethics Review Committee to be set up in institutions that perform research on life science technology. Its purpose was self-regulation by implementing support for the regulation [9].

3.4. Deregulation to Promote Life Science Research

3.4.1. Opinions of the Scientific Community after the Revision of the Bioethics Act in 2008

Since the revision in 2008, the scientific community has consistently raised concerns that the scope of research allowed on gene therapy is too narrow [9]. The Ministry of Science and ICT (MSIT) jointly held the 9th Bio Economic Forum at the National Assembly with Yong-hyeon Shin, a member of the People's Party, and discussed the direction for revising the Bioethics Act. In that forum, experts identified three major problems with the Bioethics Act: positive regulation, a comprehensive prohibition that blocked both basic research and clinical trial research, and centralized regulation. In addition, there was an opinion that the procedure for obtaining research permission was very difficult [32].

Life science researchers have pointed out that the current Bioethics Act is blocking innovative research and development (R&D). Researchers agreed that "regulation by disease" of gene therapy (clinical) research should be abolished and that it was not reasonable to limit the content of embryonic research by law. Researchers agreed on the need to allow basic research, eliminate overlapping regulations, consider changes in technology and environment, and expand autonomy at research sites. In addition, opinions suggested that "differentiated regulation" was needed according to the research topics and degree of violation of bioethics, and that the National Bioethics Committee should cooperate with IRBs of private institutions to recognize management based on autonomy [33].

There seemed to be no major disagreement about amending the provisions of the law at the time that limited the diseases subject to research on somatic cell gene therapy. Instead, some called for a system to monitor and manage risks that may appear after gene therapy is implemented. So-ra Park, a Professor of Medicine at Inha University (physiology), said, "It is necessary for the scientific community to monitor themselves, educate and train themselves, and establish guidelines such as open research. It is also necessary to operate an Ethics Committee, and it is also necessary to open the discussions of the Ethics Committee to the outside world [34]".

Seung-joon Yoo, Director of the Republic of Korea Center for Bio-Economic Research, said, "For the clinical application of medical technology, it is necessary to allow the generation of embryos for research and research at the level of major countries (of research and development). In this case, it seems necessary to take strong penalty measures such as punitive damages [34]".

At the time, research on gene-related treatments and embryos was fundamentally blocked except for 22 specified rare and incurable diseases. Scientists saw these restrictions as excessive and demanded that they be lifted at the United Kingdom, United States and Japan levels. In particular, they insisted on changing from 'positive regulation', which specifies the names of diseases allowed and restricts all other cases, to 'negative regulation', which explicitly limits only those to be restricted. Even legal scholars and regulatory researchers are generally in agreement on this point [35].

There were also criticisms about the reality of having to go through multiple approvals and reviews as the review agencies and procedures overlapped. Professor Dong-ryul Lee criticized, "If you go through the Institutional Review Board (IRB) and the National Bioethics Committee (NBC), the deliberation continues for more than a year at most, and studies that have been abandoned because of this [35]".

3.4.2. Opinions of the Bioethics Community after the Revision of the Bioethics Act in 2008

In particular, the issue of embryonic research could be amplified into a controversy over bioethics when it coincides with the religious world's view of life. Professor Jae-woo Jeong of Catholic University (Dean of the Graduate School of Life Sciences) said,

"Creating embryos for research means creating weak human beings in need of protection and nurturing to be used as a research tool, and this cannot be tolerated. It is not a matter to be decided by majority vote [34]".

Instead of allowing research, it was pointed out that strict management is needed to secure human rights and research ethics in the process of obtaining and using embryos and reproductive cells. This was because there were continuous criticisms that the IRB was performing only perfunctorily [32].

Some suggested that sensitive ethical issues should be dealt with through public debate involving experts and citizens. Professor Hyeon-cheol Kim of Ewha Womans University Law School said, "The question of how far embryos will be allowed for research is inevitably a major issue of conflict", adding, "We need a public debate with citizen participation [24]". He also argued, "The bioethics law should be left as the basic law, and the research itself should be treated separately as an individual law [35]".

3.4.3. Revision of the Bioethics Act in 2020

Conditions for permitting research on gene therapy were partially reflected in the 2020 revision, and conditions for permitting gene therapy research were alleviated. However, revisions, such as obligatory review by the institutional committee for research plans, and so on, were made. This law was proposed to ease the requirements for permitting research on gene therapy so that more diverse research on gene therapy could be conducted in the Republic of Korea, not to supplement the risks that may occur due to the relaxation of the permitting standards with the institutional committee review system (Table 3) [9].

Table 3. Comparison of the Bioethics Act and its revisions.

Act	Main Contents	Regulation Level
2004 Enactment	Establishment of the Presidential Advisory Council on Science & Technology (PACST). Establishment of the Institutional Bioethics Review Board (IRB) at institutes with embryo research, gene banks, and gene therapy institutes. The implantation, maintenance, or birth of cloned embryos in the womb for the purpose of human cloning was prohibited. The production of embryos for purposes other than conception was prohibited. Somatic cell nuclear transfer for purposes other than research for the treatment of rare or incurable diseases, etc., was prohibited.	The permissible range of research was wide and the system to prevent deviance was insufficient.
2008 Revision	Mandatory health checkup for egg donors. The frequency of oocyte retrieval was limited. Somatic cell nuclear transfer between humans and animals was prohibited. The use of stem cell lines was permitted only for purposes such as research for diagnosis, prevention, and treatment of diseases.	The permissible range of research was narrow enough to discourage research.
2020 Revision	Relaxation of acceptance conditions for research on gene therapy.	The permissible range of research was wide and a system was in place to prevent deviance.

Source: [9].

4. Discussion

4.1. Comparison of Life Science Research Regulatory Policies in the Republic of Korea and Japan

Due to Japan's unique bureaucratic nature, participation of various actors in the policy-making process is not guaranteed. Decision making is not fast either. However, it is possible to make specific decisions with expertise through the participation of experts. Life science researchers, who can be called regulated subjects, can make predictions. It has the advantage of being able to provide possible and actionable guidelines.

In the Republic of Korea, from the beginning of the establishment of the Bioethics Act, has had conflicting characteristics with confrontation between the scientific community and the ethical community. Activities of government departments to secure regulatory authority have occurred. This characteristic has made policy makers interested in whether or not to allow research in relation to life science and technology regulation. However, progress has been hampered due to the lack of specific discussions on how to allow such research.

The excessive permissibility of research led to the Woo-seok Hwang incident. In 2008, due to strong demands from civil society, the regulation of the Bioethics Act was strengthened, resulting in a decline in research. After nearly ten years of excessive regulation, criticism from the scientific community intensified again and regulations were eased in 2020. In this way, the Republic of Korea's life science research regulations have fluctuated akin to a pendulum (Table 4) [15].

Table 4. Comparison of life science research regulatory policies in the Republic of Korea and Japan.

Division	Republic of Korea	Japan
Policy actors	The range of actors is wide and diverse with the participation of government, science, and ethics.	The government and experts are at the center, and civil society participation is weak.
Policy change	At first, the level of regulation was low, but after the Woo-seok Hwang incident, it fluctuated.	Regulatory change is slow.
Advantages	▪ The participation of a large number of actors has been guaranteed, and rapid decision making has been made amid conflicting issues.	▪ Able to make professional and specific decisions. ▪ It can provide predictable and actionable action guidelines for life science researchers.
Disadvantages	▪ Rationality and expertise in the process and content leading to the policy are somewhat lacking.	▪ Due to its bureaucratic nature, the participation of many is not guaranteed, and decision making is not fast.
Implications	▪ It is desirable to maintain the strengths of our system while embracing the strengths of the Japanese system. ▪ It is necessary to enable detailed decision making with expertise through in-depth discussions centered on the government and experts. ▪ Asian countries, in particular, need to introduce organizations such as Japan's BPIS, where government officials and scientists go through a deliberation process to improve life science research regulations.	

Source: [15].

4.2. Desired Direction of Life Sciences Regulatory Policies in Asia

The advantages of the network related to life science and bioethics in the Republic of Korea include the guaranteed participation of various actors and quick decision making. Therefore, for the development of life science- and bioethics-related systems and organizations in the Republic of Korea, it is necessary to accept Japan's strengths without losing the Republic of Korea's strengths. The Republic of Korea's Bioethics Act was enacted in a way that allowed too much research. As a result, life science researchers have deviated and the level of regulation of the Bioethics Act has increased, hindering research development.

By accepting the advantages of Japan's slow but stable system, researchers will not act in a way that undermines bioethics. Asian countries, in particular, need to introduce organizations such as Japan's BPIS, where government officials and scientists go through a deliberation process to improve life science research regulations.

In-depth discussions centered on the government and experts, which are Japan's strengths, could enable concrete decision making with expertise for the development of systems and organizations related to life science and bioethics in Asian countries. Sufficient issues should be discussed and data should be provided to whole communities. Through this, it is possible for life science researchers to recognize predictable and practicable action guidelines in research and to equip religious groups, women's groups, civic groups, bioethics groups, and others with expertise for activities and sufficient monitoring.

This process will ensure bioethics and safety in Asian countries and ultimately contribute to the development of life science research.

4.3. Futher Discussion and Future Work

The Republic of Korea's rapid decision making and Japan's slow but stable decision making system research regulations were compared. It was also argued that the Republic of Korea should accept the merits of Japan's decision-making system. However, it was a limitation that this paper only compared these two Asian countries.

It was difficult to precisely compare and analyze life science research achievements and their economic effects in the Republic of Korea and Japan. In the future, these two countries will need to actively conduct such research.

However, in the Republic of Korea, the prevailing opinion is that the Republic of Korea is far ahead of Japan in science and technology. The number of Nobel laureates in the field of science symbolizes the level of basic science and original technology. Japan has 24 Nobel Prize winners, but the Republic of Korea has none. It is a lamentation that there are winners from the neighboring country, but not from the Republic of Korea, which is also an Asian country [36,37].

Since this paper only compared the Republic of Korea and Japan, comparing life science policies in other Asian countries will be an important future research task. In particular, China is a country that should be examined.

The CRISPR-Cas9 genome editing system, derived from bacterial adaptive immune strategies, is a powerful tool for precise modification of the target genome in living cells, allowing control over functional genes with high accuracy [38]. However, due to its powerful nature, this tool might raise ethical concerns, such as the loss of human dignity. Furthermore, it has the potential to lead to catastrophic events, such as the spread of unintended mutations in the human gene pool.

For example, Chinese researcher He Jiankui, known for his claim of creating genetically edited babies, was found guilty of conducting illegal medical practices and sentenced to three years in prison. He and his collaborators were found to have forged ethical review documents and misled doctors into implanting gene-edited embryos [39]. Dr. He has been found guilty of forging approval documents and deceiving couples in a trial held in Shenzhen. He claimed to have prevented human immunodeficiency virus (HIV) infections in newborns through gene editing but was found to have misled both the subjects and medical authorities. Dr. He's controversial work resulted in the birth of twin girls and an undisclosed third genetically edited baby [40].

It will be an important task to quantitatively identify the relationship between life science and technology policy regulation and socioeconomic effects. After that, we will be able to discuss the socio-economic effects of expanding our system to other Asian countries.

Some conditions must precede the introduction of such a system in Asian countries. First, the authority of scientists should be secured so that an atmosphere in which the public and policy makers can accept scientists can be created. The second is to overcome the superiority of politics and administration over the field of science and technology.

Author Contributions: Conceptualization, M.-K.L.; methodology, S.-H.H.; investigation, S.-H.H. and J.A.; resources, S.-H.H.; writing—original draft preparation, S.-H.H. and J.A.; writing—review and editing, H.-S.R. and M.-K.L.; visualization, H.-S.R.; supervision, M.-K.L. and J.A.; project administration, H.-S.R.; funding acquisition, M.-K.L. All authors have read and agreed to the published version of the manuscript.

Funding: This work was supported by Chungbuk National University BK21 program (2021).

Institutional Review Board Statement: Ethical review and approval were waived for this study due to it not involving human or animal subjects.

Informed Consent Statement: Patient consent was waived due to the study not involving human subjects.

Data Availability Statement: This research did not generate or analyze any data.

Conflicts of Interest: The authors declare no conflict of interest. The funders had no role in the design of the study; in the collection, analyses, or interpretation of data; in the writing of the manuscript; or in the decision to publish the results.

References

1. Kato, K. The ethical and political discussions on stem cell research in Japan. In *Crossing Borders: Cultural, Religious and Political Differences Concerning Stem Cell Research*; A Global Approach; Bender, W.C., Hauskeller, C., Manzei, A., Eds.; Agenda Verlag: Münster, Germany, 2005; pp. 369–379.
2. Kawakami, M.; Sipp, D.; Kato, K. Regulatory impacts on stem cell research in Japan. *Cell Stem Cell* **2010**, *6*, 415–418. [CrossRef] [PubMed]
3. Colman, A. Stem cell research in Singapore. *Cell* **2008**, *132*, 519–521. [CrossRef] [PubMed]
4. Takahashi, K.; Yamanaka, S. Induction of Pluripotent Stem Cells from Mouse Embryonic and Adult Fibroblast Cultures by Defined Factors. *Cell* **2006**, *126*, 663–676. [CrossRef] [PubMed]
5. Mollaki, V. Ethical Challenges in Organoid Use. *BioTech* **2021**, *10*, 12. [CrossRef] [PubMed]
6. Kim, H. Korea's Bioethics Law Emphasizes Nurturing Biotechnology Over Ethics. *Korea Assoc. Policy Stud.* **2004**, *13*, 45–71.
7. Kim, I. A Study on the Dilemma between S&T Regulation and Promotion and the Policy Changes: Focused on Bioethics and Safety Act. Ph.D. Thesis, Sungkyunkwan University, Seoul, Republic of Korea, 2016.
8. Kim, I.; Park, H. Science & Technology Regulatory Policy Change and Policy Network Dynamics: A Case of 'Bioethics and Safety Act' Policy Process. *Korean J. Policy Anal. Eval.* **2017**, *27*, 155–197.
9. Hyeon, S. An Analysis on the Regulatory Policy Change of The Science and Technology: The Comparison of the Enactment and Revision Process of the Act of Bioethics and Biosafety Using Game Theory. Ph.D. Thesis, Chungbuk National University, Cheonju, Republic of Korea, 2023.
10. Lee, M.; Ryoo, H. A Study on Recent Policy and Legislation Trend of the Stem Cell/Regenerative Medicine in Japan. *Korean Soc. Law Med.* **2015**, *16*, 191–219.
11. Takahashi, K.; Tanabe, K.; Ohnuki, M.; Narita, M.; Ichisaka, T.; Tomoda, K.; Yamanaka, S. Induction of pluripotent stem cells from adult human fibroblasts by defined factors. *Cell* **2007**, *131*, 861–872. [CrossRef]
12. Okita, K.; Yamakawa, T.; Matsumura, Y.; Sato, Y.; Amano, N.; Watanabe, A.; Goshima, N.; Yamanaka, S. An efficient nonviral method to generate integration-free human-induced pluripotent stem cells from cord blood and peripheral blood cells. *Stem Cells* **2013**, *31*, 458–466. [CrossRef]
13. Cabinet Office, Council for Science, Technology and Innovation. Available online: https://www8.cao.go.jp/cstp/stmain.html (accessed on 28 February 2023).
14. Cabinet Office, the Bioethics Professional Investigation Society. Available online: https://www8.cao.go.jp/cstp/tyousakai/life/lmain.html (accessed on 28 February 2023).
15. Hyeon, S.; Kim, D.; Lee, M. Regulatory Policies for Life Science and Technology Crisis Management: The Comparison of Cases between Korea and Japan. *Crisisonomy* **2023**, *19*, 41–53.
16. Kim, B. A Study on the Biotechnology Watchdog Movement in South Korea. Ph.D. Thesis, Republic of Korea University, Seoul, Republic of Korea, 2011.
17. Kim, H. *Biotechnology and Politics*; Whistler: Seoul, Republic of Korea, 2005.
18. Hong, S. A Study on the Personality Status of the Human Embryo. *J. Korea Bioeth. Assoc.* **2002**, *3*, 16–32.
19. Hong, S. An Ethical Review of the Human Embryonic Stem Cell Research. *J. Ethics* **2005**, *60*, 71–91.
20. Chin, K. An Ethical Study on the Research Concerning the Cloning of Human Embryo. *East. West. Thoughts* **2009**, *7*, 13–38.
21. Kim, H. The Stem cell research and protection of human embryo. *Law Treatise* **2010**, *32*, 239–353.
22. Huh, K. Life from a Feminist Perspective. *J. Korea Bioeth. Assoc.* **2001**, *2*, 47–57.
23. Um, Y. Ethical considerations on the use of eggs in biotechnology research. *Korean Fem. Philos.* **2004**, *4*, 95–108.
24. Kim, M. Feminist bioethics marginalized in mainstream media coverage of Hwang Woo-suk incident. *Korean J. Commun. Stud.* **2006**, *50*, 171–198.
25. Jung, K. Comments on the Bioethics and Biosafety Act-NT and stem cell research. *Korean J. Fam. Law* **2005**, *19*, 7–33.
26. Kim, E. A Comparative Analysis of Government Ethics Committees in the US, Republic of Korea, and the UK on Public Ethics Related to Embryo Research. Science and Technology Policy Institute Policy Material. Available online: https://www.dbpia.co.kr/journal/articleDetail?nodeId=NODE06286361 (accessed on 5 November 2022).
27. Kim, I.; Park, H. Bioethics Issues and Science & Technology Regulation Policy Formation and Change: The Case of Enactment Process of "Bioethics & Biosafety Law". *Korea Assoc. Policy Stud.* **2011**, *20*, 111–150.
28. Koo, Y. Ethical Problems in Human Embryo Cloning Research by Woosuk Hwang's Team. *Philos. Real.* **2005**, *65*, 62–73.
29. Koo, Y. Analysis of Hwang Woo-seok and Prof. Mun Shin-yong's case of therapeutic human embryo cloning: From the aspect of life science research ethics. *J. Korea Bioeth. Assoc.* **2004**, *5*, 59–70.
30. Kyunghyang Shinmun. Available online: https://www.khan.co.kr/article/200607201828071 (accessed on 28 February 2023).
31. Doctors News. Available online: https://www.doctorsnews.co.kr/news/articleView.html?idxno=46995 (accessed on 28 February 2023).
32. Hankyong. Available online: https://www.hankyung.com/it/article/2017120778826 (accessed on 28 February 2023).

33. Korea Harald Business. Available online: http://heraldk.com/2017/12/06/%EA%B3%BC%ED%95%99%EA%B8%B0%EC%88%A0%EA%B3%84-%EC%83%9D%EB%AA%85%EA%B3%BC%ED%95%99-%EC%97%B0%EA%B5%AC%EB%82%B4%EC%9A%A9-%EB%B2%95%EB%A5%A0%EB%A1%9C-%EA%B7%9C%EC%A0%9C-%EB%A7%90%EC%95%84/ (accessed on 28 February 2023).
34. Hankyoreh. Available online: https://www.hani.co.kr/arti/science/science_general/825792.html (accessed on 4 June 2023).
35. Dong-A Science. Available online: https://www.dongascience.com/news.php?idx=20736 (accessed on 4 June 2023).
36. Asia Economics. Available online: https://www.asiae.co.kr/article/2021081509045811822 (accessed on 5 June 2023).
37. Maekyung Premium. Available online: https://www.mk.co.kr/premium/special-report/view/2020/09/29066/https://www.mk.co.kr/premium/special-report/view/2020/09/29066/ (accessed on 5 June 2023).
38. Tavakoli, K.; Pour-Aboughadareh, A.; Kianersi, F.; Poczai, P.; Etminan, A.; Shooshtari, L. Applications of CRISPR-Cas9 as an Advanced Genome Editing System in Life Sciences. *BioTech* **2021**, *10*, 14. [CrossRef] [PubMed]
39. Science. Available online: https://www.science.org/content/article/chinese-scientist-who-produced-genetically-altered-babies-sentenced-3-years-jail (accessed on 5 June 2023).
40. New York Times. Available online: https://www.nytimes.com/2019/12/30/business/china-scientist-genetic-baby-prison.html (accessed on 5 June 2023).

BioTech

Opinion

Treatment of Rheumatoid Arthritis with Gene Therapy Applications: Biosafety and Bioethical Considerations

Zinovia Tsitrouli [1], Maria-Anna Akritidou [1], Savvas Genitsaris [2] and Gijsbert van Willigen [3,*]

1 School of Humanities, Social Sciences and Economics, International Hellenic University, 57001 Thermi, Greece; ztsitrouli@ihu.edu.gr (Z.T.); makritidou@ihu.edu.gr (M.-A.A.)
2 Section of Ecology and Taxonomy, School of Biology, National and Kapodistrian University of Athens, Zografou Campus, 16784 Athens, Greece; genitsar@biol.uoa.gr
3 Leiden University Medical Center, Department of Health, Safety and the Environment, Leiden University, 9500 Leiden, The Netherlands
* Correspondence: G.van_Willigen@lumc.nl

Abstract: Rheumatoid Arthritis (RA) is an autoimmune and inflammatory disease that affects the synovium (lining that surrounds the joints), causing the immune system to attack its own healthy tissues. Treatment options, to the current day, have serious limitations and merely offer short-term alleviation to the pain. Using a theoretical exercise based on literature, a new potentially viable therapy has been proposed. The new therapy focusses on a long-term treatment of RA based on gene therapy, which is only active when inflammation of the joint occurs. This treatment will prevent side effects of systemic application of drugs. Furthermore, the benefits of this treatment for the patient from a socio-economic perspective has been discussed, focusing on the quality of life of the patent and lower costs for the society.

Keywords: rheumatoid arthritis; gene therapy; medical biosafety; environmental biosafety; adeno-associated virus; vector

Citation: Tsitrouli, Z.; Akritidou, M.-A.; Genitsaris, S.; Willigen, G.v. Treatment of Rheumatoid Arthritis with Gene Therapy Applications: Biosafety and Bioethical Considerations. *BioTech* **2021**, *10*, 11. https://doi.org/10.3390/biotech10030011

Academic Editor: Maestri Enrico

Received: 23 April 2021
Accepted: 22 June 2021
Published: 23 June 2021

1. Introduction

Rheumatoid arthritis (RA) is a long-term inflammatory and autoimmune disease that affects the synovium (lining that surrounds the joints), causing the immune system to attack its own healthy tissues. The process starts with the release of pro-inflammatory cytokines, especially tumor necrosis factor-α (TNFα) and Interleukin (IL-6 and IL-1), followed by the production of inflammatory cytokines in the joint (TNFα, IL-6, -15, -16, -17, -18, Interferon-γ (IFN-γ)). RA starts with painful swelling, which can lead, ultimately, to bone erosion and joint deformity [1]. Symptoms appear in smaller joints first (mainly in those that attach the fingers to the hands and the toes to the feet); as the disease progresses, symptoms tend to spread to bigger joints as well. In the plethora of cases, RA symptoms occur in the same joints on both sides of the body; a great number of patients with RA also experience symptoms that do not involve the joints, such as weight loss, fatigue, and weakness. It is not known why the immune system attacks healthy body tissue in RA, although a genetic component appears likely [2] and can increase the susceptibility to environmental factors that may trigger the disease.

Despite the improved understanding of RA pathophysiology over the past 20 years and the appearance of improved treatment options, severe RA can still cause physical disabilities, while therapy with most antirheumatic drugs, such as non-steroidal anti-inflammatory drugs (NSAIDS) and disease-modifying anti-rheumatic drugs (DMARDs) is palliative [3], alleviating inflammation but leaving the disease incurable, with some patients partially or not at all responding, short-term effectiveness [4], and unwanted associated systemic complications of immunosuppression [5]. Biological-based approaches have appeared as the most promising, using mainly monoclonal antibodies, recombinant forms of natural inhibitors, recombinant soluble TNF receptors, or anti-inflammatory cytokines, counteracting the released cytokines produced in the joint [3]. However, these therapies have serious limitations, such as high expenses, side-effects (i.e., nausea, low blood pressure, skin reactions, trouble breathing), and the requirement for repeated systemic injections [6].

The aim of this paper was to outline the steps that could lead to a successful gene therapy which would tackle the abovementioned limitations. Furthermore, potential biosafety concerns that may be linked to the proposed treatment have been identified and discussed. Furthermore, ethical dilemmas that could arise when administering the proposed therapy have been pinpointed.

2. A Potentially Viable Proposal

To overcome the limitations and difficulties of the present treatments, genetic therapies for RA offer the possibility of delivery of the therapeutic gene product to the disease site and, thus, prevent side effects by systemic injections or infusion, while enhancing efficacy and achieving local long-term expression, with endogenous production of high concentrations of the therapeutic agent. The overall goal for the treatment of patients with RA should not merely be alleviating the pain, but also achieving remission or at least low disease activity for all patients and preventing irreversible damage to the diseased joints. Since most, if not all, of the forms of RA result in the inflammation of the joint, and thus, share the process of inflammation, a gene therapy approach for RA, aiming either at inhibiting proinflammatory cytokines and/or overexpressing anti-inflammatory cytokines [7], could be promising. In this context, and given the fact that the overproduction of inflammatory cytokines by fibroblast-like synoviocytes (FLSs) is believed to play a pivotal role in the development and progression of RA [8], we have proposed a therapy that would overall suppress inflammation, by expressing anti-inflammatory cytokines (see Figure 1 for a schematic representation).

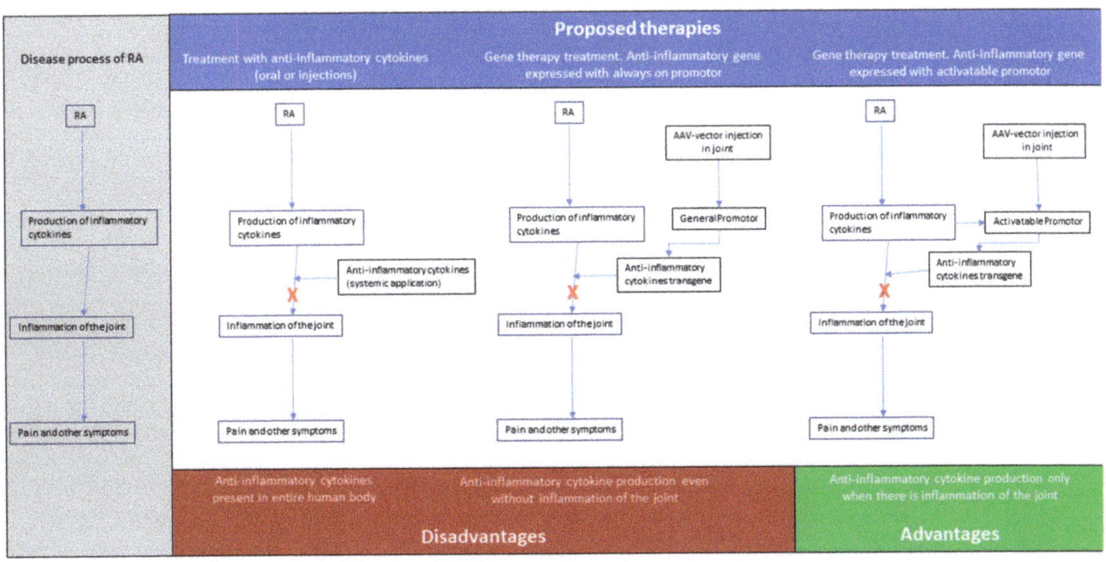

Figure 1. Schematic representation of a proposed treatment of Rheumatoid Arthritis (RA) with gene therapy applications.

Regarding the vectors of choice, the ideal vector should transfer a precise amount of genetic material into each target cell expressing the gene material, without causing toxicity. As a delivery method for the therapeutic gene, there are several choices available. The most obvious methods are plasmids carrying the therapeutic gene or viral vectors. Because a long time expression of the transgene is needed for treatment of RA, plasmid vectors are not an option, because they are known for only a short-term expression and often only suboptimal expression of the transgene, although there have been improvements made to overcome these difficulties [9]. Therefore, only viral vectors can be used to transfer the transgene. Viral vectors that will integrate into the genome or stay as an endosomal plasmid present in the cell have a preference. This limits the choice of vectors to viral vectors, such as retro- and lentiviral vectors and AAV [10]. Because the retro- and lentiviral vectors are known for insertional mutagenesis [11], the preferred vector is AAV. In the absence of a helper virus or genotoxic factors, AAV DNA can either integrate into the host genome at a predefined spot (chromosome 19) or persist in an episomal form [12]. This makes AAV the vector of choice, because it fulfils all the criteria needed for an effective therapy for RA.

Adeno-associated virus (AAV) is preferred, because it is safe, effective, and less immunogenic than other vectors. Genetic modifications of human cells can be done either by an ex vivo or in vivo approach. Both methods are possible in RA treatment and have been used in different studies [13]. The fact that modified cells were cleared shortly after intra-articular injection was the main disadvantage in several ex vivo studies [14], thus making in vivo delivery a preferable approach for RA treatment. AAV is commonly used in in vivo studies where the goal is long-term expression, as in RA, because this lowers the frequency of treatment administrations [15]. Specifically, for in vivo gene delivery to the joint by direct intra-articular injection, AAV is safer than other unsuitable-for-clinical-translation vectors that are inflammatory, immunogenic [14], and can provide more extended periods of transgene expression than non-viral vectors [16].

When it comes to the promoter, a promotor of the pro-inflammatory gene that is active during the onset of an inflammatory response in the joint is preferred, since in this way, expression of the therapeutic gene can be achieved locally and specifically when RA-related inflammation arises [17]. For this purpose, promotors of TNFα, IL-1α, Cyclooxygenase-2 (Cox2), or nuclear factor kappa-light-chain-enhancer of activated B cells (NF-kB) would all be suitable to regulate expression of the therapeutic gene, as they are upregulated during inflammation. Finally, the therapeutic gene needs to be an anti-inflammatory agent that will alleviate the phenomenon of inflammation in the joints. There are numerous choices, but IL-4 [18] and IFN-β [19] are among the best candidates due to their anti-inflammatory functions.

3. Biosafety Considerations

Using viral vector systems for gene therapy as treatment options for several diseases is promising, but viral vector delivery remains risky and is still under study to ensure safety and efficacy during clinical trials. The safety of a gene therapeutic agent can be viewed from different angles. First is the risk for the laboratory worker and medical staff, second is the risk from a medical point of view, i.e., risk for the patient, and third is the risk for the environment. This third category also includes the risk for the patients' offspring. However, and especially for AAV, the vector of choice in our case, safety concerns are limited, since AAV does not cause any known disease [20]. Furthermore, the risk for the laboratory worker and the medical staff will be negligible when standard hospital hygienic measures are in place. These will prevent contact with the AAV-particles during normal handling and during incidents. Most concerns are related to the preexisting immunity to human AAV vectors and the related integration into the host genome, which, if it happens at all, is random and could lead to accidental activation or inhibition of endogenous gene expression [21]. In this sense, medical and environmental risks are not related strictly to AAV and are considered, as already mentioned, rather safe, but mostly in relation to other parameters of the approach.

3.1. *Biosafety for Lab and Medical Staff*

In terms of laboratory precautions, AAVs are classified as Risk Group 1 [22]. Viral manipulation should be performed in a Biosafety Laboratory 1, with adequate biohazard signs, while manipulation in the same Biosafety Cabinet with other materials must be avoided to prevent contamination of the gene therapeutic agents. As already mentioned, the risk of an AAV vector for lab and medical staff is negligible. Health employees work using the standard hospital hygiene measures. These measures would prevent any direct contact with patient material, even if shedding occurred. During the injection of the AAV vector into the joint, the medical staff should wear personal protective equipment to prevent any exposure to the gene therapeutic agent. Furthermore, for the people working in the diagnostics labs, the risk of working with materials of the patient injected with the AAV is negligible. Normal working procedures in diagnostic labs are already sufficient to prevent unwanted exposure to AAV, even if shedding were to occur. The largest risk is during preparation of the syringe for injecting the AAV gene therapeutics. This procedure should be performed in a Biological Safety Cabinet Class 2 for sterile preparation, preventing unwanted exposure of the worker. In case of spills, sodium hypochlorite or quaternary ammonium compound are the recommended disinfectants, while alcohol is not an effective disinfectant against non- enveloped viruses, such as AAV [23]. Infection materials should also be decontaminated prior to disposal, generally using an autoclave, at 121 °C for 30–45 min [24].

3.2. Medical Risks

Before starting the clinical study, one of the very first questions that arises is which should be the joint in which the intra-articular injections will start. Since up to 75% of RA patients experience symptoms in the wrist [25], someone could suggest that this should be the joint of choice for gene therapy trials. However, studies have identified that injections into the wrist joint could result in complications [26]. Risk of septic arthritis following the injection of bacteria from the skin's surface can enter the joint directly with insertion of the needle, while the synovium has little ability to protect itself from infection. Misplaced injections could potentially cause tendon rupture or even, in rare cases, nerve damage [27]. An infection of, or adverse events in, the synovial tissue in the wrist is hard to treat. The synovial tissue cannot be removed without causing any damage to the joint. When the wrist joint is damaged, the only option is to fixate it in an immobile position, which will hamper the function of the wrist and the mobility of the person. Replacement of the wrist joint while keeping the function of the joint is impossible. Because of this, we propose that the wrist joint is not the best option for starting gene therapy. Another option is the metacarpophalangeal joint (MCP) or knuckle. This is a small joint and one of the first joints affected by RA. From this joint, the synovial tissue can be easily removed, and if the joint is damaged, it can be easily replaced by an implant. This joint replacement would not affect the joint function. Thus, from a medical point of view, the MCP, as a joint for testing gene therapy, would be the joint of choice, because serious adverse events in the joint do not result in loss of function of the joint.

One of the potential benefits of gene therapy is that the therapy would be long lasting, and no repeated injections or oral medication would be needed. This decreases the burden for the patient (see also below in the "Bioethical considerations" section). For AAV, it has been shown that the expression of the transgene can be long lasting in different tissues. As already mentioned before, AAV is not only present in the episomal in target cells, but it also integrates into the genome. This integration gives rise to the long-lasting expression of the transgene. Studies have revealed a transgene expression using AAV vectors that lasts up to 10 years [28], making repeated injection unnecessary. Furthermore, the episomal AAV was shown to exist over a long period of time, with the expression of the transgene lasting up to six months in the liver [29]. For the first injection of AAV, a screen for pre-existing immunity can be performed. However, if repeated injections are necessary, an immune response against the therapeutic agent can be an issue. Several studies have already shown that suppression of the immune response can be successful when repeated injections are necessary [29]. Based on this, a gene therapy based on AAV would prevent daily medication, an additional burden of the RA patient.

3.3. Environmental Risks

AAV vector genomes remain episomal in target cells and are highly unlikely to integrate. Shedding from the host could only happen in rare cases, when the AAV integrates into the host cell chromosome, if both the adenovirus (or some other helper virus) and wild-type AAV are present. When it comes to the survival of this virus on surfaces, in the case of potential spills, sodium hypochlorite or a quaternary ammonium compound could be used to disinfect the area, since they are the recommended disinfectants against AAV [23]. Specifically concerning the animals used during the clinical trials of the proposed therapy and the potential risk caused by AAV, we should mention that, in some animal models, the integration of recombinant AAV has been associated with an increased incidence of tumor formation. However, this association has not been observed to occur in humans [30]. AAV vectors can shed from the patient into the environment, but also to the gonads. Both shedding events could give rise to unwanted effects of the treatment. Shedding to the environment can give rise to unwanted contact to the AAV particles of non-patient humans. Shedding to the gonads can result in germline transmission of the transgene. As already mentioned, a joint is closed by the synovial tissue that keeps fluid in the joint. When injecting the AAV vector into the joint, the synovial tissue would also protect the human body from the injected AAV vector. If injected correctly, no shedding from the joint would be possible. In case of damage of the synovial tissue, however, there will be shedding from the joint. Due to this, the AAV particles can become systemic. The biggest risk is the transduction of gonadal cells and the subsequent risk of germ line transmission. However, in studies where AAV was injected directly into the male gonads, no transduction of sperm cells was observed. The AAV preferred other cells in the gonadal tissue, such as the Leydig cells [31]. Long-term transduction of sperm cell-producing tissue was also not observed, and after a few cycles of sperm production, AAV in sperm cells was not detected [32]. Other gonadal tissues, not involved in spermatogenesis, could be positive for AAV over a longer period [32]. From this, it can be concluded that shedding has only a minor risk for germ line transmission and can be easily prevented.

4. Bioethical Considerations

Ethical questions arising generally in gene therapy, and specifically in our case, are not new to the debate, yet they are fundamental. Regarding the administration of the treatment, ethical concerns are of relevance, especially when it comes to the specific joint which should be chosen. Bearing in mind the complications that could result from a potential administration to the wrist, already mentioned under Medical Risks, we argue against such an option, due to the nature of the joint and the difficulty of treatment, in case of potential damage during wrong administration. We would opt for other joints, where this risk is rather limited and serious adverse events in these joints would not result in loss of function.

Rheumatoid arthritis, as mentioned above, can affect patients from different ages, but the disease usually has later-in-the-life onset symptoms, which mostly appear after the age of 35–50 [33]. This means that potential volunteers will, in the plethora of cases, belong in the middle-age and above age group. With most of them already having received other therapies (which most probably have failed), this could also mean that their symptoms are not light anymore. The first question that should be answered is how we will make our choice of volunteers. Should we choose people that have already received (inadequate) therapy or others, at earlier stages of the disease, with no prior experience with treatments? Especially given that, according to several published studies, older RA patients, at later stages of the disease, most probably receive less aggressive treatments than younger RA patients, even though they experience the same or more severe symptoms [34].

In the same context, we should not ignore questions regarding informed consent and its specific content, especially in cases of juvenile arthritis, where minors are not able to consent themselves. In our proposed treatment, risk is rather low, since AAV is a rather safe vector, which cannot have detrimental health effects, and in any case, the benefits from therapy outweigh the potential risk. However, as it happens generally with informed consent in minors, the rule should be that, besides their guardian's or representative's consent, their opinion must also be taken into consideration. It is important to opt for earlier intervention, given the severe complications and pain that come as a result when the disease progresses; thus, an early intervention would be more beneficial, rather than starting treatment when minors would have reached the legal age of consent. Taking into consideration the above, patients in each stage of the disease should participate equally in the study, since there is no just way in which we can weigh the costs and benefits between different stages and the respective level of pain, which should be avoided at all costs.

Moreover, RA is known to affect women more than men [35], and the question that subsequently arises is how this fact can potentially affect our chosen group of volunteers. It is probable that the percentage of women participating in the gene therapy trial will be bigger, since women suffer from RA in a higher ratio. However, can we say that, in the name of equality among patients, we would opt for including men and women in a ratio 1:1, or would such an option not serve equality among patients, since it would take into consideration criteria not directly connected to the level of pain and the severity of the symptoms? This difficult question correlates also with the criteria that would be used for inclusion/exclusion of the patients to ensure fairness in the selection procedure. We should not forget, at this point, socioeconomic parameters. It is true that people with higher economic feasibility would be informed easier, would more easily afford the related costs, and they would, thus, more easily participate in the trial.

Finally, in the case that treatment fails, and pain persists, there would be more dilemmas arising. More choices would have to be made in such a case, with regards to who would receive treatment: those that previously received it, but it failed, or those that are new in the trial? The same dilemma could arise in the case when patients have been treated on one side, but the joint in the opposite side also starts to present RA symptoms. Equality and justice among patients should be the main principles guiding our approach in all the aforementioned different situations, but the severity of the pain and the stage of the disease should play the most important role in our final decision.

5. Conclusions

Gene therapy can be a viable alternative to treat Rheumatoid Arthritis, a long-term inflammatory disease, alleviate the patients' pain, and tackle the limitations of current treatments. The course of action we proposed here comes with biosafety concerns and bioethical dilemmas, which, should they arise, should be addressed with systematic approaches and guidelines. In particular, lab and medical stuff biosafety risks could be managed with the normal laboratory precautions, medical risks for the patient could be avoided if the suitable joint is chosen for the administration of the treatment, and environmental risks were not considered a point of concern in our proposed treatment, due to the characteristics of our vector of choice and the suggested solutions. Finally, the main ethical dilemmas to be considered included the choice of the joint for administrating the treatment, the choice of volunteers for the clinical trials, and the options of the patient, in case treatment fails. Equality among patients should guide the course of action in all the different situations that may accrue, but the severity of the pain and the stage of the disease should play the most important role in final decisions.

Author Contributions: Conceptualization, G.v.W. and S.G.; methodology, G.v.W., Z.T. and M.-A.A.; formal analysis, Z.T. and M.-A.A.; investigation, Z.T. and M.-A.A.; resources, S.G.; writing—original draft preparation, Z.T. and G.v.W.; writing—review and editing, all authors; visualization, Z.T. and G.v.W.; supervision, G.v.W.; project administration, S.G.; funding acquisition, S.G. All authors have read and agreed to the published version of the manuscript.

Funding: This work was developed during the Project with code 2018-1-EL01-KA203-047726 and title "Biosafety in Biotechnology: Connecting Academia with the Bioeconomy Market", implemented in the framework of Key Action 2 Strategic Partnerships in the fields of Education and Training of the Erasmus + program.

Institutional Review Board Statement: Not applicable.

Informed Consent Statement: Not applicable.

Data Availability Statement: Not applicable.

Acknowledgments: The European Commission's support for the production of this publication does not constitute an endorsement of the contents, which reflects the views only of the authors, and the Commission cannot be held responsible for any use which may be made of the information contained therein.

Conflicts of Interest: The Authors declare no conflict of interest.

References

1. Nakajima, A. Application of Cellular Gene Therapy for Rheumatoid Arthritis. *Mod. Rheumatol.* **2006**, *16*, 269–275. [CrossRef]
2. Nemtsova, M.V.; Zaletaev, D.V.; Bure, I.V.; Mikhaylenko, D.S.; Kuznetsova, E.B.; Alekseeva, E.A.; Beloukhova, M.I.; Deviatkin, A.A.; Lukashev, A.N.; Zamyatnin, A.A. Epigenetic Changes in the Pathogenesis of Rheumatoid Arthritis. *Front. Genet.* **2019**, *10*. [CrossRef]
3. Gouze, E.; Ghivizzani, S.C.; Robbins, P.D.; Evans, C.H. Gene Therapy for Rheumatoid Arthritis. *Curr. Rheumatol. Rep.* **2001**, *3*, 79–85. [CrossRef] [PubMed]
4. Johns Hopkins Arthritis Center. *Rheumatoid Arthritis Treatment Options*; Johns Hopkins Arthritis Center: Baltimore, MD, USA. Available online: https://www.hopkinsarthritis.org/?s=Rheumatoid+Arthritis+Treatment+Options (accessed on 8 March 2021).
5. Young, E.; Gould, D.; Hart, S. Toward Gene Therapy in Rheumatoid Arthritis. *Expert Rev. Precis. Med. Drug Dev.* **2020**, *5*, 123–133. [CrossRef]
6. Woods, J.; Sitabkhan, Y.; Koch, A. Gene Therapy for Rheumatoid Arthritis: Recent Advances. *Curr. Gene Ther.* **2008**, *8*, 24–41. [CrossRef] [PubMed]
7. Deviatkin, A.A.; Vakulenko, Y.A.; Akhmadishina, L.V.; Tarasov, V.V.; Beloukhova, M.I.; Zamyatnin, A.A., Jr.; Lukashev, A.N. Emerging Concepts and Challenges in Rheumatoid Arthritis Gene Therapy. *Biomedicines* **2020**, *8*, 9. [CrossRef]
8. Bartok, B.; Firestein, G.S. Fibroblast-like Synoviocytes: Key Effector Cells in Rheumatoid Arthritis. *Immunol. Rev.* **2009**, *233*, 233–255. [CrossRef]
9. Hardee, C.L.; Arévalo-Soliz, L.M.; Hornstein, B.D.; Zechiedrich, L. Advances in Non-Viral DNA Vectors for Gene Therapy. *Genes* **2017**, *8*, 65. [CrossRef]
10. McCarthy, H.O.; Wang, Y.; Mangipudi, S.S.; Hatefi, A. Advances with the Use of Bio-Inspired Vectors towards Creation of Artificial Viruses. *Expert Opin. Drug Deliv.* **2010**, *7*, 497–512. [CrossRef]
11. Cavazza, A.; Moiani, A.; Mavilio, F. Mechanisms of Retroviral Integration and Mutagenesis. *Hum. Gene Ther.* **2013**, *24*, 119–131. [CrossRef] [PubMed]
12. Deyle, D.R.; Russell, D.W. Adeno-Associated Virus Vector Integration. *Curr. Opin. Mol. Ther.* **2009**, *11*, 442–447.
13. Adriaansen, J.; Vervoordeldonk, M.J.B.M.; Tak, P.P. Gene Therapy as a Therapeutic Approach for the Treatment of Rheumatoid Arthritis: Innovative Vectors and Therapeutic Genes. *Rheumatology* **2006**, *45*, 656–668. [CrossRef]
14. Evans, C.H.; Ghivizzani, S.C.; Robbins, P.D. Gene Delivery to Joints by Intra-Articular Injection. *Hum. Gene Ther.* **2018**, *29*, 2–14. [CrossRef]
15. Canver, M.C. Evaluation of the Clinical Success of Ex Vivo and In Vivo Gene Therapy. *J. Young Investig.* **2009**, *19*, 1–10.
16. Evans, C.H.; Ghivizzani, S.C.; Robbins, P.D. Arthritis Gene Therapy Is Becoming a Reality. *Nat. Rev. Rheumatol.* **2018**, *14*, 381–382. [CrossRef]
17. Van de Loo, F.A. Inflammation-Responsive Promoters for Fine-Tuned Gene Therapy in Rheumatoid Arthritis. *Curr. Opin. Mol. Ther.* **2004**, *6*, 537–545.
18. Cottard, V.; Mulleman, D.; Bouille, P.; Mezzina, M.; Boissier, M.-C.; Bessis, N. Adeno-Associated Virus-Mediated Delivery of IL-4 Prevents Collagen-Induced Arthritis. *Gene Ther.* **2000**, *7*, 1930–1939. [CrossRef] [PubMed]
19. Van Holten, J.; Reedquist, K.; Sattonet-Roche, P.; Smeets, T.J.; Plater-Zyberk, C.; Vervoordeldonk, M.J.; Tak, P.P. Treatment with Recombinant Interferon-Beta Reduces Inflammation and Slows Cartilage Destruction in the Collagen-Induced Arthritis Model of Rheumatoid Arthritis. *Arthritis Res. Ther.* **2004**, *6*, R239–R249. [CrossRef] [PubMed]
20. Naso, M.F.; Tomkowicz, B.; Perry, W.L.; Strohl, W.R. Adeno-Associated Virus (AAV) as a Vector for Gene Therapy. *BioDrugs* **2017**, *31*, 317–334. [CrossRef] [PubMed]
21. Ghosh, S.; Brown, A.M.; Jenkins, C.; Campbell, K. Viral Vector Systems for Gene Therapy: A Comprehensive Literature Review of Progress and Biosafety Challenges. *Appl. Biosaf.* **2020**, *25*, 7–18. [CrossRef]
22. NIH Office of Science Policy. *NIH Guidelines for Research Involving Recombinant or Synthetic Nucleic Acid Molecules (NIH Guidelines)*; Office of Science Policy: Bethesda, MD, USA, 2019.
23. Gene Therapy and Infection Control. Available online: https://www.infectiousdiseaseadvisor.Com/home/decision-support-in-medicine/hospital-infection-control/gene-therapy-and-infection-control/ (accessed on 15 March 2021).
24. Adeno-Associated (AAV) Safety. Available online: https://sct.uab.cat/upv/content/adeno-associated-aav-safety (accessed on 15 March 2021).

25. Ilan, D.I.; Rettig, M.E. Rheumatoid Arthritis of the Wrist. *Bull. NYU Hosp. Jt. Dis.* **2003**, *61*, 179–185.
26. Farooq, M.A.; Devitt, A.T. Perceived Efficacy and Risks of Infection Following Intra-Articular Injections: A Survey of Orthopaedic Surgeons. *Ir. J. Med. Sci.* **2005**, *174*, 26–32. [CrossRef]
27. Cheng, J.; Abdi, S. Complications of Joint, Tendon, and Muscle Injections. *Tech. Reg. Anesth. Pain Manag.* **2007**, *11*, 141–147. [CrossRef]
28. Buchlis, G.; Podsakoff, G.M.; Radu, A.; Hawk, S.M.; Flake, A.W.; Mingozzi, F.; High, K.A. Factor IX Expression in Skeletal Muscle of a Severe Hemophilia B Patient 10 Years after AAV-Mediated Gene Transfer. *Blood* **2012**, *119*, 3038–3041. [CrossRef]
29. Goswami, R.; Subramanian, G.; Silayeva, L.; Newkirk, I.; Doctor, D.; Chawla, K.; Chattopadhyay, S.; Chandra, D.; Chilukuri, N.; Betapudi, V. Gene Therapy Leaves a Vicious Cycle. *Front. Oncol.* **2019**, *9*. [CrossRef] [PubMed]
30. Collins, D.E.; Reuter, J.D.; Rush, H.G.; Villano, J.S. Viral Vector Biosafety in Laboratory Animal Research. *Comp. Med.* **2017**, *67*, 215–221.
31. Rajasekaran, S.; Thatte, J.; Periasamy, J.; Javali, A.; Jayaram, M.; Sen, D.; Krishnagopal, A.; Jayandharan, G.R.; Sambasivan, R. Infectivity of Adeno-Associated Virus Serotypes in Mouse Testis. *BMC Biotechnol.* **2018**, *18*. [CrossRef] [PubMed]
32. Schuettrumpf, J.; Liu, J.-H.; Couto, L.B.; Addya, K.; Leonard, D.G.B.; Zhen, Z.; Sommer, J.; Arruda, V.R. Corrigendum to "Inadvertent Germline Transmission of AAV2 Vector: Findings in a Rabbit Model Correlate with Those in a Human Clinical Trial. *Mol. Ther.* **2006**, *14*, 893. [CrossRef]
33. Wolff, D. *Rheumatoid Arthritis*; Enna, S.J., Bylund, D.B., Eds.; Elsevier: Amsterdam, The Netherlands, 2007.
34. Innala, L.; Berglin, E.; Möller, B.; Ljung, L.; Smedby, T.; Södergren, A.; Magnusson, S.; Rantapää-Dahlqvist, S.; Wållberg-Jonsson, S. Age at Onset Determines Severity and Choice of Treatment in Early Rheumatoid Arthritis: A Prospective Study. *Arthritis Res. Ther.* **2014**, *16*, R94. [CrossRef] [PubMed]
35. Van Vollenhoven, R.F. Sex Differences in Rheumatoid Arthritis: More than Meets the Eye. *BMC Med.* **2009**, *7*. [CrossRef]

MDPI
St. Alban-Anlage 66
4052 Basel
Switzerland
www.mdpi.com

BioTech Editorial Office
E-mail: biotech@mdpi.com
www.mdpi.com/journal/biotech

www.ingramcontent.com/pod-product-compliance
Lightning Source LLC
Chambersburg PA
CBHW062035220926
51850CB00010B/2557
* 9 7 8 3 7 2 5 8 0 1 0 5 3 *